The Republic of
IRELAND

The Republic of
IRELAND

BARRY BRUNT

Lecturer in Geography,
University College, Cork

WESTERN EUROPE:
ECONOMIC AND SOCIAL STUDIES

P·C·P
Paul Chapman
Publishing Ltd

Brunt, Barry
  Ireland.—(Western Europe : economic
  and social studies).
  1. (Republic) Ireland. Economic conditions,
  1945–1987
  I. Title II. Series
  330.9417'082

ISBN 1-85396-019-5

Typeset by Inforum Ltd, Portsmouth
Printed and bound by Butler & Tanner Ltd, Frome, Somerset

For my mother, Dilys, and to the memory of
my father, Fred Brunt, who gave me so much.

CONTENTS

PREFACE

In his preface to the third edition of his major work on Ireland, Freeman (1965) writes that 'the fascination of Ireland lies in its distinction from Great Britain, its separate if related history, its population problem unique in Western Europe, its farm pattern and agriculture still in a state of evolution from the woeful fragmentation of pre-Famine times, and even in the ethos of its people' (p. x). The development of the country since 1960 adds rather than detracts from this fascination as Ireland has sought to modernize through urban-industrial development and to become more fully integrated within the international community. Ireland of the 1980s is a very different place to that of the 1950s, as its economy, society and politics have evolved to accommodate new pressures and demands from both within and without the country. And yet, history and tradition, best expressed in the rural communities, remain strong forces which direct and limit contemporary trends. The net result is a geography of contrasts, and one that well illustrates the difficulties of a small, marginalized island economy, located off the north-west coast of Europe, linking its development to a strategy of open trade and depending on foreign investment.

After a generation of independence, Ireland emerged from the Second World War largely unchanged from the rural-based and traditional society that characterized the 1930s. This was perhaps not unexpected given the policies of neutrality, nationalism and economic autarky adopted by the country in an attempt to detach itself from the long-established political and economic dominance of Britain. Thus, while the countries of war-torn Europe attempted to rebuild economies based on principles of modernization and internationalization, Ireland persisted with its fundamental belief in internal solutions to development based on self-sufficiency and cultural integrity. But these policies were not adequate to achieve the national goals of raising living standards and increasing job prospects, and throughout the second quarter of the twentieth century Ireland continued to rely on emigration, as it had since the 1840s, as a solution to internal deficiencies. Population continued to decline in the 1950s and emigration increased dramatically to provide some sort of safety valve for the rising levels of unemployment, associated with the failure of new investment to compensate for the continued erosion of agricultural employment. A second problem that had plagued the country was the unequal development between east and west. These long-established spatial inequities were fuelled rather than reduced by policies which increasingly focused on the national dimension of decline rather than its spatial or sectoral components. While Dublin's primacy was enhanced, the squalor and deprivation of many citizens were testimony to the urgent need to effect change. The optimism and sense of purpose, which were widely expressed among the largely classless rural society of Ireland's first quarter-century of independence, rapidly gave way to despair as to the future prospects of an independent nation state. It was against this background that government sought a new approach to replace the one that had patently collapsed in the 1950s. A general consensus emerged to favour a new *Programme for Economic Expansion* (1958), which emphasized modernization of the socioeconomic system based on externally promoted industrial development and a reintegration within global trade.

Ireland of the 1980s exhibits remarkable contrasts to the situation of the 1950s, yet there are also many disturbing similarities. Modernization has resulted in the development of socioeconomic structures more similar to those typical in other countries of north-west Europe. Agriculture has become more commercialized, reflected in a greater degree of specialization of production, while branch plants of foreign-based multinational enterprises have become an important new element in the economy and landscape. Overall, a greater sense of prosperity has spread into the rural communities. But Ireland is now an urbanized society, exposed to the cosmopolitan values and materialism that have spread into the country from Dublin and the other major cities. The divide between east and west is thus less stark, but the dominance of the capital remains a fundamental factor in the spatial expression of the country's human geography. Above all, perhaps, the face of modern Ireland is best reflected in the population. In place of decline, there has been growth, and in contrast to a projection made in the 1950s (O'Brien, 1954) that the national population by the end of the century would amount to only two million, more recent estimates suggest a doubling of that figure. The turnabout in demographic trends has been highly significant, and reflects the decline in emigration as new job opportunities kept many in the country. But while the proportion of young people has brought new opportunities, it has also led to certain difficulties based on their demands and expectations.

Similarities with the 1950s present a somewhat more pessimistic image of the current position. Unemployment and emigration have recently increased to levels reminiscent of the 1950s, and are particularly acute for the younger generation. Agricultural and industrial development has faltered, and a major debt crisis has emerged. Optimism has again given way to pessimism about the ability of the small nation state to maintain effectively a development momentum. This situation has furthermore been aggravated by the fact that modernization has brought new stresses in association with the more complex socioeconomic structures it has created. Spatial and sectoral divides have been exacerbated as the impacts of modernization have tended to favour disproportionately the better-off areas and growing middle-class element. A significant social gulf has emerged between blue-collar and white-collar workers, between small- and large-scale farm operators and between the employed and unemployed. This finds a spatial expression in the conflict of interests emerging between inner city and suburbs, town and countryside, more productive agricultural areas and more marginal environments, and between the dominant capital and the rest of the country.

Many processes contribute to these changed conditions, but of paramount importance have been the policies adopted by the Irish government to reflect and accommodate changes in the international political economy. After the comparatively unsuccessful flirtation with economic nationalism, a policy of modernization fundamentally changed Ireland's role in the global economy and reflected a transition from colonial to neocolonial status. Following the 1950s, Ireland traded a dependency on Britain for a dependency on international capital to bring about the social and economic transformation of the country. Thus, agricultural development became intimately related to the Common Agricultural Policy (CAP) and industrialization reflected the perceived advantages of Ireland for multinational investment. Furthermore, this new image of the country, being receptive to investment based on an international division of labour and production, favoured a much needed internal redistribution of development which partially accorded with the government goals for a more balanced socioeconomic system. The huge debt built up during the 1970s and 1980s to finance the development of a new social and physical infrastructure has, however, created a serious problem. The nation's obligations to international financial institutions have intensified and the government's freedom of action is restricted. As a result, control over external decision-making has been marginal, and the spatial and sectoral ramifications of decline, resulting from a stagnation of the world economy, have been exacerbated since they have occurred in a context which has placed little emphasis on national or regional interests.

The ability of governments of small countries to direct national development within the context of an open-trade policy is limited, and yet the response of government to the opportunities and pressures of change is of considerable importance for the quality and spatial distribution of development. Ireland's policies have largely been deferential to the needs of international capital, and have been sectoral and lacking in the coordination of development within a defined spatial context. In addition, the policies have tended to be reactive rather than formulative, and to aggravate rather than minimize the potential for internal divisions. Keynesianism has been favoured, and large-scale state expenditure has occurred to build up a system of social welfare. Consensus politics dominated in all these areas, since it was politically an easy option to spend money, especially when it was borrowed capital. The major surge in unemployment, emigration, poverty and debt, however, has witnessed a change in policies. Consensus still exists between the dominant political parties as to the urgent need for expenditure cutbacks and general restraint. Choices are now having to be made, and the appearance of monetarism and elements of Thatcherism suggest that broad socioeconomic conflicts within Ireland may be intensified, at least in the short term.

This book discusses the changing geography of Ireland since the Second World War by identifying the major social, economic and political processes that have interacted to shape the Ireland of today. These processes form a common theme throughout the book, which is organized to reflect their critical impact on the transformation of Ireland. Four main chapters are presented to focus attention on the major spatial divisions used to reflect the changes in the patterns and processes of development – national, regional, rural and urban. Within these broad divisions, the interplay of economic, social and political processes is reviewed to give a better understanding of the complexities of the contemporary position. However, although treated separately, development processes operate within a continuum, and therefore it is to be stressed that the national, regional, rural and urban dimensions form part of an interactive whole rather than existing as isolated entities. Whether the buoyant social and economic conditions of the twenty years from 1960 to 1980 were a temporary dislocation from the otherwise more traditional marginalized conditions found in this small island economy is a matter of great import to Ireland. The aim of this book is, therefore, to contribute to a basic understanding of the patterns and processes currently at work and which might offer some better appreciation of the question. Only time will adequately provide the answer.

To the outside world, Ireland frequently presents the image of a rather traditional and simplistic island economy and society. It is far from being either. Change is very much an integral element of the country's human geography. Given the constraints of both time and space, the approach taken in this book, which seeks to encapsulate the major changes, is inevitably selective and reflects a personal judgement as to what constitutes the most important ingredients of change.

In compiling this book, I am indebted to many people who have eased the difficulties of research and preparation. Connell Foley, the cartographer at the Department of Geography, University College, Cork, prepared the many illustrations with his usual cheerfulness and competence. Thanks are also due to Anne Phelan, Anne Reddy and Maura Humphries who combined to type the manuscript, and to the editors, Allan Williams and Eleonore Kofman, for their general advice on the final text. My colleagues in Cork were most supportive of my needs throughout the project, and I am particularly grateful to Professor William Smyth, and also to Pat O'Flanagan and Kevin Hourihan for their insights into topic areas that were less than overly familiar to the author. A special gratitude is due to John Winberry of the Department of Geography, University of South Carolina, for his general encouragement and advice during the completion of the work. Above all, however, my thanks and appreciation go to my family, Leigh and Christopher, who bore the brunt of this work in so many ways. While many people combined to facilitate the production of this book, any inadequacies and errors remain the responsibility of the author.

Barry M. Brunt
Cork, 1987

ONE

Ireland in the Changing Postwar World

1.1 Introduction

In the years immediately following the Second World War, the Republic of Ireland could be considered a fundamental anomaly among the countries of north-western Europe. Economic and social parameters contrasted strongly with the country's largely urban-industrialized neighbours and more closely resembled the underdeveloped Mediterranean periphery of the European subcontinent (Seers, 1979, p. 7). Furthermore, as rapid postwar economic reconstruction occurred in much of Western Europe, Ireland's anomalous position was accentuated as the country remained aloof from the process of modernization. Conservatism rather than modernization, and isolation rather than integration, appeared to be the dominant forces at work and reflected policies and goals deemed appropriate to protect the national cultural and political identity. These did little to enhance the living conditions of the population and marginalization of the economy increased, as did the traditionally high rate of emigration.

Policies and goals underwent a fundamental change in the closing years of the 1950s, and subsequent decades have witnessed the embracing of modernization as the country sought more effectively to join the community of economies of north-western Europe. An extremely open trading economy benefited from internationalization of trade and the influx of high levels of foreign capital. The economic structure was transformed and the quality of life for the majority of Ireland's small population base improved. Emigration fell away, the economy moved towards full employment and an expanded public sector programme of expenditure on social services promised not only a higher quality of life but also a more egalitarian society.

Despite significant advances made, albeit from a low base level, Ireland continues to rank lowly within Europe on most social and economic indicators. On the basis of social well-being, Ilbery (1984) has ranked Ireland as nineteenth of twenty-six European states and groups the country with Albania and Portugal. Economic potential remains low and the European Commission has designated the entire country as a disadvantaged area (Clark et al., 1969; Keeble et al., 1982).

While Ireland may be the third poorest state in the European Community, with purchasing power parity equivalent to only 70 per cent of the European norm, it ranks as a developed economy in a global setting. The image of Ireland depends very much on the spatial perspective adopted and the time period within which analysis is made. For a small nation state, the country has historically created an image and a role which are disproportionate to its size. That image, whether from the world outside or for the people living within the country, has been increasingly influenced by national development policy. The remainder of this chapter outlines the principal elements of such change in the postwar period.

1.2   From isolation to internationalism

The Anglo-Irish Treaty, signed in December 1921, created the Irish Free State as a self-governing Dominion within the British Commonwealth. Under the treaty, twenty-six counties became a politically distinct entity from the six north-eastern counties within the province of Ulster that chose to remain under British rule. Partition of the island has proven to be a highly contentious topic within the country and retains to the present day a disproportionate role in the image that Ireland as a whole presents to the world. Fundamental historical and geographical forces account for the original partition and these have retained a relevance throughout the twentieth century in shaping contemporary political and socioeconomic development.

The Irish economy evolved essentially within the context of the nineteenth-century capitalist industrial system of the United Kingdom. This bequeathed a specialist role for the economy of the north-eastern counties as distinct from the rest of the country. Centred on Belfast and the Lagan valley, the north-east became the focus of a well-integrated, urban-industrial complex specializing in engineering, shipbuilding and textiles for the export trade (Busteed, 1974). In contrast, the most crucial factor for manufacturing in the rest of the country was the minimal development associated with the industrial revolution (Gillmor, 1985a, p. 212). The dictates of the colonial system, augmented by the paucity of its mineral and energy base, therefore relegated most of Ireland to providing surplus food and labour for the British industrial system. At the time of the first census in the Free State (1926), less than 10 per cent of the workforce were engaged in industry in contrast to over one-third in the six north-eastern counties, which in turn represented some 90 per cent of total manufacturing employment on the island. Two distinct and specialized subeconomies had therefore emerged which were fundamentally independent of each other, yet were both dependent on Britain. This dependency factor was further promoted by the geographical proximity of the island's economies to the dominant colonial power.

For much of Ireland, colonial attachment to Britain had provided a hostile environment for the promotion of indigenous development. Political independence was therefore recognized as a necessary precondition for economic development, whereas the continued prosperity of the more industrialized north-east depended on it maintaining its specialized function within the British free-trade system. Based on these assessments, subsequent development in the two parts of the island economy showed markedly different trends (Walsh, F., 1979; O'Malley, 1985; Brunt, 1988).

Much of Irish nationalism had a strong protectionist bias and it was anticipated that independence would see the endorsement of that principle. Tradition and the degree of integration of the national economy within the British trade network, however, made it unrealistic to expect a revolutionary change in policy. The Free State consequently adopted a very cautious approach in establishing a new identity, and Kevin O'Higgins (the first Minister for Home Affairs) boasted that the new leaders were the most conservative revolutionaries in history (McCormack, 1979).

In 1932, the more nationalist Fianna Fáil party came into government led by Eamon de Valera, one of the leading figures in the Irish independence movement. De Valera was to dominate Irish politics until the late 1950s, and was committed to establishing a clear identity for the country based on its Gaelic, rural and Catholic traditions. A policy of wholesale protectionism was introduced, while passage of the Control of Manufacturers Acts (1932, 1934) effectively restricted foreign participation in Irish industry (Meenan, 1970; Lyons, 1971).

A new Constitution passed in the Dáil (Parliament) in 1937 emphasized the individuality of the state and declared the neutral stance that Ireland would henceforth take in international affairs. This move, plus the fact that by the same year tariff levels of up to 40 per cent provided the most protected industrial environment in Europe, largely detached the country from its satellite role as defined by British politics. Ireland was thus able to escape the physical ravages of war, but the isolationism was bought at an economic cost. Trade declined by 25 per cent in the 1930s, and plummeted a further 50 per cent during the Second World War, with the result that standards of living within the state also dropped.

Commitment to an independent economic and political role was maintained in the immediate postwar years. In 1948, a Republic of Ireland was declared and the country effectively removed itself from the British Commonwealth. An initial surge in trade, largely sponsored by agricultural exports, also encouraged a continuation of protectionism. The underlying basis of the stand-alone position in trade terms, however, was to be quickly exposed. At the start of the new decade, the commodity category of trade, which primarily refers to agricultural products, still accounted for 80 per cent of national trade as opposed to only 7 per cent from manufacturing. Furthermore, Britain remained the market outlet for 87 per cent of Ireland's exports. Apart from some success in reducing import penetration of basic consumer goods, a generation of nationalist aspirations had failed to promote an economic development to match political independence.

Terms of trade increasingly moved against the Republic in the 1950s, and self-sufficiency for the Irish economy increasingly appeared to be a delusion as the import content of GNP rose. The balance of payments position worsened into recurrent crises and inflation was rampant. High unemployment and depressed living standards caused a dramatic increase in emigration, re-emphasizing its role as a supplier of labour to the international economy.

Geographical peripherality had been reinforced by inward-looking policies which detached the Republic from many of the main economic and political movements that occurred in the decade following the war. Ireland failed to benefit from the internationalization of trade and the integrative political movements based on Europe's growing prosperity in the 1950s which culminated in the Treaty of Rome (1957). Paradoxically, however, although the small island economy attempted to achieve self-sufficiency, one of the enduring and distinctive features of the Irish economy — the importance of external transactions — remained. Protectionism and economic autarky only partially and temporarily upset this basic factor and by the late 1950s it was apparent that government policy had to address the economic necessity of formally reintegrating the economy within the international arena.

Some evidence of a movement away from what Murphy (1975, p.137) describes as an almost claustrophobic insularity emerged by the mid-1950s when Ireland secured membership of the United Nations (1955), the World Bank and the International Monetary Fund (1957). It was in the following years, however, that the country appeared to commit itself to internationalism with the publication of *Economic Development* (Department of Finance, 1958). Essentially, the deficiencies of the previous system were highlighted and radical changes proposed which focused on encouraging foreign participation and export enhancement.

The creation of a free-trade environment led to the signing of the Anglo-Irish Free Trade Agreement in 1965, followed by accession to the General Agreement on Tariffs and Trade (GATT) in 1967. Probably the most strategic decision, however, was to seek membership of the European Community (EC), which was achieved in 1973. Entry into this competitive trade arena demanded the creation of an internal environment that would be advantageous for industrial development. Since indigenous industry was not considered capable of generating the necessary employment and successfully competing in the export market (Maher, 1986), this meant enhancing Ireland's position as a base for foreign direct investment. An Employer Labour Conference was established in 1962 to help maintain the country's favourable labour costs (O'Brien, 1981), while public expenditure on physical infrastructure was increased. Above all, however, the success of the country's shift into an export-dominated strategy for growth related to the generous incentive package offered by government to induce foreign companies to locate production units within Ireland.

The primary fiscal incentive for export-orientated manufacturing enterprises was the Export Profit Tax Relief (EPTR) scheme, introduced initially in 1956 but significantly modified in the 1960s. This allowed all profits generated from export transactions to be declared free of tax for a period of fifteen years up to 1990, and allowed for total repatriation of these profits. A European Community ruling on the 'opaque' nature of this incentive caused the replacement of EPTR by a 10 per cent corporation tax in 1981. This is a low level of taxation by international standards and therefore continues to be a major inducement for industrial development. Financial incentives such as capital grants, an advance factory-building programme and labour-training grants further augmented the attractiveness of Ireland for mobile international investment.

A major inflow of foreign investment occurred, especially in the latter half of the 1960s, and was maintained throughout the 1970s as accession to the EC compounded the benefits of Ireland as a production platform for exports. With agricultural exports also benefiting from higher prices and unrestricted access to the Community market, the annual growth of Irish exports was 8.2 per cent in the 1960s and 8.0 per cent in the 1970s. This trend has continued, albeit at a lower level, into the 1980s such that the sustained level of export growth emerges as a fundamental characteristic of recent Irish economic development (Foley, 1986). Imports also continued to grow rapidly and, by 1985, imports and exports of goods and services amounted to 55 and 57 per cent respectively of total GDP. The corresponding percentage ratios for the EC were 27 and 26, which clearly illustrates the dependency on foreign trade and the openness of the small Irish economy (McAleese, 1984).

Expansion of Irish trade has been accompanied by a significant reorientation in its composition and geographical parameters. The surge in Irish exports has been largely facilitated through a marked expansion in manufacturing and, by 1985, this accounted for almost two-thirds of total merchandise trade (Table 1.1). Manufactured goods have also increasingly dominated imports, especially since most overseas enterprises have tended to

Table 1.1   Percentage composition of merchandise trade by commodity, 1961–85

	Imports			Exports		
	1961	1973	1985	1961	1973	1985
Live animals and food	16	10	11	61	41	23
Beverages and tobacco	3	2	1	4	3	2
Raw materials, fuels and oil	19	14	16	9	7	6
Manufactured goods	54	69	70	18	44	65
Other	8	4	3	8	6	4

Source: *Trade Statistics of Ireland.*

import capital equipment to initiate production and specialize in processing components and raw materials from external sources. The growth in manufactured exports therefore automatically translated itself into a growth of imports.

Accession to the EC has had a major influence on the geography of Irish trade, primarily by reducing the degree of dependence on a single market. In 1960, the United Kingdom was the outlet for 75 per cent of total merchandise exports as distinct to only 6 per cent for the remaining countries of the EC. This degree of polarization of trade was steadily eroded, and by 1985 the EC replaced the United Kingdom as the principal trading

Table 1.2   Percentage composition of merchandise trade by geographical area, 1973–85

	Imports		Exports	
	1973	1985	1973	1985
Great Britain and N. Ireland	50.7	42.7	54.7	33.0
Other EC countries	21.3	22.0	21.6	34.6
Rest of Europe	8.7	7.4	4.3	7.8
North America	8.0	17.9	11.2	11.5
Central and South America	1.3	1.1	2.9	1.3
Africa	2.2	1.8	1.3	3.8
Near and Middle East	2.4	0.3	0.9	2.6
Other Asian countries	3.1	6.1	1.3	2.8
Australasia	0.9	0.2	0.8	1.5
Miscellaneous	1.6	0.6	1.3	1.1
Total (IR £ million)	1138	9427	869	9743

Source: *Trade Statistics of Ireland.*

outlet for Ireland (Table 1.2). This shift in emphasis reflects the comparatively poor growth performance of the British economy throughout this period (Hudson and Williams, 1986), but even more so relates to the global marketing strategies of foreign direct investment attracted into Ireland. Diversification of Irish trade was also prompted by a growing trade in food products and manufactures to lesser developed countries. Changes in import sources have been less dramatic. The United Kingdom continues to dominate, although a significant degree of import penetration from the United States and Japan reflects an influx of manufactured goods and component parts.

By the late 1970s, Ireland's five-year transition period to full membership of the EC had been successfully completed. In the twenty years during which the country had shifted from isolation to increased internationalism, a positive image of the country emerged. Its support for the EC, epitomized by a referendum vote (1972) of 83 per cent in favour of membership, and general support for the principles of the Treaty of Rome, gave Ireland a positive image of being a 'good' European. Furthermore, the apparent political stability within the country and the support for free enterprise made Ireland one of the most attractive areas for foreign investment within the Community. Trade was buoyant and a general mood of optimism prevailed in relation to national identity and growth potential. However, the 1980s have cast doubts on the validity of this image.

During the 1970s, several problems began to exhibit a higher profile and were associated with the increasing openness of the economy. A dominant element of Irish merchandise trade had been its deficit character. This was maintained in the post-1960 period, when the comparatively high import content of manufactured exports made their net contribution to the balance of trade performance less than anticipated. Furthermore, as the terms of trade disimproved due to inflated energy costs, linked to Ireland's dependency on imported energy (84 per cent by 1978), and less favourable price movements with the Common Agricultural Policy (CAP), the deficit on merchandise trade continued to rise. By 1981, this peaked at IR£ 1800 million.

Invisible trade earnings had traditionally offset part of the deficit, but conditions also worsened in this sector. Irish tourism performed poorly when higher inflation rates reduced the attraction of Irish holidays, as did 'the troubles' within Northern Ireland which deterred large numbers of British holiday-makers. By 1980, Irish tourists were spending more overseas than did visitors to Ireland. While conditions have improved and tourist receipts have again become a surplus item in the balance of trade since 1982, the Irish tourist industry is operating well below its potential and has one of the lowest growth rates within Europe (see Section 3.5).

Table 1.3   National indebtedness as a percentage of GNP for selected years, 1973–85

	Total debt	Foreign debt	Debt service	Balance of payments deficit
1973	60.0	6.2	5.6	0.3
1975	74.2	15.4	6.5	0.5
1979	88.5	20.9	8.4	13.9
1981	96.5	46.6	9.5	15.3
1983	120.1	65.9	12.5	6.5
1985	133.6	67.9	14.5	3.5

Source: Central Bank of Ireland, *Quarterly Bulletins.*

Internationalization of the economy did, however, secure a significant inflow of transfer payments from the EC. In spite of this, by 1979 a deficit equivalent to 13.9 per cent of GNP had appeared on the current account (Table 1.3) and can be related to the fiscal management policy adopted by the government during this period.

Inflationary pressures increased throughout the 1970s with consumer prices advancing on average by 14 per cent per annum. This was substantially higher than most other industrialized economies although it closely followed British conditions. A continued dependency on British imports and the parity link with sterling contributed to a transmission of British inflation into the Irish economy. In 1978, however, an opportunity presented itself to break the parity link and currency union with Britain that dated back to 1826. The European Monetary Union was proposed and came into effect in 1979. Britain opted to remain outside this arrangement, but Ireland chose to enter in the belief that by associating with stronger European currencies, exchange rate fluctuations would stabilize and imported inflation would be reduced (Walsh, 1984). After initial problems, some success in these areas has been achieved, although omission of Britain from the system is recognized as a particular problem for Ireland's financial market.

Public expenditure continued to rise in the 1970s as government sought to provide the physical and social infrastructures required by modern economies and expected by a population who anticipated a continued increase in their living standards. In order to satisfy this outlay, government resorted increasingly to foreign borrowings. Thus began the government's initial flirtation with foreign borrowing which by 1979 equalled 21 per cent of GNP (Table 1.3).

Ireland entered the 1980s as part of the international economy whose powerful external forces were beyond the effective control of the national government. Dependency on the external environment remained as critical as during the pre-independence era, although the form of the relationship changed. The open-trade policy merely accelerated the transition from a colonial to neo-colonial system in which international banking interests and multinational business organizations dominate the direction, possibilities for, and extent of national development.

In 1985, for the first time in more than forty years, Ireland achieved a surplus on its merchandise trade with the rest of the world. However, this achievement, together with a surplus gained from internationally traded services and a transfer of some IR£ 1000 million into the national economy via the EC and other sources, failed to generate an overall balance of payments surplus. The paradox of a substantial trade surplus accompanied by a balance of payments deficit is accounted for by a huge outflow of profits, dividends, royalties and interest from the country.

Ireland's favourable tax incentives clearly favoured a predominance of export production and have allowed multinational enterprises to average an 18 per cent return on their total investments. While this is clearly an impressive performance, concern has been expressed at the extent to which these profits reflect the use of transfer pricing policies to maximize declared profits in the low tax haven of Ireland. Thus, it is estimated that between 50 and 75 per cent of profits declared by foreign multinationals located in Ireland are lost to the national economy. In 1985, this amounted to some IR£ 1000 million, and the mechanism of its loss gave rise to the term 'Ireland's black hole'.

A second 'black hole' has also been identified through which large quantities of capital leave the country. By late 1985, rising problems of unemployment, growth of public debt, high rates of personal taxation and marginal growth within the economy all served to discourage investment. Interest-securing deposits dropped sharply as private individuals, financial institutions and business looked for more secure and rewarding investment opportunities overseas. Losses amounted to more than IR£ 1000 million in 1986.

While the country experienced a major outpouring of money on both the current and capital accounts, Ireland's commitment to borrowing increased. The sharp rise in world interest rates in the 1980s, however, placed the country within an international debt trap (Tables 1.3, 1.4). In 1985, Ireland had the highest debt burden of any country in the industrial world and this was to place a major constraint on national development.

By the mid-1980s, Ireland's global image and the internal self-confidence manifest in the 1970s had undergone important changes. The flight of

Table 1.4   Public sector borrowing requirement, its components and balance of payments as a percentage of GNP, 1975–85

	Current budget deficit	Exchequer borrowing for capital purposes	Borrowing by state-sponsored bodies and local authorities	PSBR
1975	6.9	9.1	2.0	18.1
1977	3.8	6.2	2.9	12.9
1979	7.1	6.7	3.0	16.8
1981	7.8	9.0	4.7	21.5
1983	7.2	6.0	4.1	17.3
1985	8.4	5.0	3.0	16.4

Source: Walsh and O'Leary (1984), p. 152; Central Bank National Income and Expenditure Tables.

domestic capital, rising foreign indebtedness, high unemployment, budget deficits and a poor growth performance caused some commentators to question whether the country was becoming Europe's first banana republic (Tansey, 1986). In addition, a 'begging bowl' attitude towards the EC replaced the earlier, more positive inputs by Ireland to European integration. This has tarnished EC perception of Ireland, although much goodwill remains and could be harnessed for development. Certainly, coverage of the 1987 general election by the international press focused heavily on the financial and economic problems and, according to the Industrial Development Authority (IDA), generated the worst image of Ireland since independence.

Internationalization of the economy brought rapid gains to Ireland, although its failure to emerge from the 1980–82 recession points to the problems faced by small, open economies, especially when important decision-making functions are largely externalized. The degree of dependency and type of economic policy that have emerged within the country caused Crotty (1987) to suggest that Ireland could be regarded as Europe's only capitalist colony. Ireland's neo-colonial situation is not, however, without several offsetting elements that offer prospects for growth. Based on a strong export potential, the country continues to possess a triple-A credit ranking, while foreign direct investment is being maintained. Furthermore, its geographical proximity to, and involvement within, the EC has conferred important benefits on Ireland, not least in terms of its enhanced locational characteristics and large financial transfers. It is anticipated that the successful ratification of the Single European Act (1987) will further support the country's attempts to adjust to the pressures of international capital. Ultimate success, however, depends on the Irish government's ability to implement policies which more realistically address the consequences of internationalism.

1.3 Government economic policy and the reshaping of the national economy

Ireland's postwar economy has experienced major changes in its composition and character as the dominant position of the rural-agricultural component has been replaced by an urban-industrial system. While the process is far from complete, and the country's economic and social status still lags behind that of most other European countries, Ireland in the 1980s finds itself in closer harmony with its neighbours than in former times. Central to this have been government policies introduced to accommodate the national goals of full employment, enhanced standards of living and cessation of involuntary emigration. The initial success which attended policy reappraisal in the 1960s and the general consensus of the government approach tended to mask, however, the fact that success was conditioned by strategies of international investment which temporarily complemented government aims. The difficulties of the 1980s point to a greater divergence in the strategies of international capital from the requirements of small nation states, such as Ireland. The following section reviews the policies implemented by the government to promote internal development within the context of a changing global economy.

1.3.1 1945–59: The failure of nationalist economic policy

The economic depression within Ireland during the Second World War was quickly replaced by a rapid recovery of economic activity after 1945. Food shortages in Britain ensured buoyant agricultural exports, while internal demands for consumer products boosted indigenous industry. By 1949, postwar recovery was complete and the country enjoyed a more rapid increase in national output than had been experienced at any time since independence. Thus, although the Fianna Fáil party had been replaced by an interparty coalition government in 1948, the belief that protectionism was a practical means of ensuring development had firmly established itself across the political spectrum.

State-sponsored bodies also emerged as a major feature of Irish economic development during the protectionist phase, and have maintained a high profile to the present. Given the political philosophies of the two dominant parties – Fianna Fáil and Fine Gael – direct investment within the market did not reflect a commitment to state socialism, but rather a realistic assessment of the problems of a small economy in generating and maintaining essential infrastructure and strategic industries. The Electricity Supply Board (ESB), established in 1927 to ensure an adequate power base for development, was the first state-sponsored body, while a national public transport authority, Coras Iompair Eireann (CIE), was established in 1945. Institutional arrangements were also made to facilitate important spheres of activity such as industrial and agricultural credit, tourism and labour training. These public bodies proved critical for the successful take-off of the economy in the 1960s.

The comparative ease with which postwar expansion was achieved created a climate of opinion in which a radical review of existing policies found no place, and the Republic drifted into the 1950s unconscious of the many difficulties it was creating for itself. Fitzgerald (1968), in fact, suggests that it was not until the early 1950s the independent Irish economy settled down to more normal conditions in which the merits of protectionism could be tested. For some thirty years following independence, civil war, global depression, trade war with Britain, global conflict and postwar reconstruction quickly followed on each other and prevented a true assessment of the new state's potential.

If the 1950s saw the first assessment of the experiment with protectionism and economic autarky, then the results indicated a failure. Despite two

Figure 1.1 Components of population change, 1930–83 (after Kennedy and Giblin, 1987).

Ireland in the Changing Postwar World   13

Table 1.5 Percentage changes in employment, standard industrial classifications, 1926–85

| | Percentage change | | | | | Absolute numbers |
	1926–51	1951–61	1961–71	1971–79	1979–85	1985
Agriculture, forestry and fishing	−23.5	−23.6	−27.9	−18.8	−24.0	168,500
Mining, quarrying and turf production	489.8	−2.9	8.1	17.1	−16.4	10,200
Food	60.9	2.2	13.4 ⎫	17.1	−24.4	45,300
Beverages and tobacco	11.5	−8.2	−1.5 ⎬			
Textiles	180.9	19.8	15.5 ⎭			
Clothing	13.4	−18.6	−3.1 ⎫	−22.8	−34.1	27,500
Footwear	53.8	−17.4	−20.1 ⎭			
Wood and wood products	−3.6	−21.9	14.8	−14.4	−1.4	13,700
Paper, printing and publishing	81.8	17.3	12.9	−2.7	−1.8	16,600
Chemicals, rubber and plastics	206.8	42.2	44.1	51.6	−22.5	17,900
Glass, cement and pottery	777.8	13.1	65.0	47.0	−24.1	12,900
Metals, machinery and engineering	56.2	17.0	54.9	48.0	22.6	57,600
Transport equipment	2.9	−10.0	30.3 ⎫	13.4	−42.7	13,000
Other manufacturing	104.2	57.3	47.6 ⎭			
Building and construction	133.2	−29.9	41.9	19.6	−25.1	75,700
Electricity, gas and water	311.1	0.5	39.2	−1.2	7.9	15,100
Commerce	31.2	3.9	3.6	8.7	4.7	168,700
Insurance, finance and banking ⎬	31.2	17.0	68.5	52.6	10.4	40,400
Transport and communications	45.9	−4.5	11.0	13.9	1.2	67,700
Public administration and defence	−46.8	0.1	20.4	43.4	4.4	73,200
Professional services	112.2	4.0	26.9	36.1	15.8	171,900
Personal services	−34.0	−25.1	−14.0	4.9	6.5	60,800
Recreation	195.2	1.4	−1.2	18.1	2.4	17,200
Total all industries	−0.3	−13.7	0.2	9.0	−6.6	1,073,900

Source: Census of Population, 1926–71; *Labour Force Surveys*, 1979, 1985.

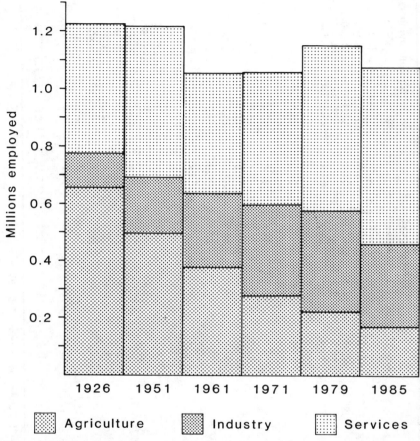

Figure 1.2   Changing structure of the Irish economy, 1926–85.

changes of government in 1951 and 1954, the country persisted with its policy of protectionism and did not attempt to reorientate industry to the buoyant export markets of Europe. The net result was that, from 1950 to 1958, the volume of GNP declined by 0.3 per cent per year and Ireland exhibited the most sluggish economy in Western Europe, being described as a 'capitalist country without capital' (quoted in Kearns, 1974a, p. 301).

The pursuit of this inward-looking policy was beset by fundamental problems which were clearly exposed in the 1950s (Walsh, F., 1980). Preference for the small domestic market ensured that the industries which developed behind high tariff barriers were small scale, poorly capitalized, highly priced and ill-equipped to exist outside a protected home environment. In addition, the inadequacies of the domestic market were being emphasized by the continuous decline in total population (Figure 1.1).

Agriculture lost its dominant employment role in the 1950s and, by 1961, had declined by some 43 per cent of its 1926 level (Table 1.5, Figure 1.2). Progress to create a modern, productive sector was limited by the traditional role of the family farm and the conservative approach to agriculture. The volume of output in the early 1950s only slightly exceeded that of the 1920s and it was not until 1960 that the total number of livestock units exceeded the 1922 level (Gillmor, 1985a, p. 171). Mining and turf production did increase, however, associated with state involvement in mineral exploration and the establishment of the state-sponsored Bord na Mona (BNM) in 1946 to work more effectively the country's extensive peat deposits.

Protection of indigenous manufacturing achieved a significant increase in both output and employment within Ireland until 1951. With the exception of wood and wood products, all industrial groups registered important gains in employment and a diversified employment structure was created in marked contrast to the highly specialized economy that still persisted within Northern Ireland. The dramatic early gains were not repeated in the 1950s, however, as opportunities for expansion were curtailed and import penetration increased. This ensured a more differentiated response by the component industrial groups. In aggregate, manufacturing employment increased by only a little over 3000 during the intercensal period, 1951–61.

The highly dispersed rural society, limited commercialization of the agricultural economy, poor industrial base, weakly developed urbanization and the lowest population density of any country in Western Europe, other than Norway and Sweden, presented a poor environment for the emergence of a well-developed service sector. The positive performance of manufacturing until the early 1950s, however, did achieve important multiplier effects within services. Unfortunately, the economic recession of the 1950s slowed down this growth performance. Personal services exhibited the greatest decline during the decade, and the growth of private transport is reflected in a marginal decline in transportation services. Professional services continued their early growth, albeit at a much lower rate, and this reflects the growing commitment to the principles of a welfare state. Finally, evidence of an emerging commercialization of the economy and the growth of office employment is illustrated by the expansion of financial services.

Total employment declined in the 1950s and by 1961 was substantially below the level of 1926. The positive performances achieved in some sectors of manufacturing and services had been nullified by the losses within agriculture. The government aspiration of full employment conditions within the state to reduce the traditionally high rates of unemployment and thereby limit the necessity for emigration remained unfulfilled.

Associated with the overall decline in employment, population also declined, emphasizing the unique demographic experience of Ireland since the mid-nineteenth century. In 1841, just prior to the Great Famine, the population of the counties that now constitute the Republic was 6.53 million. Since that date, the population total has consistently fallen, apart from a marginal increase between the census years 1946 and 1951. By 1961, the total population was 2.82 million.

In the post-independence period, the country's high rate of natural increase failed to translate into a growth of total population (Table 1.6, Figure 1.1). Emigration offset natural increases and played a particularly important role in the 1950s when the perceived disadvantages of remaining in Ireland, as opposed to emigrating, especially to Britain or North America, were highlighted. The declining national economy contrasted strongly with full employment conditions and greater income-earning potential overseas, and stimulated a large exodus, particularly of the younger and more enterprising people. As the state of the national economy declined, so the rate of emigration increased and, by the late 1950s, an average of 42,000 people were leaving the country annually.

Despite the removal of large numbers from the potential workforce, unemployment remained high. Furthermore, underemployment within agriculture and a low participation rate among females made the reality of the limited success in job creation even more apparent. Passage of the Social Welfare Act in 1952 extended coverage to a wider spectrum of the population and helped mitigate some of the financial problems faced by the unemployed. It could not, however, remove the increasing sense of despair felt by the population.

In 1957, de Valera was returned to government at a time when the national economy had 'plumbed the depths of hopelessness' (Whitaker, 1973, p. 415). As chief architect of the protectionist policy, de Valera was faced by the dual failure to provide work and to offset the traditional role of the country as a supplier of labour to the centres of international capital. His vision of Ireland perhaps was summarized in the St Patrick's Day speech of 1943: 'The Ireland we dreamed of would be the home of a people who valued material wealth only as the basis of a right living, of a people who were satisfied with a frugal comfort and devoted their leisure to the things of the spirit' (quoted in Murphy, 1975, p. 84). This idyllic vision of a rural, Gaelic society based on self-sufficiency became increasingly out of touch with reality and the demands of the international economic system. In 1959

Table 1.6   Components of population change, 1926–86

	Births	Deaths	Natural change	Migration	Population change
	Average annual rates per 1000 population				
1926–36	19.6	14.2	+ 5.5	− 5.6	− 0.1
1936–46	20.3	14.5	+ 5.9	− 6.3	− 0.4
1946–51	22.2	13.6	+ 8.6	− 8.2	+ 0.4
1951–61	21.3	12.1	+ 9.2	−14.1	− 4.9
1961–71	21.6	11.4	+10.2	− 4.6	+ 5.5
1971–81	21.6	10.3	+11.2	− 3.2	+14.4
1981–86	19.1	11.2	+ 9.7	− 4.3	+ 2.7

Source: Census of population, 1926–86.

de Valera resigned as leader of the Fianna Fáil government and was replaced by Sean Lemass, who came to symbolize a new image for Ireland. Economic progress was henceforth to become the main priority, and this was to transform both the economy and society of Ireland.

1.3.2   Modernization policies, 1959–79

The publication of *Economic Development* in 1958 (Department of Finance) marks a watershed in Irish economic development. The optimism expressed within the suggested programme contrasted with the prevailing pessimism and was taken up by Lemass as the basis for projecting Ireland into a phase of modernization (Kennedy and Dowling, 1975, p. 254). Full employment, cessation of involuntary emigration and enhanced standards of living remained central objectives of policy, although the means of achieving them were to be fundamentally different.

In an attempt to guide and coordinate national development, indicative planning was introduced within the context of three programmes for economic expansion. These programmes covered the periods 1959–63, 1964–70 and 1969–72 and, although all targets were not obtained, they proved remarkably successful in reorientating the economy and preparing it for the competitive trade environment of the EC. Thus, the 1960s were to emerge as a decade of unprecedented growth, with national output increasing annually by 4 per cent, industrial output by 7 per cent and industrial exports by 18 per cent. Although less marked, progress in agriculture was a substantial improvement on the comparatively depressed conditions of the 1950s.

During this reorientation of national economic policy, the country was favoured by general growth conditions within the global economy. In addition, Ireland enjoyed stable government since Fianna Fáil had an uninterrupted term of office from 1957 to 1973. It was, therefore, able to guide effectively its policy programme, although broad political consensus had been reached on the necessity of modernization.

The successful take-off of the economy appeared to demand both an increase and a change in the nature of government involvement. In addition, therefore, to embracing the principles of free trade, the 1960s witnessed a fiscal policy for sustained economic growth. A general increase in public expenditure occurred to create a more efficient social and physical infrastructure within which modernization could effectively function. Public sector expenditure consequently rose from 28 to 36 per cent of GDP between 1960 and 1972 (see Figure 1.4). The real growth of the national economy, high rates of foreign industrial investment and taxation increases funded much of the government public programme such that debt concern was of marginal importance.

If 1958 marked a watershed year, 1973 was to highlight the culmination of the shift to internationalization. Accession to the EC was achieved, bringing with it greater obligations and opportunities than any previous economic arrangement since independence (Stationery Office, 1972; Drudy and McAleese, 1984). At the same time a coalition of Fine Gael and Labour replaced the Fianna Fáil government. During this period of office to 1977, which broadly corresponds to the five-year transition to full membership of the Community, the economy underwent some important modifications in its fiscal management. Keynesian principles of demand management had been gathering momentum throughout the 1960s, but they appeared to gain more widespread acceptance in the 1970s. Public sector expenditure continued to rise in an attempt to provide a range and quality of services comparable to those of other European states and also to meet the demands of a rapidly growing population (Gould, 1981). Capital programmes to encourage industrial and agricultural performance further contributed to the surge in government expenditure, as did the marked increase in unemployment (Table 1.7). This expansionary fiscal approach meant that, by 1978, public expenditure had risen to the equivalent of one-half of GNP.

Prior to 1972, governments had been averse to substantial budget deficits, preferring to accommodate growth through prudent fiscal management. Following the negative impact of the first oil crisis on the economy, however, Keynesian solutions to the recession were sought and current budget deficits emerged in an attempt to insulate the national economy from the impact of external pressures. From 1975, current budget deficits became endemic, as did borrowing on a substantial scale to finance current

Table 1.7   Expenditure of central government by purpose of expenditure and economic category, 1965–84

	IR£ million, current prices				
	1965–66	1970–71	1975	1980	1984
Defence	14.1	22.4	67.1	176.3	262.6
Other central government services	23.3	37.9	126.3	320.9	607.8
Education	39.8	81.3	222.2	553.7	980.3
Health	15.6	42.7	213.6	697.3	1102.4
Social security and welfare	57.6	119.1	389.6	925.4	2133.9
Housing	21.9	37.0	139.1	371.3	626.0
Other community and social services	4.6	8.1	26.7	71.5	142.1
Agriculture, forestry and fishing	60.7	107.4	179.4	330.0	509.1
Mining, manufacturing and construction	15.7	32.0	82.9	261.5	361.0
Transport and communications	25.6	42.4	131.9	345.9	359.3
Other economic services	6.9	15.9	183.8	168.8	302.5
Public debt	38.0	88.6	217.4	1082.9	2367.7
Total expenditure	323.9	634.8	1980.1	5305.6	9754.6

Source: National Income and Expenditure Tables.

expenditure (Dowling, 1978; Walsh and O'Leary, 1984; Tables 1.3, 1.4). As the economy recovered from recession, however, government introduced some deflationary measures although these were generally considered inappropriate for an economy in which balance of payments deficits were of secondary importance to the prime objectives of job creation and expansion of output. They were also politically difficult to sustain.

The final coalition budget illustrated this point when its commitment to deflation contributed in no small way to a landslide victory by Fianna Fáil in the 1977 general election. The new government adopted a highly expansionary programme, creating a new Department of Economic Planning and Development to guide and promote national development. This, in itself, was a notable departure from the preceding five years when no national development programme existed, and suggested a belief in the ability of external growth impulses to transfer easily into the Irish system. A White Paper, *National Development, 1977–80*, was published in 1978, and together with a 'give-away' budget in the same year, created boom conditions within Ireland. The reheated economy, however, had been bought at the cost of rapidly building up the PSBR and the country's foreign and total debt burden. Thus, from being in the position of a net creditor nation in the early 1970s, Ireland's foreign debt rose to the equivalent of 21 per cent of GNP by 1979.

A fiscal policy of expansion boosted living standards, national output and employment. Visible benefits in the shape of higher child benefits, social security payments and enhanced medical and education facilities were all politically attractive. Unfortunately, however, much of the debt burden was created by promoting current consumption rather than by investing in long-term productive capacity. Easily available finance from international banks, especially within Europe, created an illusion that public service development was cost-free since payment could be deferred. This approach made effective government response very difficult in the more recessionary trade conditions of the 1980s.

If the Irish economy was to modernize successfully, specific policies to improve the agricultural and manufacturing base were required. State support for agriculture had been comparatively weak, but this altered in the 1960s as its growth potential was increasingly appreciated, especially within the context of the EC. The national economic programmes of the 1960s outlined some main policy objectives for the sector, although these seemed increasingly to conform to those existing under Article 39 of the Treaty of Rome. Integration into the CAP was thus comparatively easy and the perceived advantages to be gained from higher guaranteed prices, financial support from guidance funds and enhanced market outlets for farmers proved to be a major contributory factor in influencing the national level of support for membership. Thus, from 1973 to 1979, 86 per cent of the total of IR£ 1611 million in grants and subsidies received by Ireland from the EC, was allocated to farming. Optimistic forecasts prevailed and suggested a future of unprecedented demand for agriculture (NESC, 1977c).

Agricultural output increased markedly through state support, which rose to the equivalent of 41 per cent of the income arising in agriculture in 1972. The growth momentum was maintained within the CAP (Table 1.8) (Walsh, J.A., 1976; Gillmor, 1977a; Horner et al., 1984). Agricultural employment, however, continued to fall as off-farm opportunities increased and capitalization of production reduced the high levels of manpower associated with a more traditional farming system. State subsidies encouraged this transition, although Pratschke (1982) stresses the crucial role of

Table 1.8   National trends in selected agricultural indices

	Percentage change		Absolute levels (000s)
	1960–70	1970–80	1980
Area of cereals (ha)	15.0	17.1	446.5
Area of pasture (ha)	8.1	−12.4	2929.0
Cattle (no.)	25.7	16.0	6908.9
Breeding cattle (no.)	45.4	20.7	2321.8
Livestock units (no.)	5.5	11.1	5814.6
Total holdings > 2 ha (no.)	−15.3	−6.6	241.1
Average size of holding (ha)	34.0	8.6	23.7
Holdings < 20 ha (no.)	−24.1	−10.7	153.5
Holdings > 20 ha (no.)	3.4	2.3	87.6
Tractors (no.)	92.3	72.4	144.9
Fertilizer distributors (no.)	163.1	107.0	60.4

Source: Horner et al. (1984), Agricultural Statistics (1960).

higher CAP prices. These fundamentally changed the relationship between input and output prices for farming and, given preferential terms of trade, high capital investment became a notable feature of farming in the 1970s (Attwood, 1983; Boyle and Kearney, 1983). By 1976, only 6 per cent of gross output was used on a subsistence basis in comparison with over one-fifth in 1956.

By the late 1970s, however, the potential for conflict emerged between Irish interests and the CAP. Surplus production and mounting costs resulted in the EC attempting to curtail price advances and unlimited guarantees for agricultural output. Ireland strongly opposed such measures since the underdeveloped nature of its farm sector indicated a significant capacity for further increase, especially if productivity levels were to be moved closer to the European norm.

The drive for higher productivity in Ireland, however, faced fundamental structural difficulties that seemed inherent to the system. The Irish Constitution contains explicit reference to the value attached to family farms and dictates that, in general, any increases in production should be achieved through a maximum number of such enterprises. Partly as a consequence of this, although more fundamentally due to the passage of various Land Acts between 1880 and 1920, which effectively transferred land from the large landlord estates to the tenant class, Ireland has the highest proportion of owner-occupied land in the EC (92 per cent in 1977). This imparts considerable social and cultural prestige to land. Mobility of land is consequently extremely low, with annual transfer rates averaging only 3 per cent between 1950 and 1977 (Kelly, 1983). Family transfer is the dominant means of exchange, with the open market contributing only one-fifth of total transfers.

The identifiable trends towards intensification and consolidation of farming (Walsh, J.A., 1980) did not initially improve the incomes of farmers relative to other sections of the workforce (Gillmor, 1972). Benefits under the CAP, however, resulted in farm prices increasing at a rate in excess of inflation and, from 1971 to 1978, average farm incomes per family worker increased more than those for industrial workers. By 1978, parity had almost been achieved between farm and non-farm incomes (Matthews, 1984, p. 310).

Despite positive aggregate trends, modernization of farming within the context of the CAP tended to exacerbate the inequality within Irish agriculture. A price policy, by supporting output, favoured those enterprises better able to maximize production and had less impact on small-scale operations. The narrow basis on which Irish agricultural growth depended was highlighted by the farm classification system of the Farm Modernization Scheme (FMS) introduced within the CAP. By 1978, only 4 per cent of farmers participating in this scheme were classified as commercial and 18 per cent as development farmers. More than three-quarters were therefore deemed to be transitional (Cahillane and Lucey, 1983). Duality of Irish farming had emerged as a pressing problem that needed to be confronted if the agricultural community was to contribute more effectively to national development in the 1980s.

The end of the transition period in 1978 marked the high point for recent Irish farm development. Comparatively easy trade conditions and price gains were to be replaced by more competitive conditions. Readjustment would not be easy, especially for the large traditional element within farming, and would require sensitive and continued supportive policies from the national government and EC. This would not always be possible in the 1980s.

Although some preparatory changes in manufacturing policy had emerged during the 1950s, a new policy was to crystallize in 1959 within the First Programme for Economic Expansion. The Industrial Development Authority (IDA) had been established in 1949 and given statutory responsibility for the promotion of manufacturing. Industrial development grants were made available through An Foras Tionscal (AFT) while Córas Trachtála (CTT) emerged as a government body designed to foster export trade. While government agencies were therefore in place, the policies and general environment for industrial take-off needed to be changed. This was to be partly achieved in the 1960s.

Attraction of export-orientated foreign enterprise through a range of financial and fiscal incentives became the central element of the new policy (Donaldson, 1966; NESC, 1980c; 1982a). The Export Profit Tax Relief (EPTR) scheme was particularly important, although membership of the Community was also recognized as being crucial for the promotion of the country's industrial base. Success, however, demanded a more coordinated approach and to this end the IDA was reorganized in 1969 to act as an autonomous state-sponsored body with overall responsibility for administration of grants and the promotion and planning of industrial development. With its array of incentives and more efficient organizational structure, Ireland quickly emerged as one of the most attractive locations for foreign investment in Europe (Stanton, 1979; Yuill and Allen, 1980).

Comparatively little consideration was given to indigenous industry and, despite its absolute importance, no real policy emerged for import substitution activities. Adaptation and re-equipment grants of up to 35 per cent of the cost of new plant and machinery were introduced to encourage some reorientation of indigenous enterprise in the face of more competitive trade conditions. In essence, however, indigenous enterprises geared to serving the domestic market were ignored due to their perceived lack of job potential after operating for up to thirty years behind high levels of protection.

The 1960s and 1970s were decades of significant expansion for industrial employment within the Republic (Gillmor, 1982). Closures and rationalization affected this sector, but job losses were greatly exceeded by expansions and more particularly by new openings. By 1979, 242,300 were employed in manufacturing industries, an increase of 36 per cent since 1961. While expansion throughout the 1960s was common within Europe, the recessions of the 1970s made employment growth far more difficult. Continuation of the growth in Irish manufacturing employment was thus a notable achievement, and the country was the only member of the EC to exhibit such a trend during the 1970s.

While several major processes have contributed to the contemporary manufacturing performance in Ireland, the role played by government policy is considered to be of central significance (Brunt, 1988). Moore et al. (1978) substantiate this for the 1960s, when changes in government policy were considered to have generated an additional 75,000 jobs between 1960 and 1974. Grant-aided industries under the government's New Industries Programme were particularly important, and detailed surveys by O'Farrell (1975, 1984) point to their rapidly growing significance. By 1973, 45 per cent of national manufacturing employment was due to this programme, and by 1981 this had risen to 52.5 per cent.

Table 1.9 highlights the increasing role played by foreign companies, and

Table 1.9   The changing role of foreign manufacturing employment, 1973–85

Source	Employment			
	1973	1980	1985	1973–85
Britain	26,932	22,652	14,100	−12,832 (47.6%)
USA	14,935	32,563	36,500	+21,565 (144.4%)
All foreign	58,892	81,968	78,373	+19,481 (33.1%)
Indigenous	158,400	166,300	134,857	−23,543 (14.9%)
Total	217,292	248,268	209,841	− 7451 (3.4%)
% Foreign	27.1	33.0	37.3	

Source: Brunt (1988).

especially those from the United States of America, in Ireland's employment structure. As a result, the country quickly became a component in the international division of labour favoured by multinational enterprise (Perrons, 1981; see Section 2.2.2), with the vast majority of output entering global trade (McAleese, 1977). Indigenous industry performed poorly in comparison, and the success of manufacturing clearly depended on the perceived advantages of the country for foreign direct investment.

Overseas investment was primarily orientated to growth-related sectors such as light engineering (especially electronics) and chemical manufacture. This helps explain their significant increase in employment during this period (see Table 1.5). In contrast, indigenous industry was disproportionately represented in the declining sectors such as textiles and clothing. The failure of domestic-controlled industry adequately to shift emphasis into growth sectors which could compete successfully in international trade removed an essential dynamism from the domestic economy (NESC, 1983). It further enhanced dependency on foreign capital for future growth potential.

In spite of increased manufacturing employment and the continued ability of the IDA to achieve its gross job targets in the 1970s (IDA, 1972, 1979), elements of concern were emerging. A self-sustaining industrial base had not been created, and continued growth came to depend increasingly on the ability of new openings to offset job losses. As trading conditions disimproved in the late 1970s, and internal inflation and labour costs increased, foreign companies began to review more critically their branch plant operations in Ireland. Rationalization and closures became more commonplace, and the rates of closure for foreign-owned enterprises became noticeably higher than for indigenous enterprises (O'Farrell and

Crouchley, 1983). This contrasts with the position in the 1960s and early 1970s when no discernible difference existed between the two categories of ownership (O'Farrell, 1976; McAleese and Counihan, 1979). Linkages between foreign-based industry and the national economy were also weak, and the indirect creation of wealth and employment through a multiplier effect was not as great as had been anticipated. Characteristic elements of a dual economy emerged, with many companies operating as enclaves largely detached from their immediate environment (Stewart, 1976a, b). A more recent study showed that only 16.4 per cent of raw materials purchased by the non-food sector originated in Ireland (O'Farrell and O'Loughlin, 1980).

Major development in manufacturing was also translated into a significant growth of the services sector which, by 1981, accounted for over one-half of all employment. In contrast to the cyclical nature of expansion in industry, the service sector experienced steady growth throughout the period and, during the 1970s, accounted for 77.8 per cent of net new jobs created outside agriculture (Bannon, 1985). The increasing complexity of Irish society and economy, together with the rising standards of living of the growing population, favoured growth in most service sectors. Employment in marketed producer services was especially buoyant and reflected the growth of the national economy (Bannon, 1979). Private and public consumer services also developed strongly as public expenditure increased within the health and education services. Finally, increasing state involvement in the management of the economy and society accounts for a large increase in service employment, particularly in public administration and defence, as government attempted to rectify major deficiencies in the public service infrastructure (Sexton, 1982).

The growth of service employment is further emphasized by the occupational shift within the Irish economy which witnessed rapid increases in clerical, professional/technical and managerial occupations. Thus, white-collar employment increased by 20 per cent during the 1960s, and this rate doubled in the 1970s. While the trend is indicative of the developing nature and diversification of the Irish economy, it is also associated with an increase in the number of women in the workforce. In spite of this, female involvement in the labour force remained low by West European standards and relates primarily to the low participation rates among married women. In 1981 women still accounted for only 28.3 per cent of the labour force.

The changes in government policy, which favoured modernization and greater integration within the global economy, had a significant influence on the overall employment trends. After a long period of decline in the level of total employment, demand for labour stabilized in the 1960s and a small annual increase was recorded. This gathered momentum in the 1970s when the overall level of employment grew at an annual average rate of 13,000

Figure 1.3   Changes in Ireland's labour force and levels of unemployment, 1961–85 (Labour Force Surveys).

(Figure 1.3). It appeared that growth in non-farm employment had finally succeeded in more than compensating for the heavy, continued losses in agriculture. In spite of this positive trend, unemployment rates failed to adjust downwards and by 1979, 6.9 per cent of the workforce was unemployed compared with only 4.6 per cent in 1971.

Central to the movement in unemployment are major changes in the demographic characteristics of the country. Unemployment problems traditionally had been partially mitigated by two important elements which were largely removed after 1960 (Walsh, B.M., 1978). An historically low marriage rate was replaced by a more typical European pattern and, given high fertility rates, Ireland emerged as the only EC country to exhibit a constant rise in its natural rate of increase from 1961 to 1981 (see Figure 1.1). By the latter date, 74,000 births were recorded, the highest this century, and the rate of natural increase exceeded the EC average tenfold.

Traditionally, emigration had more than offset natural increase but,

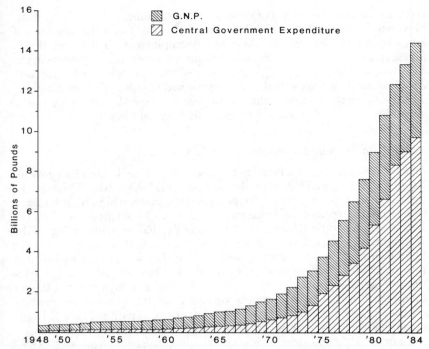

Figure 1.4   GNP and central government expenditure, 1948–84 (National Income and Expenditure Tables, Central Statistics Office).

during the 1960s, enhanced employment prospects at home, contrasting to more depressed conditions in Britain, reduced the outflow (see Table 1.6). The net result was an overall increase in population which further seemed to endorse the shift in economic policy. These trends were maintained in the 1970s but were compounded by the fact that Ireland's economic prosperity converted it into a country of net in-migration (Horner and Daultry, 1980). This was a unique state of affairs for a country that had traditionally exported its youth overseas.

There was an increase in total population in the 1960s and 1970s, particularly within the younger age-groups. Over this period, there was a rise of 55 per cent in those aged 15 to 24, and of 32 per cent among 25- to 44-year-olds. This factor, together with some increase in overall participation rates and feminization of the workforce, resulted in the labour force increasing at a rate of 2000 per annum in the 1960s and 18,000 a year during the 1970s. Expansion in the labour force therefore greatly exceeded job creation. During the period of the coalition government (1973–77), unemployment increased by over 33,000 to reach 109,000 when the new Fianna Fáil government was elected. Although unemployment had emerged as a pressing issue, the rate of increase in Ireland was lower than elsewhere in the EC. This was due to expansionary fiscal policies in Ireland which, while encouraging growth, also led to an unsustainable public finance position. The 1980s were to expose the fragility of a system based on excessive dependency on foreign capital to maintain internal growth.

1.3.3   The 1980s: the emergence of monetarism

Charles Haughey's ascendancy to the leadership of the Fianna Fáil government in 1979 coincided with the second world oil crisis. This set the international economy into a 'stagflationary' spin in which high levels of inflation and depressed market conditions were quickly imported into the Irish economy. Inflation rose to 20 per cent by 1981 as membership of the European Monetary System (EMS) failed to cushion the economy from the falling value of the Irish punt against sterling. In addition, unemployment rose to 123,000 as deterioration in labour demand coincided with a continuing increase in its supply (Figure 1.4). Full employment and higher living standards remained central objectives of the government, yet increasingly they appeared to be beyond the control of national policy. In the meantime, the financial position worsened.

Between 1978 and 1981, public sector expenditure rose from 49.6 to 69.8 per cent of GNP. This primarily reflected the rising cost of public service provision in a high-wage inflation economy and also the mounting costs of social security and foreign debt repayments (see Tables 1.3, 1.4). Further fiscal stimulus of the economy did not appear to be practical and the government was forced to acknowledge the constraints imposed on national development by the legacy of the indebtedness built up in the 1970s. Restraint and deflation appeared inevitable.

Unfortunately for national development, the two elected governments of 1981 and 1982 were of such short duration and of unstable character that no discernible policies emerged. General fiscal and economic conditions deteriorated further and by the time a new Fine Gael–Labour Coalition was elected in November 1982, the national debt exceeded GNP. 'The judgement of economic historians on Ireland's experimentation with fiscal and monetary expansion (1975–83) is (thus) likely to be very unfavourable' (Walsh and O'Leary, 1984, pp. 165–6).

The Coalition budget of 1983 introduced a severe dose of deflation and appeared to suggest a commitment to reducing inflation and controlling the balance of payments. A national economic plan, *Building on Reality*,

1984–87, offered the prospect of some growth in the economy, although no immediate fall in the high levels of unemployment was envisaged. A rupture with the full employment policy had emerged, and in future greater emphasis would be placed on the stability and value-added content of job creation, rather than on absolute levels of employment creation. Strict financial management was to be an essential element of the plan.

Unemployment continued to increase, however, and the attempt to control expenditure was an abysmal failure. Government appeared incapable of taking the unpalatable political step of cutting back expenditure, particularly on the current account. The link between government expenditure and revenue, vital for sound financial management, had been broken in the 1970s and persisted unabated into the 1980s. Current expenditure increased from 45.3 to 49.4 per cent of GNP between 1981 and 1985, despite major increases in revenue derived from taxation. In order to support public services and the rising outlay on social welfare, foreign borrowing remained unacceptably high, averaging IR£ 2000 million annually between 1984 and 1986. As a result, overall debt servicing approached 15 per cent of GNP, and the PSBR showed little improvement by 1985 (see Tables 1.3, 1.4).

The deflationary effect of the debt burden and of restraint on capital programmes severely depressed economic conditions. Such problems were not unique to Ireland, but were facing many other recently industrialized and small, open economies at the start of the 1980s. Ireland's response, however, has been less than effective as its options increasingly became constrained by indebtedness, and the lack of a coherent economic policy as distinct from a financial policy (Wrigley, 1985). While other European countries pulled out of the 1980–82 recession, Ireland has experienced only a marginal increase in its GNP in real terms since 1981. By the time of the 1987 general election, the spiral of decline associated with indebtedness and escalating expenditure on current consumption had impressed themselves sufficiently on the main parties to allow for a consensus position to be reached. Reductions in the budget deficit and government expenditure were embraced as policy objectives. During 1987, the budget deficit was reduced to 6.9 per cent of GNP compared with 8.6 per cent in 1986, while Exchequer borrowing requirements for central government purposes fell from 13.2 to 10.4 percent of GNP. This has been taken by some economic commentators to suggest that the government has finally taken the difficult political step of moving to a more balanced budget. Although some ten years behind Britain, it appeared that monetarism was about to be accepted as a panacea for the country's economic problems.

Economic recession and increasing pressures from external sources in the 1980s also began to influence the emphasis — if not the direction — of government policies with respect to both agriculture and manufacturing. After the high point of 1978, Irish agriculture became fully integrated within the CAP but subsequent modifications to the policy began to affect the sector adversely (Conway, 1986). Limitation of price advances, deemed necessary to resolve a European-scale problem, meant that Irish farmers were unable to recoup through higher prices the higher input costs resulting from inflation. In addition, quota restrictions, especially on milk output, have severely affected many smaller-scale dairy enterprises which anticipated raising their herd size and milk throughput. The real level of agricultural income and volume of net output declined in the early 1980s and, with comparatively little incentive to remain within farming, the agricultural labour force is declining at a rate which is at present almost twice the Community average.

Despite a White Paper on Land Policy in 1980 and the creation of the Council of Development in Agriculture (ACOT) to assume responsibility for education and advisory services for the sector, the complicated issues involved in securing an effective reform of land structure were virtually ignored. 'Ireland failed to introduce measures which were obviously needed . . . consequently we are left with the present configuration of Irish farming in which agricultural modernization has accentuated the emergence of a two-tier farming economy' (O'Hara, 1986, p. 51). Thus, immediately prior to the cessation of the Farm Modernization Scheme in 1983, 70 per cent of Irish farmers remained in the transitional category.

Marginalization of a majority of Irish farmers has persisted into the 1980s (Kelleher and O'Mahony, 1984). In the 1984 National Farm Survey, 57 per cent of all farms (110,000) had family farm incomes of less than IR£ 3800, which is deemed by the state to be the minimum income for a basic family unit. This indicates the potential deprivation that exists on the majority of Irish farms. Under the existing conditions of income opportunity, there were simply too many people on the land. This has to be recognized as a major policy issue.

The dilemma facing the Irish government was that to encourage movement off the land and further commercialize production would only aggravate overall levels of unemployment and exacerbate public expenditure difficulties. The National Planning Board document, *Proposals for Plan 1984–87* (1984), thus focused on the need to improve the value of output and to minimize production costs as a more effective way to enhance farm income. This was echoed in proposals by the European Commission (Commission of the European Communities, 1985a, b) which stressed the need for efficiency on existing farms while reaffirming the traditional role of the family farm unit.

Ultimate success of any agricultural policy, however, will depend on recognition of the need to incorporate agriculture within a broader policy framework. To date, the EC has tended to function in a sectoral manner, dealing with agriculture in a largely isolated context. Irish approaches to planning have also been predominantly sectoral and have exhibited little appreciation for integration between economic sectors and the environments within which they function. Recent approaches advanced by the EC, however, offer some prospect for encouraging integrated rural development as the basis for effecting farm change. These will involve greater coordination with tourism and forestry, and the provision of off-farm employment in rural areas (see Sections 3.3, 3.4). The multidimensional approach offers the best prospect for Irish agriculture, although the history of integrated planning and the conservatism of many farmers may make its application difficult. Concern with financial cutbacks will also prove problematic for a coordinated approach, since its success will be conditional on the availability of adequate funding from both the EC and within Ireland.

By the late 1970s, significant changes in the international and national economic environment necessitated a review of Ireland's industrial programme. This was undertaken by the National Economic and Social Council (NESC), which published six major reports between 1981 and 1983, most notably that by Telesis, an American consultancy group (NESC, 1982a). Telesis was highly critical of existing policy, considering that the fiscal and financial incentive package was unnecessarily generous and favoured capital formation rather than employment. Indigenous enterprise and adequate promotion of the country's natural resources were largely ignored.

In essence, government policy succeeded in attracting foreign investment and creating employment, but it failed to address the constraints which hampered further development of manufacturing within Ireland. With the economic recession of the early 1980s significantly reducing the amount of international investment, however, government was forced to tackle more urgently the constraints facing self-sustaining development within manufacturing.

A government White Paper on Industrial Policy (1984) reflected the recommendations of Telesis and the NESC (1982b), as well as recognizing some of the reorientations already stressed by the IDA in their policy goals for the 1980s (Boylan and Cuddy, 1984). Basic policy objectives were reformulated, but a discretionary industrial policy utilizing generous fiscal and financial incentives remained dominant (Ruane, 1984; Foley, 1986).

Two important differences emerged, however, between the proposed objectives and those within existing industrial policy. First, employment creation was no longer the sole objective of policy. Instead, policy should focus on maximizing net domestic value added which would itself induce additional employment through its multiplier effects. The second shift in emphasis was to focus attention on the international competitiveness of the whole industrial sector, rather than its export component. This finally recognized the value of indigenous enterprise and the major loss of employment and wealth creation through import penetration and the poor linkages of foreign plants in Ireland.

Greater selectivity of incentives became a central element in the new policy. Indigenous enterprises have been given a higher profile, and the Company Development scheme and the creation of a National Development Corporation have focused attention on the need to identify and encourage potentially successful Irish ventures. The promotion of a greater number of internationally traded industries is a clear priority and an export development scheme has been instituted to overcome weaknesses such as poor marketing and technological inadequacies. Import substitution activities have not been ignored, and a National Linkage Programme was introduced in 1985 to encourage the development of subcontracting industries.

The attraction of foreign investment must remain a high priority, however, if the required total employment levels are to be achieved. Emphasis is directed more to encouraging international growth industries, especially those which are prepared to adopt a total business development programme. Location of administration and research and development within the country, as well as production, is considered essential not only for the higher-quality employment created, but also because this enhances company stability and has potentially greater indirect benefits for the rest of the economy.

The policy aims to achieve a more integrated development pattern, both within manufacturing and between this sector and the rest of the economy, as well as between indigenous and foreign enterprise. In theory the approach appears to have great relevance for a small, open, trading economy, but in practical terms it may be difficult to implement. Integrated planning on this scale requires a long-term commitment whereas the issues of high unemployment and economic stagnation demand more immediate political responses. In such circumstances, the needs of absolute job creation, rather than of employment stability and value creation, will be hard to ignore.

The 1980s have proved to be a difficult period for Irish manufacturing and employment in this sector has declined. Stagnation of the global economy clearly affected all areas of manufacturing, with the notable exception of expanding metals and engineering (see Table 1.5). The electronics sector continued to grow, and by 1985 employed some 23,000 people and contributed one-quarter of the total value of manufactured exports (O'Brien, 1986).

Despite the decline in the amount of footloose international investment, Ireland continued to attract foreign-based development, although the high rate of new openings failed to compensate adequately for job losses. Overall decline in foreign enterprises was marginal, however, in comparison with the major erosion of indigenous industry. As a result, dependency on foreign-based employment rose to 37 per cent by 1985 (see Table 1.9). The failure of indigenous enterprise to secure a share of newer growth industries stresses the urgency of the policy modifications belatedly put into effect in the 1984 White Paper. By 1985, for example, the IDA estimated that 81 per cent of all jobs in the electronics sector were externally controlled.

In contrast to manufacturing, employment within services continued to rise, albeit at a slower rate than in the 1970s. This was due to negative multiplier effects conditional on the decline in manufacturing activities, and also to the imposition of an embargo on public sector employment. The net result of the latter was a marked decline in the rate of growth of employment in public administration and defence. Marketed producer services, however, continued to grow strongly.

Despite the increasing importance attached to the service sector, no coherent policy has emerged to guide future developments. This is a serious omission, since national policy needs to take greater account of the role of services and the importance of an information-rich environment for the creation of wealth and employment. Some recognition of the crucial need to promote services to ensure success of a more integrated development programme has appeared, however, in more recent government pronouncements (Bannon, 1985). The IDA has extended its brief to include the attraction of internationally mobile service firms, and the export of a range of technical and professional services is now recognized as an important aspect of national development. Import substitution of services currently being purchased abroad also forms part of the government strategy. While some success has been achieved in these spheres, the peripherality of the country, its relatively small population base and underdeveloped urban and physical infrastructure militate against major development. The current expenditure crisis suggests that major capital expenditure will not be forthcoming for a significant upgrading in national infrastructure.

Aer Lingus, the national airline, provides an early, and successful, example of the emergence of an internationally traded service. Established in 1936, the airline expanded rapidly after the Second World War, and by 1958 introduced a transatlantic service to complement its comprehensive series of routes to the rest of Western Europe. This helps reduce the problem of Ireland's peripherality, and generates an important source of foreign revenue. In addition to passenger and freight traffic, however, Aer Lingus offers facilities for flight crew training at Shannon and ground crew maintenance operations for other airlines. Its role in the direct and indirect promotion of the tourist industry in Ireland is also of great significance. Other state bodies, such as the ESB, have also increased their role in the arena of international services. One interesting recent development is the government decision to build an International Financial Services Centre at the Customs House Docks area in Dublin (see Section 4.6).

The growth of service employment failed to compensate for decline in other sectors of the economy, and the result was a loss of over 76,000 jobs between 1979 and 1985. In effect, the significant gains made in the 1970s were largely wiped out and no net employment growth occurred in the decade to 1985. The reorientation of the economy, however, was differentially to affect male and female job prospects. In a comparison of 1971 and 1983 employment data, Gillmor (1985b) clearly illustrates the increasing feminization of the workforce. This was almost exclusively related to the tertiary sector, most notably professional services. By 1983, however, their participation rate of 31 per cent was still well below the European average and suggests a continuation of the trend is likely, providing jobs are made available.

While total employment declined, the labour force continued to increase resulting in continued growth in unemployment (see Figure 1.3). By the end of 1986, over 250,000 were registered as unemployed, almost one in five of the workforce. Recent demographic trends contributed to the problem by emphasizing the youth component in unemployment totals (Walsh, B.M., 1985). This demanded the introduction of several direct measures to alleviate this problem such as the Youth Employment Agency in 1982 and the creation of a Youth Employment Levy to fund training and provide temporary employment. These have achieved limited success, although the scale of the problem in the present recession ensures that youth unemployment remains a pressing social and economic concern (Corcoran, 1985).

Population continued to increase during the 1980s reaching a little over 3.5 million by 1986. The rate of increase had dropped markedly, however, in spite of continued high rates of natural increase, reflecting the re-emergence of emigration as a safety-valve for Irish people faced with declining opportunities at home (see Figure 1.1). Net emigration loss from 1981 to 1985 was 75,000, but the annual rate accelerated strongly as the recession in Ireland deepened. Thus in 1985–86, an estimated net loss of 31,000 occurred in contrast to only 1000 in 1981–82. Emigration — the oldest Irish solution to the oldest Irish problem — is reasserting itself.

The year 1986 marks a significant new watershed in recent Irish economic history. For the first time in twenty-five years, total population fell. Furthermore, it is estimated that the decline will continue and in the decade to 1996 it is projected that some 242,000 people will have emigrated (NESC,

1986; Davy Kelleher McCarthy Ltd, 1987). Even this substantial loss of potential workers will not cause a fall-off in the growth of Ireland's labour force. With approximately one-half of the population under the age of twenty-five years, the growth momentum of the population is considerable and illustrates the dramatic need to reverse the recent trend of a decline in total employment (Couniffe and Kennedy, 1984). This will be difficult to achieve, since the recently elected Fianna Fáil government (1987), strongly supported by the main opposition party (Fine Gael), has made its primary policy goal the resolution of the problem of public finances. An austerity budget was introduced to cut spending and foreign borrowings, and reduce the budget deficit to 6.9 per cent. The government, in November 1987, also proposed to implement the most severe cuts (IR£ 485 million) in public spending for thirty years. This will make a tripartite national agreement worked out between the government, unions and employers in October 1987, and covering a three-year period, difficult to implement. This Programme for National Recovery reaffirms the key issue of financial control, and projects a reduction in the Exchequer borrowing requirement from 10.4 per cent to between 5 and 7 per cent, while also stabilizing the national debt/GNP ratio. Pay increases at a level not exceeding 2.5 per cent have been accepted by the unions in return for tax concessions, a commitment to maintain levels of social welfare payments and a more active programme of job creation. In manufacturing, for example, the aspiration is to employ 100,000 more people, while for the economy as a whole it is hoped to create approximately 20,000 extra jobs each year over the next ten years. This contrasts with a net job loss of 71,000 from 1981 to 1986, and is clearly an ambitious target, especially since precise mechanisms for job creation are not included in the programme. During the twelve months ending August 1987, however, Ireland's trade surplus exceeded IR£ 1000 million for the first time and exports topped IR£ 10,000 million. This can be taken as some indication of an underlying resilience to the economy and, if public finances can be effectively managed, observers are more confident that economic growth can be translated into positive employment trends.

1.4   Social policy and changing living conditions

Changes in the economic policies of the Republic have profoundly influenced the structure of Irish society which, in turn, has helped to shape the direction of economic change. Diversification of the economic base and a shift in emphasis away from primary activities have broadened the opportunities for entry into the workforce, while also encouraging the emergence of a more complex class structure. A stronger middle class has been one important consequence of growing industrialization and urbanization within

Ireland, and the demands of this group have been crucial in shaping contemporary social policy. In addition, an industrial and urban-orientated working class has emerged to replace the more traditional rural labourers. This has had major implications for living conditions and lifestyles, since the expectations of the urban workers are significantly different from the more conservative values of agricultural labourers and small farm operators. Internationalization of the economy has furthered this process of social change by introducing more cosmopolitan values into the country. These elements have almost inevitably strained the long-established understanding between the Catholic Church and government, as policies of modernization have brought Church and State into conflict over issues such as divorce and family planning. In addition, the strongly conservative role of the Church in Irish society is being questioned increasingly, especially within the growing urban centres.

Commercialization of the economy and the availability of more remunerative employment have ensured that consumerism and materialism have become integral elements of modern Irish society. Average per capita real disposable income and consumer expenditure have increased and standards of living have generally improved. Feminization of the workforce has increased the number of two-income households in the country. In addition, the increasing number of working married women has begun to break down the traditional male-orientated society, more especially in the 1980s when growing numbers of male unemployed resulted in the female partner often becoming the principal wage-earner for the family. While living standards have been increasing, however, Ireland remains one of the poorest countries within the European Community. The recession of the 1980s and current commitment to deflation suggest that the relative ranking will not show much improvement in the near future.

Government has played a principal role in creating the social infrastructure within which the quality of life in Ireland has improved. Despite recent problems, social services are well developed with respect to income per head and the degree of industrialization exhibited nationally. While growth of social services was well under way in the late 1950s, welfarism came comparatively late to Ireland and only emerged as a powerful force during the 1960s. This suggests that the advances in social service provision required a period of sustained economic growth. Certainly, Gould (1981, pp. 130–31) supports this contention and argues that Ireland's need to catch up in social welfare standards, as well as in industrial development, with its trading partners was the biggest single factor responsible for the surge in public expenditure after 1959. In addition, a powerful shift in attitudes to state involvement in welfare provision occurred. Prior to the 1960s, a strongly anti-interventionist philosophy prevailed, reflecting the position of the Catholic Church (Whyte, 1971). Given the dominant position of the Church within Irish society, McCashin (1982), for example, argues that it was only with a dilution of this anti-state ethos that substantial state intervention could occur. During the 1960s more relaxed social teachings emerged within the Church, which recognized a central role for the state in providing welfare services. This point can be overstated, but there seems little doubt that this changing philosophy complemented growing popular demand for welfare facilities.

Cultural, historical and economic changes overlapped to encourage a commitment to a form of welfare state. Political consensus also emerged to favour state involvement in social welfare matters as well as economic development. Social policy issues rarely emerged in general election campaigns, and the ideological squabbles that typified the contrasting stances taken by the Conservative and Labour parties in Britain over issues such as education, public housing and the health service (Hudson and Williams, 1986) have notably been absent within Ireland. Essentially neither major party adopted a monetarist approach and advocated cuts in expenditure on social services (Coughlan, 1984), with the result that both parties have attempted to outbid each other in the provision of social services and public expenditure has soared (see Figure 1.4). Recent problems, however, have seen the emergence of a more monetarist stance, and continued growth in welfare services is unlikely. Clear evidence of this emerged in the 1987 budget and estimates for public expenditure in 1988, both of which point to major cuts in housing, health and education services.

In the remainder of this section we examine change in the patterns and provision of housing, health and education under the direction of general policy guidelines which have emphasized the principles of universalism, professionalism and centralism (McCashin, 1982). Important advances have been made in all aspects, but they have generally failed to bring about a marked reduction in social class inequalities (Joyce and McCashin, 1982). (Redistributive social policy is far from achieving an egalitarian society and some identifiable public expenditures and policies have worsened rather than reduced the extent of inequality. Finally, a review of changes in private consumption patterns will be addressed.

1.4.1 *Housing policies and changing patterns of supply and demand*

Adequate provision of shelter has long been recognized as a basic human necessity, and the availability of housing of the right type and amount to satisfy changing demand has consequently emerged as a sensitive social, economic and political issue. Increasingly, housing has come to occupy a central position in society, effectively linking economic performance to changing conditions of lifestyle. Increases in personal incomes and the emergence of a stronger middle class have increased pressure on the government to implement policies which would ensure easier access to the housing market, and at a level which would reflect their aspirations for better living conditions. The 'catch-all' character of the dominant political parties has ensured a positive response to this pressure with little discernible difference between the approach of the various governments. Generally, they have adopted a dual approach to housing, although the emphasis has changed according to the pressures on public expenditure.

Viewed historically, the housing system has steadily improved the average standard of accommodation available. Successive census figures have shown a substantial decline in overcrowding and a significant improvement in the provision of such services as electricity, sanitation and water supply. Following independence, however, a major housing crisis existed within Ireland, especially within the larger towns and cities. A vigorous house building programme was undertaken which gathered momentum with the first Fianna Fáil Housing Act of 1932. This greatly increased state subsidies for housing development and, from 1933 to 1942, 81,000 houses were built compared with only 26,000 during the first decade of Irish independence. The housing drive could not be sustained at this level, however, and wartime shortages of raw materials and concern with a rising national debt led to a fall-off in new completions and reconstructions.

A government White Paper in 1948 reviewed previous housing policies and suggested that despite significant advances made in meeting the housing problem, an estimated 100,000 houses were still required. Subsidies to local authorities were increased to encourage public housing, while grants for private housing were also advanced. These financial incentives, together with the elements of postwar economic growth, encouraged a major increase in the building programme which peaked in 1953 (Figure 1.5). Local authority housing provided the bulk of the new units, reflecting the direct involvement of the state.

The onset of economic recession in the 1950s and the re-emergence of a severe balance of payments crisis necessitated an economy drive within the public sector, affecting housing. There was also a shift in policy towards greater encouragement of the private sector, and by 1960–61 only 22 per cent of new houses were built by local authorities. This contrasts with more than one-half in the early 1950s.

Since the start of the 1960s, the general trend in house building has been strongly upwards reflecting the growing national economy and, even more so, the changing demographic conditions. Employment in the construction industry rose significantly during the 1960s and 1970s. The initiative in meeting the increased demand for housing clearly passed to the private

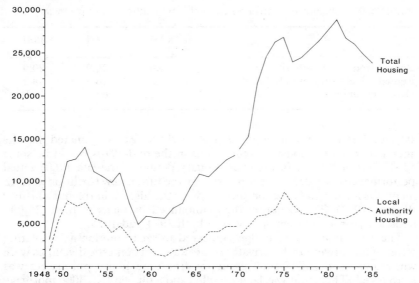

Figure 1.5   New house building in Ireland, 1948–85 (*Quarterly Bulletin of Housing Statistics*, 1970–85, and *Annual Abstract of Statistics*, 1948–70).

sector, due to a series of Housing Acts offering ever-more attractive terms for private building. This was partly due to a shift in philosophy to favouring free market forces in the housing market, but more especially was a response to facilitating owner-occupancy as the preferred form of tenancy. A commitment to local authority housing was maintained, however, to satisfy the needs of lower-income groups. By 1964, the target of 60,000 new local authority houses laid out in the 1948 White Paper was achieved, although by this date the private sector had produced almost double the initial projection of 40,000 houses.

The 1966 Housing Act emphasized privatization of the housing market. Although subsidization of local authority housing was retained, a commitment was made to facilitate tenant purchase of public housing. Rented accommodation has not been especially favoured within Ireland and the 1966 Act simply encouraged an established trend (Table 1.10). By the mid-1980s, over 70 per cent of housing units were owner-occupied, a level which is the highest within Europe.

The demographic turnabout in the 1960s, which was accentuated in the following decade, dramatically increased the rate of new household formation in Ireland and consequently placed increasing pressure on the housing

Table 1.10   Percentage of private households by nature of occupancy

	1961	1971	1981
Rented from local authority	24.6	26.0	20.9
Rented other than from local authority	17.2	10 9	8.2
Owner-occupied	53.6	60.7	67.9

system. The 1969 White Paper *Housing in the Seventies* estimated that the aggregate need for housing completions in the mid-1970s would be some 15–17,000 each year. In the expansionary period of the late 1960s actual performance exceeded these forecasts. By the time a new Coalition government was formed in 1973, completions were the highest in Ireland's history (Roche, 1982). The Coalition then announced its plans to build 25,000 houses a year — a target achieved in both 1974 and 1975.

The 1977 Fianna Fáil budget appeared to set in motion an escalating series of incentives for the private sector. Rates on domestic dwellings were withdrawn, and a IR£ 1000 grant for first-time house purchasers was introduced. This grant was later doubled and a phased IR£ 3000 mortgage interest subsidy added. By 1986, this was converted into a IR£ 2250 grant payable to the builders of new houses. Despite these escalating incentives, the recessionary conditions of the 1980s and the slower growth rate of population caused housing completions to fall away from the postwar peak of almost 29,000 achieved in 1981. New completions remained high, however, given the continued commitment in favour of site clearance and greenfield development rather than general rehabilitation. In 1985, the Coalition introduced an incentive partially to address this bias when a grant of IR£ 5000 was offered for home improvement of houses built prior to 1940. This covered 44 per cent of all houses enumerated in the 1981 Census.

Expenditure on local authority housing also increased during the early 1980s to accommodate the rising number of low-income families. This has quickly been reversed, however, and in the period 1982–87 capital spending on local authority housing was more than halved. The downward trend, moreover, is set to continue with a major reduction in government grants for local authorities projected for the late 1980s.

By the 1980s a tolerably efficient system of housing provision and allocation had emerged. Yet Baker and O'Brien (1979) strongly assert the continued inequity within the housing market and point in particular to the 'deficiencies in catering for the needs of a substantial minority of the population' (p. 3). Encouragement of home ownership via tax relief on mortgage interest payments, abolition of domestic rates and purchaser grants all favour the more advantaged sector of society. Even the tenant purchase scheme is weighted in favour of those best able to respond to the opportunities of home ownership, leaving a rump of low-income families concentrated within the more inferior local authority housing areas. The state-influenced nature of the market and the overriding concern with ownership of property, however, suggest that governments will continue to favour the better-off sections of society despite the retrogressive social character of such policies and loss of revenue to the state.

1.4.2 Welfare provision and collective consumption

The public provision of social security benefits, health care and education is recognized as being central to the achievement of social democratic principles enshrined within the Welfare State. Within Ireland, while government has become increasingly involved in the provision of these essential services, significant elements of privatization remain; this is perhaps best reflected in the health service.

A separate Department of Health was established in 1947, thus beginning the trend towards greater state participation in the control of the service. Until then, local rates had constituted the major source of finance for the provision of health facilities, the state providing approximately 16 per cent of the total costs. Under the Health Services (Financial Provisions) Act of 1947, however, the state's share increased to one-half of total costs (Hensey, 1980). Dr Noel Browne, the Minister of Health, recognized inadequacies in the provision of health services for the lower-income groups and was especially concerned with infant mortality. However, proposals under what became known as the Mother and Child Scheme to provide maternity treatment and free medical care for children up to the age of sixteen, met with opposition from the medical profession and the Church. Together, these two powerful pressure groups played a central role in rejecting this state incursion into the provision of welfare services and ultimately led to the resignation of the Minister. The Health Act of 1953 did succeed in improving access to the health services, although the anti-interventionist views of the Church made difficult the effective promotion of social welfare.

The tensions between the forces of centralization and decentralization have continued to be strong, although state involvement in the health services has increased greatly (Zimmerman, 1981). Demand for better health facilities together with high labour costs and the need for expensive infrastructure have ensured greater state involvement with this service. The net result has been a major increase in the commitment of funds to the provision of health services (see Table 1.7). All governments have contributed to this trend, which was considered quite acceptable during the expansionary decade of the 1970s (McDowell, 1982). The demand for maintaining a high level of commitment to health care was not modified, however, when recession replaced economic growth. Thus, from 1971 to 1986 employment in the health services increased from 38,250 to 63,000, and the real cost of the health services rose fifteen-fold. By 1986, 19 per cent of government expenditure was on the health services. Difficult political choices are needed if expenditure is to be reduced. Some evidence of this has appeared in the policies of the Fianna Fáil government elected in 1987. Under the 1987 budget estimates, a cut of IR£ 79 million was proposed for the health services. Of a total of 50 hospitals, 43 will face significant cuts and there are suggestions that nine units will be phased out completely. Approximately 2000 jobs are expected to be lost as a result of the financial cutbacks. These proposals have met with a great deal of opposition and will test the political skill of government to effect this programme of rationaliz-ation. The 1988 Book of Estimates, however, proposes a further cut of IR£ 88.5 million in expenditure on health services and clearly signifies the government's intention to persevere with rationalization.

Despite important developments, the number of general practitioners for every 100,000 of the population (147 in 1982) remains one of the lowest in the EC. From 1851 to 1971, general practitioners were organized in over 600 dispensary districts. Within these districts, salaried doctors were centrally located to attend the medical needs of eligible, lower-income groups, while competing freely for fee-paying patients. In 1972, however, a choice of doctor scheme was introduced, and subsequently public sector patients have operated within the same 'free market' environment as private patients. Under the scheme, doctors are paid fees for each medical card patient from a central fund. A little over one-third of the population are eligible for free medical treatment at this level. The new scheme has caused some difficulties in remoter areas as doctors' surgeries have moved into the towns, where group practices have also increased in importance. Although a centralized service may be more effective, it frequently creates problems of accessibility for those with low personal mobility (Curry, 1980).

Although the majority of the population did not have free access to medical treatment, a state-sponsored health insurance scheme was initiated in 1957 under the Voluntary Health Board. This was established primarily to deal with the cost of hospital care for those income groups not covered by the 1953 Health Act. An initial membership of 23,000 rose to some 800,000 in 1979, when compulsory health contributions were extended to these groups. This meant that all members of society became eligible for free public hospital care. In spite of this, membership has continued to rise to a little over one million in 1985 as both higher-income, and an increasing number of lower-income, groups sought to ensure better access to less-congested private and semi-private hospital facilities.

The problems of reconciling efficiency with equity in the government health programme have been highlighted in hospital planning. Major deficiencies relating to the inability of too many small hospital units to support specialist staff suggested the need for a major reorganization. The Fitzgerald Report (*Report of the Consultative Council on the General Hospitals Service*, 1968), following on from the 1966 White Paper on Health, advocated rationalization of the hospital system based on a four-tier structure. At the highest level, four regional hospitals with at least 600 beds would be located in Dublin (two), Cork and Galway and would be associated with university medical schools within those centres. A further nine general hospitals were proposed, each with no less than 300 beds, and would service a population of at least 120,000. As far as possible, nobody should live beyond a 96-km radius of a major hospital facility. The conclusion reached clearly indicated that the best service could be provided from twelve urban centres possessing specialized hospital units. Horner and Taylor (1979) confirmed that this represented a highly efficient solution to the goal of maximizing accessibility. Community health centres and district nursing homes would constitute the lowest two levels of the hierarchy, providing more routine medical treatment.

The downgrading of many county hospital facilities provoked considerable opposition, and in 1973–74 the Hospital Board proposed an eighteen-centre solution for the rationalization of hospital services, with general hospitals to function over a 48-km radius, serving a population of 100,000. In 1975 the Coalition government extended the number of general hospital centres to twenty-three. Clearly, the demotion of hospitals not listed for development was a political 'hot potato' and no party was prepared to be identified with centralization, even if efficiency parameters required such an approach (NESC, 1977b). Fianna Fáil retreated even further from the Fitzgerald Report; expenditure on health programmes increased by 70 per cent between 1977 and 1979, the decision to restrict centres of development was largely reversed and virtually all county hospitals were retained.

During the 1970s, while a commitment to large, specialized hospitals emerged as an integral element of government hospital policy, comparatively little alteration occurred to the structure of hospital provision at the lower level. Across-the-board expansion was permitted in staffing levels and equipment and contributed to the marked escalation in costs. Until 1987 no government seemed able to address the problem of spiralling costs (Tussing, 1985).

While expenditure on the health services increased from 3.7 to 7.5 per cent of GNP between 1970 and 1986, the increasing entitlement to free health services and government subsidization of the service have generally favoured the better-off. For example, the 50 per cent tax relief on Voluntary Health Insurance (VHI) contributions and government subsidies to the private health system lower the real cost of private health care. This has resulted in significant growth of private facilities while public hospitals face cutbacks. The rural and urban poor, although benefiting from advances in health provisions, are still faced with greater problems of physical accessibility. Yet standards of health have risen markedly and life expectancy has increased (Pringle, 1982, 1986).

Public expenditure on education has also increased considerably during the period of modernization of the Irish economy. This relates partly to a desire to extend equality of educational opportunity to all sections of society. But it was also a pragmatic response to the turnaround in population trends, and to a perceived need to create a better educated workforce to meet the demands of modern industrial development. Greater selectivity of investment has occurred during the 1980s, however, which is in part a response to the pressures of expenditure constraints, but also reflects an attempt to concentrate on more technologically orientated skills. This has particular relevance in the colleges and universities.

The Church has traditionally had a strong influence in Irish schools and most were the property of diocesan authorities or religious orders. An apparent marriage of convenience existed between the State and the Church; while the Church provided the facilities, the government was responsible for the bulk of the capital costs and teacher salaries. By the 1960s, however, the State adopted a more activist approach and began to impose policy and financial norms on what had previously been mainly a private educational system. Changing church attitudes to the role of state intervention, together with a decline in religious vocation in Ireland, facilitated what Coughlan (1984) refers to as 'nationalisation by stealth' (p. 41). The extent of centralization of the education services in Ireland is further emphasized by the fact that, unlike most countries, local authorities are not charged with the administration of education, apart from that of technical and vocational schools.

At the primary level, the numbers attending national schools declined until 1947, but since then has increased, more especially following the rejuvenation of the country's demographic profile in the 1960s and 1970s. In 1961, a joint OECD/Department of Education study of the Irish education system was instigated and the subsequent report, *Investment in Education* (Department of Education, 1965), advocated a programme of rationalization based on the creation of larger schools. Enrolment of 300–400 pupils was to be the preferred norm and this resulted in the closure of many small rural schools. Free school transport partially eased the problem of longer journeys to school, but social disruption of community life and adverse effects on children resulted in the rationalization programme being abandoned in 1977 (Curry, 1980). The economic arguments of centralization versus the cultural and social benefits of a dispersed primary school system remain. In aggregate, however, the number of such schools has declined from almost 5000 in the 1950s to 3400 in the mid-1980s, and closed national schools in remoter rural areas bear visual testimony to the forces of rural depopulation and centralization.

Rationalization and the preference for larger, more centrally located schools to accommodate a growing intake of children also typify the secondary sector. Enrolment increased from only 45,000 in 1945 to 320,000 by the mid-1980s, and placed great demands on the provision of adequate numbers of qualified teachers and facilities within the schools. The introduction of free, post-primary education in 1967 significantly influenced this positive trend, since it allowed greater satisfaction of educational aspirations to be brought within the reach of a wider spectrum of society. In addition, free transport was also made available for post-primary pupils living more than 4.8 km from the nearest school, and this has helped to offset the cost disadvantages for lower-income groups. New community and comprehensive schools have also been built in an attempt to combine vocational courses with more academic subjects. This replaced the traditional demarcation of such curricula between vocational and secondary schools in Ireland.

MacKeogh (1983) suggests that prior to the 1960s, the function of Irish education was generally to provide moral, religious and intellectual training, but modernization led to education being perceived as having a role in providing the labour requirements of economic development. This is reflected, above all, within the tertiary division of education. Teacher training colleges and the five university colleges have all increased their intake to meet the demand for places and to satisfy the more diversified employment market. The belief that Ireland lacked an adequate supply of suitably qualified people with the technical proficiency to facilitate economic development also led to the creation of nine Regional Technical Colleges (RTCs). These would provide technical courses and would be located in areas previously unserviced by higher education. A more effective and dispersed resource base of skills has therefore been created and acts as a stimulus to economic development. Continued belief in the need for a more technologically orientated education system has led to increased pressure on the established institutions of higher education to give more emphasis to science-based courses, to the comparative detriment of the liberal arts. Funding reflects this preference, especially within the context of expenditure cutbacks.

As in housing and health care, expansion of education facilities and opportunities have not removed inequities within the system. The 1965 report, *Investment in Education*, pointed to differences in educational participation rates among different socioeconomic groups; twenty years later, the same problems persist. Achievement levels of working-class children continue to fall below those of the children of higher socioeconomic groups (Breen, 1986). Recent research has also indicated that children of poor parents are ten times more likely to drop out of school after the primary level than children of better-off parents. Very few of the former group obtain a Leaving Certificate (Breen, 1984; Whelan and Whelan, 1984). Discrimination on entry to some secondary schools, which are able to select pupils on the basis of fees and/or ability, further weakens the option for many working-class children to avail themselves of better quality education and thereby to escape the poverty trap. For example, a survey of youth unemployment has indicated that the sons of semi-skilled and unskilled manual workers have a one in four probability of being unemployed. The probability drops to one in fourteen for the children of the professional-managerial classes (Whelan and Whelan, 1984). Youths who drop out of the education system are at serious risk of being unemployed, and often for a long period of time. Thus, a National Manpower Survey in 1983 indicated that 43 per cent of those with no qualifications remained unemployed one year after leaving school (National Planning Board, 1984). The large number of unqualified and unemployed young people is a pressing social problem.

Elitism is carried further into higher education, with only 1.2 per cent of children of unskilled workers and 3.9 per cent of those of skilled manual workers having attended tertiary colleges in 1981. The comparable figure for professional classes was 38 per cent. Within this minority, 67.9 per cent of the total university intake belongs to families of upper socioeconomic groups, while only 15.7 per cent comes from lower-income groups (Clancy, 1982). Establishment of the RTCs has helped to remedy this inequity to some degree, the comparative percentage figures for these institutions being 39.5 and 30.8. This suggests that decentralization has made education accessible to a more geographically and socioeconomically varied population. In general, however, there seems little doubt that the system of educational financing favours the middle classes (Tussing, 1978). Egalitarianism has therefore by no means been the strongest outcome of the creation of the Irish welfare system, especially where some of the central institutions and programmes help to exacerbate or sanction existing inequities. The political and economic muscle of the middle classes clearly finds expression within a government system that exhibits little tradition of socialist principles.

Similar to the health and education systems, the provision of social insurance and assistance has been upgraded since the Social Welfare Act of 1952 laid the foundation for the present system of welfare benefits. Initially, benefits were comparatively small, but enormous strides were achieved from the 1960s onwards, with new services and benefits appearing such as a child allowance scheme (1966) and free travel for old-age pensioners (1967). Real value of payments also continued to rise and the coverage of the social insurance system extended to 85 per cent of the labour force by 1979. Social welfare payments have continued to rise in the 1980s and, given the scale of the social crisis, it is difficult to see how this can be checked. The number of beneficiaries of social welfare rose from 20 to 37.5 per cent of the population between 1966 and 1985, while the cost, as a proportion of GNP, doubled in a decade to 14 per cent in 1985. This is another dilemma for central funding; if expenditure is not to increase then priorities have to be reassessed for a sector of society who are already experiencing declining standards of living.

Despite a high level of expenditure on social policy, poverty remains a real issue in Ireland. Several studies conducted in the early 1980s concluded that approximately one-fifth of the population lived in some form of poverty (Ó Cinneide, 1980; Kennedy, 1981; Joyce and McCashin, 1982). It has been recently estimated that at least 811,000 people in the Republic live in poverty (Commission on Social Welfare, 1986). Existing social welfare programmes have reduced the extent of serious poverty, yet the patterns of deprivation are ominous, especially within the current climate of reductions in state expenditure. Certainly, the neo-liberal position advanced in Britain to reprivatize the social services or to introduce more effective charges for health services is seen as an option worthy of consideration within Ireland. Major cutbacks in the provision of education and health care are already under way, and despite promises to the contrary, it is difficult to see social welfare benefits retaining their real value as laid out in the Programme for National Recovery. The late 1980s are likely to be a bleak time for the social services and the weaker members of society who depend disproportionately on their availability.

1.5 Patterns of private consumption

Private consumption patterns have changed markedly during the postwar period in response to a commercialization of the economy which brought with it enhanced purchasing power and a desire for changes in personal lifestyles and living conditions (Table 1.11). While total personal expenditure has increased significantly, personal taxation has risen disproportionately, especially since the 1970s, and has impacted adversely on consumer spending power during the current recession.

Expenditure on food, although declining as a proportion of total personal

Table 1.11   Expenditure of personal income in Ireland, 1953–84

| | Percentage of total expenditure | | | | |
	1953	1960	1970	1979	1984
Food, beverage and tobacco	52.9	49.9	33.7	34.8	34.0
Food and non-alcoholic beverage	37.3	34.5	26.7	22.6	20.8
Alcoholic beverage	7.8	7.8	10.4	9.2	9.3
Tobacco	7.8	7.6	6.0	3.1	3.9
Clothing and footwear	12.0	9.9	9.5	6.3	4.6
Fuel and power	4.7	4.6	3.8	4.3	4.6
Rent	4.9	5.7	5.8	4.4	5.2
Household equipment and services	9.8	11.0	12.2	6.3	4.5
Durable household goods	4.9	5.5	7.2	4.7	2.9
Transport and communication	6.6	7.8	8.7	11.0	9.4
Recreation, entertainment and education	4.4	5.3	4.8	8.0	6.9
Miscellaneous	3.9	5.3	5.3	7.4	6.1
Tax on personal wealth and income	5.1	5.3	11.1	17.6	25.2
Total	100.0	100.0	100.0	100.0	100.0
Total personal expenditure (IR£ million)	408	525	1,294	6,275	12,379

Source: National Income and Expenditure Tables.

outlay, remains the largest item. Dairy products, meat and potatoes have traditionally formed a major element of the national diet, although entry into the European Community and integration within a wider trading network have resulted in the availability of a greater range of food products. The critical dependence on the potato for sustenance by the bulk of the rural population, which resulted in the great famines of the mid-nineteenth century, is very much a thing of the past. In fact, a high proportion of potatoes consumed in Ireland is now imported. There is no doubt that, in general, the Irish population are well fed, their average daily calorie intake being 163 per cent of that required for a healthy diet. This is one of the highest levels in the industrial world.

The role of the pub in Irish social life is clearly reflected in the comparatively high expenditure on alcohol. Neighbourhood bars and rural pubs are almost ubiquitous to the Irish landscape, and their dual function as a focal point for social interaction or entertainment makes them attractive for both locals and tourists. Consumption of stout continues to dominate alcohol sales, although sales of lager, spirits and wine have increased strongly. This is partly the result of a liberalization of Irish society, which has seen greater numbers of females within licensed premises, but is also due to what some consider to be increasing sophistication of the growing middle class.

Within the home, purchases of labour-saving equipment and services have increased. This reflects both the increasing number of married women entering the workforce, but also a desire by those remaining at home to ease their household duties, thereby contributing to improvements in their personal quality of life. Washing machines, refrigerators, vacuum cleaners and deep freezers have become increasingly prevalent within Irish households. The failure of the economy to pull out of the 1980–82 recession has particularly affected expenditure on these items, especially within the context of high unemployment and deflationary policies. A 'self-service' economy has been boosted by this environment, and greater shared responsibility for household work has been assumed. This, however, is still in its infancy in Ireland, which remains a male-orientated society. Nevertheless, social and economic forces are at work to achieve a greater degree of equality between the sexes, both within and outside of the home (Hannan and Katsiaouni, 1977).

A traditional low level of personal mobility and a well-integrated kinship system operating throughout the large rural areas have resulted in much of Irish life revolving around the local community and the extended family. This continues to be the case in the more rural areas, and especially within the Gaeltacht, or Irish-speaking communities, that are located primarily along the western seaboard. These relatively restricted areas are vital outposts of traditional Irish culture and are of major importance for the national identity. Government subsidies encourage the preservation of the language within these areas, and also help to maintain standards of living through job creation (see Section 3.7.3). Elsewhere, lifestyles are being modified substantially, especially within the more urbanized areas. The establishment in 1960 of Telefis Eireann, the Irish television network, has been one of the most powerful agents of change; it transmits into almost every household values largely determined by external sources. New attitudes are being framed, especially among the young, and parish and family identities are being modified. Certainly, the role of the Catholic Church as the arbitrator of social values has been reduced by new media forms.

Car ownership has increased from less than 100,000 at the end of the Second World War to some one million at present. Despite a vehicle ownership rate of only 0.26 per capita, which lags substantially behind that of other north-west European economies, personal mobility has increased.

While private transport has improved, public transport provision has been adversely affected; the rail network has been halved since independence and major rationalization has occurred in public bus routes. Rural areas have been particularly affected as part of the spiral of decline associated with rural depopulation. Access to personal transport has thus become almost essential for those living within many rural communities. Availability of a car, however, only partly solves the problems of family mobility. The head of the household is facilitated in the journey to work, but the remainder of the family is constrained by the removal of the car for much of the week. Compounding this problem has been the increasing centralization of service provision on towns. The closure of local shops and the increasing tendency for supermarket developments to occur on the peripheries of larger population centres (which assumes access to a car) can make even basic shopping problematic (Cawley, 1986). Similar problems arise for the 'transport poor' within towns, although the compact nature of Irish towns and the recent attempts to revive town-centre shopping facilities suggest that the degree, if not the type, of problem is different (Parker, 1980b).

This increased prosperity resulting from economic modernization finds expression in greater expenditure on recreation. A greater range of restaurant facilities now attracts a growing proportion of Irish people, especially the younger generation. In addition, a variety of outdoor sports are played throughout the year and still attract a large number of direct and indirect participants, despite the lure of television. Above all, however, the car has extended recreation possibilities for many families. In a study of Dublin city and county residents, two-thirds of the respondents undertook day trips to coastal or inland areas during summer weekends (Mawhinney, 1975).

Approximately one-half of the Irish population takes an annual holiday, and 60 per cent of the main holidays are spent within Ireland. This latter percentage is likely to increase as income availability restricts the choice of holiday to visits to friends and family within the country. Domestic tourism in 1986 involved 3.2 million trips and was valued at IR£ 217 million. This contrasted with an external tourist revenue of IR£ 476 million from 2.5 million visitors. Overseas holidays have become more popular among those who have enjoyed rising real incomes. The package holiday industry, in particular, has been instrumental in promoting holidays 'to the sun', and given the vagaries of the Irish weather, a convincing argument appears to have been made. Reduced economies of scale can be passed on to the Irish consumer compared, say, to those offered by British tour companies, reflecting the smaller market and high transport costs. Thus, for many Irish working-class families, overseas holidays remain a vision conjured up by the media rather than a practical option.

1.6 The changing face of Irish politics

The party system in Ireland is possibly unique in post-1945 Europe in that the two dominant parties, which have consistently polled at least 80 per cent of the vote since the 1960s, do not reflect either social or economic cleavages within the country. The basis of the contemporary party system has its roots firmly established within the Civil War fought over the ratification of the Treaty which established the Irish Free State. For more than a generation, the bitterness of this conflict ensured a polarization of Irish politics around constitutional matters, and largely ignored social and economic considerations.

The present Fianna Fáil party, which was organized in 1926, has its roots in those who principally opposed ratification of the Treaty, which effectively divided the island into two political entities. Supporting the Treaty and forming the government for the first decade of the state's history were Cumann na nGael, the forerunners of Fine Gael, which was reorganized into its present form in 1933. the Fianna Fáil party therefore claims to be the more nationalist and, on achieving government in 1932, it applied nationalist policies to the economy. This found support from factory workers and small farmers who stood to gain most from an attempt to achieve self-sufficiency. In addition, the party's attack on housing problems boosted its popular support among both these sectors of society, which continue to form the basis of its electoral support. Settlement of the dispute with Britain and maintenance of free trade, however, appeared more central for Fine Gael, and this attracted support from the merchant class and wealthy farmers. While some claim is made, therefore, that Fine Gael represents the conservative element in Irish society, the ideological differences today between the two parties in matters of social and economic development are not significant. In no way could Fianna Fáil be considered a party of the Left as it could perhaps partially claim to be in the 1930s.

Despite the existence within Ireland of comparative poverty, high unemployment and class distinction, the Labour Party has never emerged as a powerful force. The conservative rural vote, the strong influence of the Catholic Church, a property-owning small-farm economy and the absence of an urban-industrial proletariat all worked against a socialist party. In any event, the popularist, national policies of Fianna Fáil appeared to satisfy the immediate aspirations of the working class.

The general election results for the postwar period are shown in Table 1.12. Ireland's voting system is based on proportional representation within multi-seat constituencies (Paddison, 1976; Parker, 1986). First preference votes provide a general indication of party support, but transfer of votes within constituencies proves critical for the final seat count. In the 1980s,

Table 1.12   General election results, 1944–87

| | Number of seats and percentage of first preference votes | | | | | | | |
| | Fianna Fáil | | Fine Gael | | Labour | | Others | |
	Seats	Vote	Seats	Vote	Seats	Vote	Seats	Vote
1944	76	48.9	30	20.5	12	11.5	20	19.1
1948	68	41.9	31	19.8	19	11.3	29	27.0
1951	69	46.3	40	25.7	16	11.4	22	16.6
1954	65	43.4	50	32.0	19	12.0	13	12.6
1957	78	48.3	40	26.6	12	9.1	17	16.0
1961	70	43.8	47	32.0	16	11.6	11	12.6
1965	72	47.8	47	33.9	22	15.4	3	2.9
1969	75	45.7	50	34.1	18	17.0	1	3.2
1973	69	46.2	54	35.1	19	13.7	2	5.0
1977	84	50.6	43	30.5	17	11.6	4	7.3
1981	78	45.3	65	36.5	15	9.9	8	8.3
1982	81	47.3	63	37.3	15	9.1	7	6.3
1982	75	45.2	70	39.2	16	9.4	5	6.2
1987	81	44.1	51	27.1	12	6.4	22*	22.4

* Progressive Democrats 14 seats (11.8%); Workers' Party 4 seats (3.8%).

for instance, the formation of government has often depended on decisions made regarding transfers to elect the final member from a few marginal five-seat constituencies. This is causing some concern with the system since it appears to give undue weight to what are often the most marginal of votes.

Fianna Fáil has largely dominated government since 1945, yet on only one occasion has the party obtained more than one-half of the first preference votes. No other single party approached the popular support of Fianna Fáil until the 1982 election, and thus Fine Gael, the second largest party, has had to seek support from the Labour Party to enter government. With the gradual erosion of small parties up to 1961, elections have generally revolved around these three main parties. The marriage of Fine Gael and Labour in coalition is ideologically surprising, but a pragmatic response to achieve power. The conservative inclinations of the more dominant partner are therefore somewhat muted by Labour portfolios for key ministries such as health, housing and social welfare. In this context ideological differences between postwar governments have been marginal in social and economic matters, occupying a central position within the political spectrum. Consensus politics have also frequently emerged on several key issues such as entry into the EC, international neutrality and the recent acceptance of the Single European Act. Ratification of the Anglo-Irish Agreement did cause some problems for the more republican Fianna Fáil but, even here, acceptance has been general.

The Anglo-Irish Agreement represents an important and symbolic breakthrough in the relationships between the Republic, Britain and Northern Ireland. Since the political division of the island in 1921, the majority Protestant community in the six north-eastern counties of Ulster have fervently expressed their separate identity, while Republican communities on both sides of the border reject division and seek reunification as a dominant goal. Consensus within the Agreement between British and Irish governments therefore reflects a growing and deeper awareness in the Republic of the complexity of the sociopolitical arena of Northern Ireland. The eruption and continuation of violent conflict in Northern Ireland since 1969 have forced all political parties to reassess carefully their long-established and often diverging ideological positions in relation to 'the north'. The long-term goal of getting all the people of Ireland to agree by peaceful means to embrace a single island state remains a central policy objective of most southern political parties. However, there is now a deeper appreciation of how deeply entrenched are Unionist fears about such an eventuality. In the middle term, therefore, strategies of governments in the south are geared mainly to achieving as much social, economic and political progress as possible for the minority community in the north, while protecting and developing the well-being of society within their own country.

Since the 1970s some interesting developments have changed the character of Irish politics. With the emergence of Garret Fitzgerald as the new leader of Fine Gael in 1977, the party acquired a leader who appeared to possess the charisma and political vision to combat effectively the long tradition of popular leaders within Fianna Fáil. A clash of personalities became inevitable with the succession of Charles Haughey to lead Fianna Fáil in 1979 but, while the polarization of individuals envigorated political debate, it has often detracted from the real issues. On forming a coalition in 1982, however, Fine Gael achieved its highest ever level of electoral support. The image of a traditional conservative party was changing and was reflected in what became known as 'Garret's crusade' whereby attempts were made to adjust the Constitution through referenda on divorce and abortion, and by legislation on family planning, which indicates a shift in party policy to reflect the interests of the growing younger, urban and middle-class voter.

At the same time new elements appeared within the political system. The Labour Party had traditionally failed to attract significant urban working-class support but, in the 1980s, The Workers' Party emerged to secure a rising share of this vote. This party was formed after the split in Sinn Fein in

1969 between the Provisional and Official wings of this republican movement designed to effect a reunification of Ireland. Official Sinn Fein has
gradually transformed itself into a far more centralist, Marxian-based party
and retitled itself the Workers' Party in 1982. This has threatened the role of
the Labour Party as the mouthpiece for the working class in Ireland, and is
further reflected in the election of independent members of the Dáil
(Parliament) from inner-city constituencies. The lines of political debate
have been further complicated by the emergence of yet another centre-right
party, the Progressive Democrats, formed in 1986 by Desmond O'Malley
after his expulsion from Fianna Fáil. The Progressive Democrats have
attracted dissidents from both major parties and in the 1987 election gained
14 seats and polled almost 12 per cent of first preference votes. A proliferation of parties and the emergence of minority and unstable governments
are the last thing needed by the national economy, but the ideological
similarity expressed by the dominant parties for the past two generations
inevitably meant there was ample room for alternatives to appear.

Although the Labour Party is politically comparatively weak, the trade
union movement is strong with two-thirds of employees in the Republic
affiliated to the Irish Congress of Trade Unions (ICTU). Increasingly, the
ICTU and the employers' counterpart, the Federated Union of Employers
(FUE), have been brought into discussion with government to help shape
national policy via national understandings on wage agreements and social
and economic policies to benefit the workers and achieve national growth.
The agricultural sector is represented by two powerful bodies, the Irish
Farmers Association (IFA) and the Irish Creamery Milk Suppliers Association (ICMSA), and their lobbying in Dublin and Brussels has direct bearing
on the shape of national policy as it affects agriculture.

Many pressure groups have emerged in recent years in response to issues
such as environmental protection, pollution, the Irish language and the
national heritage, and to more specific areas such as revitalization of the
inner city in Dublin, and the building of an international airport in County
Mayo. Environmental issues have not traditionally held a high profile in
Ireland, largely due to the underdeveloped nature of the economy and the
overriding concern with job creation. This has been partially modified in
more recent years as toleration of environmental degradation has declined
and stricter planning controls applied to development proposals. An
Taisce, an organization concerned with environmental protection, has a
current membership of some 5000, although recession and rising unemployment have reacted adversely on its paid-up membership. Green politics
has yet to make any significant impact within Ireland, however, and
although a Green Alliance was formed to contest some Dáil seats in the 1987
general election, the fragmentary nature of the Alliance, poor funding and a

lack of coherent policies resulted in an extremely weak performance at the polls.

Talking and politics have long been — and still remain — an integral part of the Irish national character. Individualism, in particular, is cherished within the country, although this makes effective government planning difficult to implement. Increasingly, therefore, there appears to be a need for the populace to accept a more disciplined response to political leadership if government policy is to be translated into effective action. The current economic crisis and problems over public expenditure clearly emphasize the importance of a more responsible interaction between government and people.

TWO

The Regional Expression of Ireland

2.1 Introduction

Even in a country as small as Ireland (70,000 km^2), there exists considerable internal diversity of landscape, culture and socioeconomic development. In particular, marked differences have traditionally been recognized between what is broadly referred to as the west as opposed to the east although, more accurately, the major regional division lies between the north-west and the south-east. This has been the focus of much debate over the mechanisms best suited to remove long-established geographical imbalances. An overriding concern with the promotion of national development, however, has generally had greater priority than regional matters. This was especially the case in the formative decades of the State's existence, and has resurfaced as a priority during the economic recession of the 1980s, following a brief interlude of enhanced regional planning in the 1970s.

The twenty-six counties and the five county boroughs form the basic administrative units of the country and have responsibility for local government and planning. However, as practical units for planning for an increasingly complex society, their boundaries are unnecessarily restrictive. Some attempts were, therefore, made in the 1960s to recognize the need for larger planning units within which a greater degree of coordinated planning would be possible.

The Local Government (Planning and Development) Act of 1963 established the legal basis for physical planning, but this focused primarily on urban development and not on the areas of social and economic development. Some provision for coordination of local plans was made, however, and it was hoped that this could act as the basis for coordinated national development. Despite the establishment of nine planning regions in the following years (Figure 2.1), an effective intermediate tier of regional administration has not emerged. Although the Industrial Development Authority (IDA) uses these official planning regions as a basic spatial unit, the National Economic and Social Council (NESC, 1976) has identified some 200 public organizations which are involved in various aspects of regional development. The majority of these do not operate within this defined regional context, and the lack of territorial consistency makes data

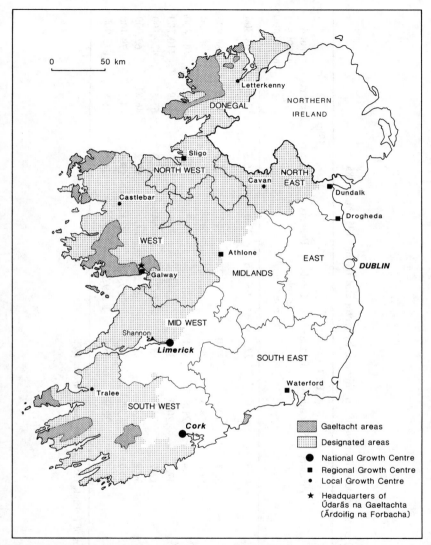

Figure 2.1   Planning regions, designated areas, the Gaeltacht and proposed growth centres.

analysis extremely difficult and coordinated planning almost impossible (O'Neill, 1971; Paddison, 1983; Johnson, 1987). With an extremely strong

Table 2.1 Percentage distribution of employment by sector and region, 1951 and 1985

Planning region	1951				1985			
	Primary	Secondary	Tertiary	Total employ-ment (no.)	Primary	Secondary	Tertiary	Total employ-ment (no.)
North-West/Donegal	63.3	14.0	22.7	98,236	22.0	26.8	51.2	58,300
West	68.6	10.4	21.0	126,624	34.1	25.3	40.6	86,900
Mid-West	51.6	18.5	29.9	111,712	20.7	31.7	47.6	96,000
South-West	44.4	21.8	33.8	188,568	19.2	28.3	52.5	160,800
South-East	47.4	20.0	32.6	134,981	21.6	31.5	46.9	110,700
East	11.7	34.9	53.3	367,565	4.4	30.0	65.6	420,100
North-East	50.2	22.5	27.2	82,630	24.0	29.2	46.8	62,000
Midlands	60.2	15.5	24.3	109,406	26.3	29.6	44.1	79,100
State	41.5	22.9	35.6	1,219,722	15.7	28.5	55.8	1,073,900

Source: Census of Ireland, 1951; *Labour Force Survey*, 1985.

tradition of local and county identities set against a background of growing centralization at the national level, regional considerations remain under-emphasized within Ireland. Yet, this is an important dimension for evaluating effectively social, economic and political changes within the country. This chapter sets out to examine such changes.

2.2 Regional variation in economic activities, employment and population

2.2.1 Regional development under protectionism

At the time of the 1951 Census, the sectoral distribution of employment among the planning regions revealed the underdeveloped status of much of the country (Table 2.1). In the western regions and the Midlands, over half the employed population still depended on the primary sector, reflecting the paucity of alternative employment opportunities. Only in the East region, centred around Dublin, was there a more diversified economic base, with dependency on agriculture being substantially below the national average. This regional pattern evolved in relation to three dominant conditions: the historic legacy of British colonialism, the physical and human environment and, finally, the influence of contemporary economic policy and market forces.

The regional character of Irish agriculture is strongly rooted in the country's colonial history (Duffy, 1980). By the late seventeenth century, British capital interests in Ireland had succeeded in creating a well-defined land-owning élite. The more fertile lands of east Munster and Leinster proved particularly attractive for the development of large estates orientated to the commercial dictates of trade in grain and cattle between Britain and Ireland. In contrast, the landscape of the far west is more rugged and the soil less fertile, much of the land being raised or blanket bog with a low carrying capacity for agriculture. Less opportunity for commercial farming, together with geographical isolation from Dublin and Britain, caused absentee estate owners in such regions to opt out of farming and sublet land as a means of achieving a suitable return on their property. A multiplicity of small peasant holdings therefore emerged in an environment of limited physical opportunities and a poorly developed urban base. The historical legacy and the inverse relationship between farm size and soil quality lie at the base of the regional definition of agriculture that emerged in the post-independence era (Freeman, 1965; Walsh, J.A., 1976).

The creation of a land-owning peasantry and the endorsement of the central role for the family farm did little to change the nature and regionalization of agriculture in post-independence Ireland. If anything, the attempt to create a more self-sufficient economy and the protectionist policy which disrupted trade in the 1930s emphasized the primary contrasts between the south-east and the west/north-west (Stamp, 1931; Freeman, 1945).

Industry was poorly represented in the majority of regions, the dictates of the colonial system and the inadequate resource base contributing to its failure to develop outside the East. Only in this region did industrial development occur on a significant scale, relating to the activities of its port and its dominant market position within the national economy. This region, together with outliers of manufacturing around the port cities of Cork and Waterford, accounted for almost 70 per cent of national manufacturing employment in 1926. What little industry occurred in the remaining regions was generally craft orientated or based on food processing.

Under the policy of protection, concern was expressed regarding the need to effect some spatial redistribution of manufacturing from the dominant core region. Few objective criteria were established to guide such development, apart from the aim of securing a better match between employment opportunities and regional population distribution. Far from accelerating a regional dispersal of manufacturing, the initial policies, designed to promote national development, further emphasized the large port-city regions of the east and south coast, where the majority of the population was concentrated, the infrastructure best developed and prevailing standards of living created a higher than average demand for consumer goods. Some state-sponsored industry was located in the more rural areas, but apart from areas surrounding major cities, industrial development was small scale and highly diversified. Regional uniformity rather than differentiation was typical of the early Irish industrial landscape.

Comparatively little regional variation existed with respect to service employment. The nature of the rural society in, and the poor industrial base of, most regions generated comparatively weak multiplier effects for the tertiary sector. Social services had yet to emerge as a high national priority and the paucity of producer services reflected the underdeveloped nature of the economy. The East region, however, was distinctive, for the tertiary sector dominated regional employment. As a former colonial administrative centre and capital of the new state, the control activities of government, amplified by trading and financial functions, resulted in a polarization of service provision in Dublin. By 1951, 45 per cent of the country's service employment was located in this region.

In 1952, the existence of a regional problem was recognized officially with the passage of the Undeveloped Areas Act. This clearly established a marked spatial divide within the country between an undeveloped west and a somewhat more prosperous east and south-east. Although originally defined to promote industrial development, its relevance as a basic divide between contrasting farming systems ensured that it was used also to designate areas in need of special agricultural assistance.

Agricultural employment continued to fall throughout the 1950s in all the regions, and particularly acutely in poorer regions with a high labour content of farming. Poor development prospects for agriculture in these areas resulted in surplus labour being released as farm owners endeavoured to maintain living standards. Less severe problems were experienced in the richer agricultural areas, although even here increased mechanization inevitably resulted in a further reduction of farm labour.

The exodus of labour from the land and the appreciation of a need for an alternative employment base in the western regions prompted the introduction of a new locational incentive for manufacturing under the 1952 Undeveloped Areas Act. This regional dimension to the policy of promoting manufacturing, however, was gradually eroded in the latter half of the 1950s as governments became increasingly concerned with inadequate national growth performance. As a result, grant incentives were gradually extended to industrialists who were prepared to locate anywhere in Ireland. A differential was maintained in respect of the maximum grant levels payable which favoured Undeveloped Areas but, by and large, there was considerable regional uniformity in incentives by the end of the decade. This aspatial approach to development had clearly been influenced by a shift in state policy to encouraging foreign investment. Any attempt to enforce too radical a spatial limitation on such investment might have resulted in rejection of Ireland as a production base for export markets. In total, grants were approved for the creation of approximately 6000 jobs in the 1950s (Gillmor, 1982).

A regional approach to the development of manufacturing, albeit diluted, did result in some decentralization of new projects. In aggregate, however, the success was very limited since many of the new projects remained undercapitalized, were concerned with the domestic market and had comparatively little dynamism. Furthermore, the inducements generally failed to deflect most development away from the established industrial regions and the larger towns (O'Neill, 1971). Dublin and its adjacent counties therefore continued to dominate manufacturing trends in the 1950s (O'Farrell, 1972). Finally, many craft-orientated industries located within the regions were coming under increased pressure from rising costs and import penetration of standardized goods. The net result was that the small net gains in national manufacturing were strongly focused on the more favoured regions. In contrast, employment fell in the weaker regions.

In the period 1926–61, spatial inequity within manufacturing increased.

62   *Ireland*

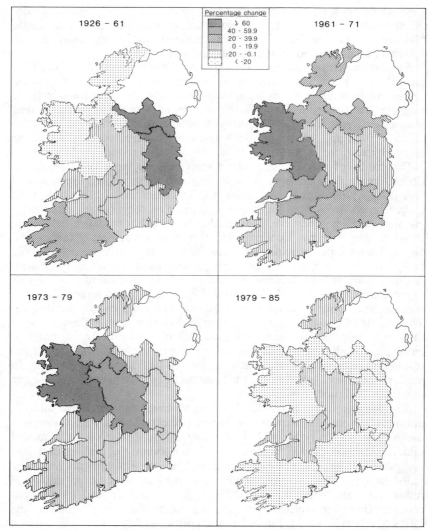

Figure 2.2   Regional manufacturing change, 1926–85 (Census of Population and Labour Force Surveys).

The Dublin region doubled its base of manufacturing employment and increased its share of national industrial employment from 40 to 53 per cent (Gillmor, 1982). In contrast, apart from the adjacent and urbanized North-

Table 2.2   Regional percentage share of national population, 1926–86

Planning region	1926	1951	1961	1971	1981	1986	Percentage change 1926–86
Donegal	5.1	4.4	4.0	3.6	3.6	3.7	−15.1
North-West	4.3	3.4	3.1	2.6	2.4	2.3	−34.8
West	11.5	10.2	9.7	8.7	8.3	8.3	−14.3
Mid-West	9.9	9.4	9.3	9.1	9.0	8.9	6.7
South-West	17.3	15.8	15.9	15.6	15.3	15.2	4.2
South-East	12.2	11.5	11.4	11.0	10.9	10.9	6.5
East	23.0	30.0	32.2	35.7	37.5	37.7	95.1
North-East	7.1	6.4	6.1	5.8	5.6	5.6	− 5.8
Midlands	9.6	8.7	8.5	7.8	7.5	7.4	−11.1

Source: Census of Population, 1926–86.

East, all other regions declined or grew more slowly than the national rate of manufacturing change (Figure 2.2). Polarization of manufacturing activities had thus been accentuated rather than reduced, which clearly called for a new policy package.

The contrasting trends within manufacturing were largely replicated in the tertiary sector during the 1950s. Polarization of industrial development in Co. Dublin and its adjacent area resulted in a positive multiplier effect for services, which was reinforced by continued growth of government employment. Depressed conditions in agriculture, and the erosion or slow growth of industry elsewhere in the country, translated itself into a general decline of service employment. By 1961, the East controlled 60 per cent of all office workers in the Republic (Bannon, 1979) and was an important element in the continued prosperity of the capital region.

The availability of employment directly impacted on regional population trends, especially in view of an absolute and relative decline of population over much of Ireland (Figure 2.3, Table 2.2). Population losses were particularly severe in the more western and agriculturally dominated regions and reflected the migration of large numbers who saw little opportunity for self-advancement in their depressed communities. While many left Ireland, large numbers still followed a long-established internal migratory flow which focused on the Dublin region. The enhanced employment prospects of the capital city were particularly attractive to the younger and more enterprising, and further enhanced the market status of this region. In contrast, the selectivity of migration from the peripheral areas further eroded their prospects for development of an alternative industrial base.

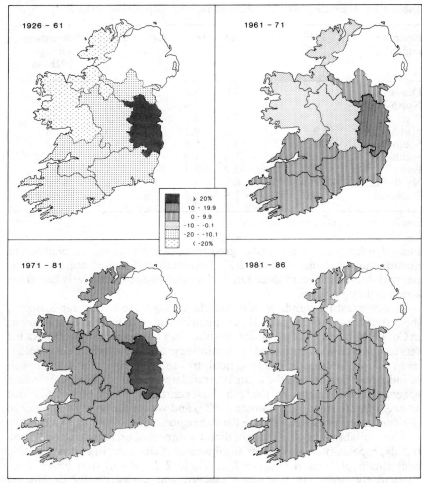

Figure 2.3 Regional population change, 1926–86 (Census of Population).

Between 1926 and 1961, the East was the only region to increase its population base and, by the latter date, almost one-third of the State's population resided in this core region. Thus, by the late 1950s, not only had prevailing policies failed to effect a national rejuvenation of the economy, they had also failed to reorganize the imbalanced spatial order of economic activities. The pressing needs of the peripheral regions and of national development were to be more successfully addressed in the following decades.

2.2.2 Modernization and regional change: 1959–79

The 1960s witnessed the introduction of policies which emphasized modernization and free trade as the panacea for underdevelopment and to achieve a more balanced, spatially equitable, distribution of prosperity. Large-scale public expenditure was directed at improving the social and physical infrastructure of the country — an essential prerequisite for the successful establishment of a growth-orientated economy. Active state support of agriculture and manufacturing had a notable effect in reducing the degree of inequality and differentiation that existed between regional economies.

During this period, agricultural employment in rural communities continued to decline. In contrast, enhanced market opportunities, especially within the context of membership of the EC, encouraged developments in terms of both specialization and intensification of production. This, in turn, influenced farm size and the income potential of farmers, since higher prices and guaranteed markets promoted a more commercial view of land as a factor of production. Modernization of agriculture, however, impacted differently on the diverse agricultural regions of the Republic and, as Jim Walsh (1980, p. 91) noted, the ability and the propensity to intensify production became the major differentiating characteristic between the two

Table 2.3 Provincial percentage shares of national agricultural production, 1960 and 1977

	Leinster		Munster		Connacht		Ulster	
	1960	1977	1960	1977	1960	1977	1960	1977
Milk output	24.1	20.0	56.2	62.4	12.4	8.0	7.3	9.6
Cattle output	34.4	32.1	36.7	38.8	20.9	20.3	8.1	8.8
Sheep output	37.5	37.0	21.3	16.8	31.9	38.5	9.2	7.7
Pig output	30.9	27.9	48.9	42.8	9.4	8.9	10.9	20.4
Poultry output	26.6	27.5	31.3	29.9	27.7	11.0	14.5	31.5
Tillage area	45.8	54.9	32.2	31.1	12.3	8.1	9.6	6.0
Gross agricultural output	32.7	30.2	40.0	44.7	19.0	16.0	8.3	9.1

Source: Gillmor (1985a).

66   *Ireland*

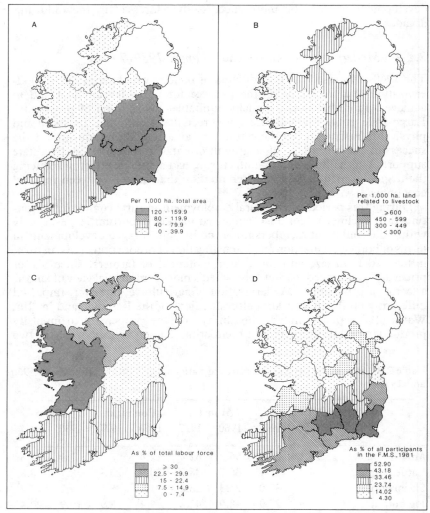

Figure 2.4   Regional distribution of selected agricultural elements. A, Cereals per 1000 ha of total area, 1980 (Horner et al., 1984). B, Breeding cattle per 1000 ha land related to livestock, 1980 (Horner et al., 1984). C, Persons in agricultural occupation as a percentage of total labour force, 1981 (Horner et al., 1984). D, Development farmers as a percentage of all participants in the FMS, 1981 (Walsh, 1986).

Table 2.4   Percentage change in selected characteristics of agricultural production, 1970–80

	North-West	West	Midland and East	South-West	South-East	State
Cereal area	−19.1	−30.5	37.4	− 2.6	29.8	17.1
Total cattle	15.6	19.7	8.5	17.9	17.4	16.0
Dry cattle	17.4	27.3	10.1	16.2	15.2	17.0
Breeding cattle	16.9	12.3	9.5	27.3	26.8	20.7
Tractors	83.6	173.6	45.0	66.9	40.8	72.4
Employment	−37.4	−35.7	−27.0	−29.7	−27.4	−31.8
Average size of holding (ha)	8.2	7.0	6.0	5.7	5.2	6.6

Source: Horner et al. (1984).
Note: Regions are based on those used by the Agricultural Training Authority (ACOT).

primary agricultural regions. The essential east–west divide of agriculture was thus reinforced and complemented the sectoral duality that had clearly emerged at the national level (see Section 1.3.2). Some of the major changes in the composition of agricultural output and structure support this analysis (Gillmor, 1977b; Horner et al., 1984; Tables 2.3, 2.4; Figure 2.4).

The share of arable cropping in total agricultural output fell from 20 to 14 per cent between 1960 and 1980 as the benefits of intensive grassland production were vigorously promoted. Within the context of decline, however, there was a marked locational shift to those areas best suited to tillage. The dominance of the East and South-East regions was thereby enhanced, based on the more favourable environmental conditions for cereals and the large field patterns which facilitated large-scale, mechanized farming techniques.

Improved market prospects within the EC encouraged a further commitment to dairy and cattle enterprises and their contribution to the total value of output rose from 52 to 70 per cent between 1960 and 1980 (Gillmor, 1987). High guaranteed prices encouraged a doubling of milk output and much of this development focused on the intensive dairy farming region of Munster. Almost two-thirds of the national milk output originate from the lush pasturelands of this province. The Cavan–Monaghan area of Ulster also increased its share of milk output, although specialization of farming in this border area is more closely associated with large-scale, commercial rearing of pigs and poultry.

Cattle rearing remained a common farming activity throughout much of the country, although rearing of dry cattle focused more strongly on the western regions. Here, tradition, poorer environmental quality and low labour inputs favoured extensive farm practice. The more commercial and financially rewarding fattening stage of the beef industry is concentrated on the richer grasslands of the east Midlands.

There are marked regional differences in farm size and structure. Decline in the number of holdings has been least in the more developed eastern regions where farm structures have been comparatively stable for much of the twentieth century. Medium-sized holdings of between 20 and 30 ha are most common, in contrast with the West and North-West regions where the average is between 11 and 20 ha (Walsh, J.A., 1986). The Irish Land Commission was created to implement policy on the reform of land structure. Its early role emphasized rent fixing and facilitated tenant purchasing of land but, increasingly, the Commission focused attention on consolidating the fragmented nature of much farmland, especially in the west, and enlarging existing units to create viable enterprises. It achieved some notable impact on structural improvement, although its influence declined in more recent years as the cost of land increased (thereby limiting its potential to purchase land) and less land was released on to the market. In 1985, the government abolished the Commission and structural change in farm size is now essentially left to free market forces.

The small farm holdings that typify much of the rugged western area offer little opportunity for mechanization. Yet the high capital investment in Irish agriculture throughout the 1970s found expression even in more marginal farming regions as expectations of higher income levels persuaded farmers to invest in capital equipment. Over one-half of the total number of new tractors purchased in the 1970s were located in the West and North-West regions, where mechanization had previously been lowest. Capital equipment and mechanized farming, however, remain more common in the east and south where proximity to urban centres emphasizes the need for commercial operations (O'Carroll et al., 1978).

The gradual emergence of barley as the dominant cereal crop (for fodder) and the increasing emphasis placed on dairying and cattle rearing have replaced much of the diversity that formerly characterized an agricultural economy geared to self-sufficiency. Increased specialization has had differentiated regional income effects since there is considerable variation in the profitability of different farming systems, the type of farm enterprise, the size of farm and the quality of land (Heavey et al., 1984). While almost all areas exhibited an increase in the real income of male members of farm families between 1960 and 1977, the highest gains were recorded in the east and the south. This is largely attributable to the high profitability of dairying and tillage, augmented by the greater productivity achieved on predominantly better quality soils. The larger average size of farm also has a bearing on higher income levels, since a direct relationship clearly exists between the size of farm and the income achieved per labour unit (Foras Taluntais, 1986). Lower incomes in the more western areas are largely due to a greater reliance on extensive cattle and sheep rearing, the poorer quality of the land and the small average size of farm units. Changes in regional farm income levels have, therefore, tended to accentuate the prevailing east–west divide in Irish agriculture (Attwood and Bateman, 1981).

One final feature appears to have contributed to the maintenance of a spatial division in Irish agriculture. Classification under the Farm Modernization Scheme (FMS) clearly points to the greater potential of the south and east of Ireland where the majority of development farmers are located (Figure 2.4d) and future strategy was designed to increase the allocation of support to these potentially viable enterprises. More regionally sensitive schemes were obviously needed to reflect the severe problems of farming communities living within the less favoured areas (Gillmor, 1977c).

Manufacturing was regarded as the key element in national economic growth and in the period of vigorous industrial development, important quantitative and qualitative changes occurred at the regional level. The concentration and polarization of manufacturing in the East were modified and a more dispersed pattern of industrial location emerged (see Figure 2.2), reflecting both government policy and the locational preferences of private investment. Between 1960 and 1973, there were disproportionate shifts of manufacturing employment, industrial floorspace and capital grants to the more peripheral regions. As a result, while all regions experienced an absolute growth in manufacturing, employment in the East grew only a little above one-half of the national rate of change. The Designated Areas (known as Undeveloped Areas until 1969) attracted 168 successful manufacturing establishments between 1960 and 1973, which provided over 14,000 jobs. Despite the impressive relative gains, however, most new employment — some 31,000 jobs between 1960 and 1973 — still located outside the Designated Areas (O'Farrell, 1975).

By 1979 the core region accounted for only 40.3 per cent of national manufacturing employment compared with 52.7 per cent in 1961. While the more peripheral regions continued to experience above average rates of growth, the East lost over 12,000 jobs in manufacturing between 1973 and 1979. The adjacent North-East also experienced a minor decline, while slow growth characterized the Mid-West and South-West economies.

Industrial development and regional development became synonymous in Ireland. While government industrial policy initially had a somewhat indirect impact on the regions, it came to have increasing spatial relevance.

No explicit spatial policy was formulated for the Republic in the 1960s. A general dispersal of industry was encouraged, but there was a notable lack of any clearly defined goals and objectives (O'Farrell, 1970a). Criticism of this vagueness gathered momentum and centred around two contrasting viewpoints of effecting regional development. On the one side were the proponents of growth centre strategies who favoured the economic arguments of concentration (Walsh, F., 1976). They were opposed by those who considered the social merits of dispersal to be more important for rural Ireland (Newman, 1967).

The political and social ramifications of concentrated development caused the government repeatedly to retreat from growth centre strategies. In an attempt to achieve a more balanced view, the government commissioned three programmes for regional study in 1964 to identify planning options for the Dublin region (Wright, 1967), the Limerick region (Lichfield, 1967) and all regions (Buchanan, 1968). The latter report, in particular, was contentious due to its emphasis on a limited number of growth centres and demanded a positive response from government as to their preferred spatial strategy. None of the three programmes of economic and social development which had formed the basis of government planning in the 1960s had included a regional dimension. In 1972, however, government finally issued a statement on regional development which advocated a policy of dispersal to 'minimize population dislocation through internal migration'. No other statement has appeared on regional development since this date. Despite the absence of any coherent spatial policy, however, employment trends had already begun to suggest that dispersal was proving acceptable to private investment. This was not lost on a government anxious to maintain electoral support in more rural constituencies.

In the 1970s, the Republic opted for a more explicit spatial policy, and the IDA was empowered to enact a suitable location policy for the country. It published the first of two five-year plans (1973–77 and 1978–82) in 1972, thus in effect ending the national flirtation with growth centre policy (Breathnach, 1982). In place of the nine growth centres advocated by Buchanan (1968), 47 clusters of towns were selected for job targets, clearly implying a strong level of direction was available to the IDA. The plans favoured a disproportionate degree of development for the more marginal regions and a reasonable degree of success was achieved in meeting the projected targets (Table 2.5). Differential grants favouring the peripheral areas, a programme of site acquisitions and advance factories, and a carefully selected itinerary of sites to show to potential industrialists seem to have worked well for the IDA.

Although the 1970s constitute the most highly articulated period of regional development (Boylan and Cuddy, 1984), it would be a major error

Table 2.5   IDA regional targets and achievement, 1973–77 and 1978–82

Planning region	Net job target	1973–77 % 1973 base	% achieved	1978–82 Gross job target	% 1978 base	% achieved
Donegal	2000	31.3	40	2800	66	71
North-West	1300	41.9	85	3000	68	48
West	4200	48.8	123	7250	62	71
Mid-West	3800	21.2	0	4500	47	107
South-West	7000	19.8	14	10450	31	83
South-East	3200	15.9	86	8500	33	103
East	10300	9.4	−107	19000	20	103
North-East	3400	20.2	− 29	6000	35	81
Midlands	2800	30.8	113	6500	53	86
State	38000	16.7	5	68000	30	89

Source: IDA (1972, 1979).

to assume that this was the only process at work which effected internal spatial redistribution. Perrons (1981), for example, advocates that changes in the international division of labour and production were central elements in the success of the country's industrial programme. Decision-making has become increasingly centralized, while mechanization and automation have given a new degree of locational choice for production units. Standardization of product output has reduced the spatial requirement for large concentrations of highly skilled workers and has emphasized instead the importance of an adaptable, low-cost labour force. In this way, capital has gained a more effective control over labour, and decentralization of production is recognized as being both technically and politically beneficial to the business enterprise. Perrons (1981, p. 94) thus points to several factors in the Republic's social formation that make it conducive for international investment: weakly developed indigenous industry; a surplus of a low-cost and inexperienced industrial workforce which lacked a militant tendency; existence of coastal sites and land for development; lax laws on pollution and working conditions; a dominance of small rural towns with access to an extensive rural labour supply; an improving infrastructure; and, finally, a stable political system with both major parties committed to attracting foreign capital. As a result, even the more peripheral regions were able to benefit from these changed circumstances since their locational attributes no longer inhibited the development of production units primarily concerned with minimization of basic input costs.

Foreign-based industry, which led Ireland's comparatively late industrialization, showed an above-average preference for locating in the more disadvantaged areas rather than in the core (Blackburn, 1972; O'Farrell, 1980). In the East, only 30 per cent of the regional industrial workforce was in foreign-controlled enterprise and the comparative absence of such investment contributed to the region's relative decline. Another problem for the core region and large urban centres is their dependency on older indigenous firms, often in declining sectors of manufacturing and serving the national market. Substantial decline in manufacturing has occurred due to its poor technological base and failure to overcome the higher costs of production generated through inflated labour and land costs within core areas. The more footloose nature of modern growth industries, largely controlled by foreign enterprise, enables their location in peripheral regions, thereby creating more diversified employment bases.

Although the introduction of modern growth industries created badly needed employment and wealth in marginal regions, several aspects of the branch plant economy began to provoke increased concern. The dominance of factories utilizing simple production line technology generated mainly unskilled or semi-skilled assembly work with little decision-making or research and development capacity within the regions. Diversification of the employment base, increasing employment opportunities for underemployed farm workers and an enhanced role for females all therefore emerged within the context of regional deskilling. This was to be the paradox faced by marginal communities in the 1970s.

Analysis of the components of change of regional employment trends from 1973 to 1981 highlights the situation for Ireland (O'Farrell, 1984). New plant openings were a more important source of new jobs in every region than were expansions of existing plants. In addition, regional differences in the rates of job gains were far greater than those for job losses, indicating that employment creation was the essential factor in accounting for inter-regional employment differences. With the poorer industrialized regions doing particularly well in terms of job creation, it is perhaps understandable that comparatively little thought at this stage was given to the quality of the new jobs. In contrast, the East, North-East, Mid-West and South-West accounted for 81 per cent of total job losses. The East region alone lost over 41,000 jobs, 51 per cent of the national total, while generating only 30 per cent of all new jobs. For these regions, the type of industrial structure, as well as total job creation, had emerged as serious considerations for future planning.

The positive performance of manufacturing throughout the regions had important knock-on effects in the service sector. Increased demand for producer services, in particular, contributed to diversification of the economy and ensured a better infrastructural base for further development.

Another important factor was the turnround in demographic patterns that began in the 1960s. Previously, population decline typified all regions outside the East, but during the 1960s, the more developed urban-based regions of the east and south exhibited population increases. By the 1970s, this positive trend had diffused into the west and north-west (Figure 2.3). Demands for services to meet the rising population base and a government expenditure programme to provide enhanced public and social services were inevitably translated into a general increase in the provision of services throughout all regions. By 1981, no region had less than 40 per cent of its total employment in this sector.

However, the East increasingly came to dominate service employment. During the 1970s, over 55 per cent of 130,000 new service jobs were located in the East, and by 1981 this region controlled almost one-half of the national total of such employment (Table 2.6). Apart from the West, which had enjoyed a significant increase in public administration and defence, plus the positive multiplier effects consequent on strong manufacturing growth, all other regions showed a decline in their share of national service employment (Bannon, 1985; Dineen, 1985).

Of particular importance has been a polarization of higher-quality occupations involving control and decision-making functions in the economic core. A clear qualitative as well as quantitative shift in services has therefore occurred. The infrastructural base, proximity to government decision-making and better promotion of research and development facilities have all made the East, and especially Dublin, the obvious location for both public and private headquarter functions. While industrial policy advocated decentralization of manufacturing, no policy directives emerged for services, and the operation of free market forces worked counter to the idea of a balanced regional development. Decentralization of services was marginal at best and mostly related to more routine office employment. Polarization of service employment was incompatible with the government's continued vague reference to balanced growth and suggested that no clearly articulated policy for overall regional economic development had emerged. Industrial decentralization was only one component of a far more complex set of processes involved in regional development (NESC, 1977a).

The contrasting sectoral performances in the various regions had important repercussions for both total employment changes and the proportion of females employed within the regional economies. In the North-West/Donegal and the West regions the growth of manufacturing and services did not compensate fully for the heavy losses in agriculture, and total employment declined. Elsewhere, apart from in the North-East, modern developments succeeded in more than offsetting the erosion of the agricultural base. Of the total increase in national employment of 80,000 in the 1971–81

Table 2.6   Regional percentage shares of employment in services and white-collar*
occupations, 1971–81

Planning region	Services			White-collar		
	1971	1981	Total 1981	1971	1981	Total 1981
Donegal	2.6	2.4	14325	2.4	2.5	3859
North-West	2.0	2.0	11961	2.0	2.0	2942
West	6.3	6.5	38367	6.1	6.6	11710
Mid-West	7.7	7.6	44428	7.5	7.5	11463
South-West	14.2	13.7	80523	14.0	13.4	18197
South-East	9.4	8.5	49960	9.0	8.6	10928
East	47.2	49.0	288059	48.5	49.2	76021
North-East	4.7	4.6	26815	4.8	4.5	5903
Midlands	5.9	5.7	33807	5.7	5.7	8402

Source: Bannon (personal communication, 1987).
* White-collar occupations include clerical, commercial, insurance, finance, professional, technical and other occupations.

period, however, the East still accounted for 79 per cent. The dynamic performance of the service sector was clearly instrumental in this, since both agriculture and manufacturing declined in this region. By 1981, two out of every three persons employed in the East were engaged in some form of service activity.

Feminization of the regional workforce was particularly encouraged by the new job opportunities created by modernization. Traditionally, the strongest representation of females within the workforce had been in the more urbanized regions, primarily the East. Following the decline of the male-orientated agricultural sector and the enhanced employment opportunities in services and branch plants in the 1970s (Figure 2.5), female employment increased in all regions, although 42 per cent of the national gain between 1971 and 1983 was still located in the East (Gillmor, 1985b). The expansion of the tertiary base in the core more than compensated for a one-third decline in female manufacturing employment and, by 1983, 82 per cent of the region's female workers were in the tertiary sector. In general, services were mainly responsible for promoting a higher profile for female workers in the other regions, although manufacturing also played a role. 'Thus although tertiary employment became more concentrated in the East, the strong reverse tendency in manufacturing led to a somewhat greater dispersion of female employment . . . (and) the effect of spatial change in women's jobs . . . was to lead to a greater regional dispersal of total employment' (Gillmor, 1985b, p. 72).

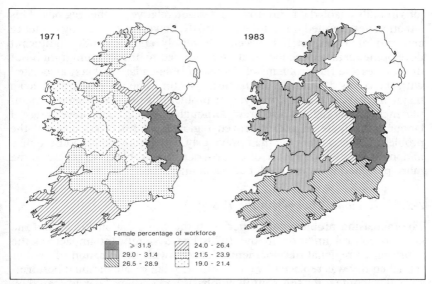

Figure 2.5 Regional distribution of female employment, 1971 and 1983 (Gillmor, 1985b).

Changes in the pattern of labour demand also influenced population trends. While total population increased in all regions, the East experienced an above-average growth and was the only region to increase its relative share of total population (see Table 2.2). This trend again contradicts the concern of regional policy to achieve greater decentralization. Internal migration to the East contributed to this shift, as perceived employment opportunities, particularly in offices and professional careers, induced many younger, more educated people to leave peripheral regions (Hughes and Walsh, 1980). The age-selective nature of migration contributed to the East's growth performance, since its more youthful population encouraged higher rates of natural increase than in the marginal regions. However, enhanced job prospects within such regions finally succeeded in reducing rates of emigration below those for natural population increase. In addition, some return migration generated by the better job prospects in the western regions and the movement of retirees to such areas all contributed to their improved demographic trends in the 1970s.

Unemployment has remained a problem for most regions although its spatial expression has changed. Traditionally, the Dublin region exhibited comparatively low levels of unemployment and its capacity to create new jobs initially enabled it to improve its position relative to other regions. This situation deteriorated during the late 1970s, however, as growing evidence emerged of a mismatch between job supply and demand. Significant developments in service job creation continued to attract immigration but did not resolve the problems of displaced blue-collar workers, associated with the core's declining manufacturing sector. The net result has been a major increase in the unemployment problem of the core region. Unemployment in the regions also grew, although out-migration, lower rates of labour force increase and improved regional job prospects ensured the problem was less dramatic than previously. Unemployment had become a national issue, with the core often experiencing problems as severe as the more peripheral, lesser developed economies.

2.2.3   Regional changes in the 1980s

The increasing problems identified with the rising national debt and the need to control inflation in the 1980s had a significant impact on the approach to regional development. Concern with the creation of greater spatial equity was replaced by a concern with aggregate national performance. The context for this shift in emphasis had perhaps been prepared by the EC when the entire state was designated as a single region eligible for aid under the European Regional Development Fund. As the regional dimension was downgraded, therefore, discussions on the implications of Community membership for the regions were stifled (Lee, 1984). Increasing economic difficulties caused government to focus on promoting sectoral interests as a basis for reviving the economy, and *Building on Reality, 1985–87* clearly supported this approach. Even the country's industrial development policy, which had established quite close formal links with regional policy objectives, was reorientated under the 1984 White Paper on Industrial Policy. In place of the grant system designed to divert mobile resources to Designated Areas was a new system which favoured supporting defined industrial sectors and areas severely affected by the recession. Short-term support rather than longer-term commitments also formed a basis of the new programme. All of this was likely to have an uneven impact on regions that had come to rely on a high level of government aid for their development.

After the optimism expressed about agricultural development in the 1970s, and the belief that agriculturally dependent regions would benefit from inclusion within the CAP, the 1980s proved especially disappointing. Despite the introduction of Directive 268, which designated the western regions a Less Favoured Area, and the establishment of more spatially sensitive programmes such as the Western Drainage Scheme and the

Table 2.7   Selected characteristics of 'full-time' farms* in the East and 'part-time' farms in Less Favoured Areas, 1984

Characteristics	'Full-time' farms (East) (%)	'Part-time' farms (LFA) (%)
Family farm income less than IR£ 5000	17.5	91.0
Size less than 20 ha**	16.6	58.6
Dairying	67.2	15.5
Cattle	21.1	66.9
Operator has off-farm job	12.5	28.4
'Young' household†	90.1	62.0
'Well-developed'‡	56.5	6.3
Estimated number of farms	44,000	92,000

Source: O'Hara (1986).
* Farms with a labour requirement of at least 0.75 standard labour units are regarded as 'full-time' farms. 'Part-time' farms are the remainder.
** Excludes hill farms which account for 30 per cent of farms in LFA.
† Households with some members aged 45 or under.
‡ Based on adoption of recommended farm practices.

Western Package for Ireland, the preferential treatment achieved little in promoting a more viable agriculture in such areas.

Production patterns did not change significantly in the 1980s apart from exacerbating the two-tier nature of agriculture. High-output farms remained concentrated in the East, geared to satisfying the demands of commercialized agriculture and focusing primarily on dairying and cereal production. In contrast, low-output farmers predominated in the less favoured western areas, where their fortunes were closely associated with cattle rearing. Table 2.7 illustrates some of the fundamental contrasts that exist between 'full-time' farms in the East compared with 'part-time' farms in the Less Favoured Areas (LFA) of the country.

The 1980s have been particularly difficult for manufacturing, as the previous growth performance gave way to national decline from 1979 to 1985. The decline in manufacturing employment spread from the eastern core region to affect regions of the west that previously had enjoyed significant gains (see Figure 2.2). A loss of over 15,000 jobs in the East indicated the continued erosion of the core's industrial base, and by 1985 this region controlled only 37 per cent of the national industrial workforce. In addition, employment in the South-West also declined precipitously, due largely to the difficulties experienced in the Cork area (Brunt, 1984). These severe job losses in the two largest and traditional industrial areas contributed in no small way to a fundamental reassessment of what constituted the problem areas of Ireland.

In essence, the differential performance of manufacturing within the regions reflected three primary influences: the continued erosion of the indigenous sector and its comparative failure to come to terms with the international trading economy; the poorer growth performance of foreign-based industrial investment; and, finally, changing industrial policy and its interpretation of regional priorities.

Indigenous industry declined in all regions, and most severely in the South-West and East, where employment fell by 21 and 25 per cent respectively between 1980 and 1985. Many of the older industries in these urban-based regions did not restructure adequately, failing not only to establish an export platform but, more especially, to combat increasing import penetration in the free trade environment of the EC. Elsewhere, losses within indigenous manufacturing were comparatively minor and reflected a greater stability in the more rural regions.

In only three regions — the Midlands, Donegal and the Mid-West — did total employment increase due to a significant influx of foreign industry. The Mid-West, in particular, emerged strongly as a focus of foreign investment in the growing electronics sector, which was intimately associated with the establishment of a National Institute for Higher Education in Limerick. Elsewhere, the ability of the regions to attract new investment to compensate for job losses was less marked. In addition, in the more competitive trading environment of the 1980s, multinationals had to rationalize their operations in order to maintain profitability.

Changing government industrial policy has played an important role in regional performance in the 1980s. As conditions for attracting additional new jobs disimproved, strategy switched to attempting to maintain existing employment and to exploiting more effectively the existing industrial economy. Essentially, this meant a greater concern with retaining wealth creation by limiting leakages through effecting a stronger linkage programme within the regions. The Small Industry programme of the IDA, which had been established in 1967 to promote a greater dispersal of employment into the more rural areas, was to be particularly important in this respect. Small industries were to be encouraged to link more effectively with established industries in the various regions and thereby reduce the necessity for external supplies of components and services. The scale of the problem (but equally the extent of the opportunities) for this attempt at greater import substitution within open regional economies was illustrated by an input-output study of the West region. This indicated that, between 1971 and 1980, the import ratio for manufacturing industry had increased from 46.6 to 61.4 per cent (Boylan and Cuddy, 1984).

This change in emphasis also indicated a shift in spatial preference for new development. The growing concern with the problems of the East region, particularly in Dublin, caused government to reduce its commitment to industrial decentralization from the core. The higher profile given to established industrial regions found clear expression in the 1984 White Paper on Industrial Policy. Areas designated for industrial development were not simply based on need, but also on the potential for maximizing growth. Since the IDA was committed to attracting high-quality and growth-orientated business activities, this suggested the business environment would become increasingly important and this favoured the core region. Within this context, the paucity of an urban base throughout much of the country, the apparent lack of a policy for urban development, and restrictions on investment in the infrastructure will have an increasingly important role to play in the future promotion of regional industrialization.

Service employment continued to increase in all regions, albeit at a reduced rate. The comparatively poor performance of the East was due in part to the decline of the region's industrial base, which inevitably induced some downward multiplier effect on the demand for services. In addition, a very modest decentralization of services had been effected in the 1970s, with some sections of government departments being transferred to the West and Midlands in particular. This was to have been continued in the 1980s but, despite the transfer of a new vehicle licensing centre to Shannon, this has not gained much momentum. As a result, a government decision in 1980 to disperse 3210 civil servants to twelve different towns was cancelled in 1982. Financial constraints were advanced as the main cause of this, although the reluctance of senior civil servants to displace themselves undoubtedly added to this failure. However, more significant has been a general embargo on public service employment introduced in the early 1980s and thus removing one of the East's major sources of new jobs.

Counteracting the less satisfactory absolute growth in service employment in the core region was its continued dominance as a centre of decision-making and high-level office occupations. The interrelated office complex of this region, based on access to government institutions, well-developed social and physical infrastructure and the ease of face-to-face contact, is likely to reinforce the high degree of centrality that typifies Irish quaternary activities — unless government initiates a more active decentralization programme, which is unlikely. Furthermore, recent concern to attract international services to Ireland endorses the primacy of Dublin, since most of these services have already gravitated to the capital, with some secondary developments occurring in Cork, Limerick and Galway. In contrast, the underdeveloped quality and range of services in the peripheral regions are causing serious concern, especially as this sector will increasingly influence the ability of regions to attract and support more effectively an industrial base.

While employment declined, population continued to rise in all regions, as did the supply of labour. The net result was a conspicuous increase in regional unemployment, particularly in the South-West and North-West/ Donegal. However, 40 per cent of all unemployment is within the East region (32 per cent in Co. Dublin), illustrating the need to address the absolute scale of the problem in the core area. Compounding this problem were the differential effects on males and females, as the sectoral opportunities for employment changed. In marked contrast to males, females continued to find increased employment opportunities within newer factories and the expanding service sector, resulting in increased proportions of females within the workforce of all regions. The disproportionately high rate of male unemployment presents a serious challenge for future job creation schemes and emphasizes the need for more effective retraining of displaced male workers.

By the mid-1980s major changes had been achieved in the sectoral composition of the regional economies (see Table 2.1). The role of manufacturing had increased in all regions with the exception of the East, thus reducing the differentiation between core and periphery. The extreme variation in agricultural dependency had also been reduced, although contrasts remained substantial. Large-scale and generalized losses within primary activities, however, ensured that the tertiary sector had emerged as the dominant employer of labour in all Irish regions. Integration of Ireland within the international economy, the locational preference for branch plant activities and government policies had all worked to effect an apparent reduction in regional contrasts between east and west.

While polarization of industrial activity had been reduced, the integration of Ireland into the global economy enhanced the central role of the core as a gateway through which innovation diffused and linkages were established to international centres of control. The East was the only region to illustrate continuing growth in aggregate employment throughout the postwar years. Core–periphery relationships may have been modified, but they remain fundamental in any appreciation of contemporary regional development patterns within Ireland.

2.3 Regional variations in income levels

Changes in economic structures and in population inevitably had a profound influence on the regional levels of per capita income. Since income levels are intimately associated with living conditions, an analysis of their spatial variation allows a better understanding of a vital dimension of

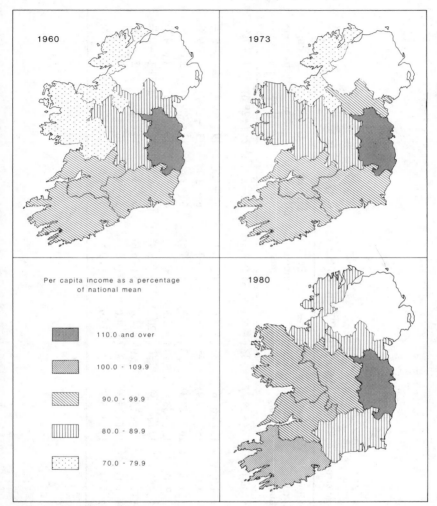

Figure 2.6 Regional income patterns, 1960–80 (NESC, 1980a).

regional development: the quality of life enjoyed by the regions' populations. This is discussed in the following section. In addition, given the
paucity of regionally disaggregated data on government public expenditure
programmes, an evaluation of regional income sources provides some

Table 2.8 Percentage structure of regional income in 1977 (percentage changes, 1973–77, in brackets)

Planning region	Agriculture, forestry, fishing	Manufacturing and mining	Services	Self-employ-ment	Interest, dividends, rent	Govern-ment transfers	Foreign transfers
Donegal/North-West	21 (+ 0.8)	11 (+28.7)	33 (+ 8.1)	5 (−8.3)	6 (−1.2)	21 (+29.6)	4 (−7.5)
West	22 (− 4.9)	11 (+66.6)	35 (+ 4.0)	4 (−6.1)	5 (−4.9)	19 (+29.4)	4 (−9.7)
Mid-West	24 (+ 4.6)	15 (+ 7.9)	35 (+13.5)	5 (+0.2)	6 (−3.7)	13 (+29.2)	2 (−9.4)
South-West	24 (+15.3)	16 (+20.3)	33 (+ 7.9)	5 (−4.5)	6 (−3.6)	13 (+29.0)	2 (−6.9)
South-East	29 (+ 9.4)	17 (+33.8)	29 (+ 5.3)	5 (−4.4)	6 (−3.4)	12 (+29.3)	2 (−4.8)
East	4 (+ 3.5)	17 (+ 1.9)	50 (+20.2)	6 (+6.4)	12 (−5.3)	11 (+28.7)	1 (−0.5)
North-East	23 (+12.4)	21 (+13.7)	29 (+ 4.4)	5 (−6.6)	6 (−3.2)	14 (+29.5)	2 (−9.8)
Midlands	27 (− 1.4)	12 (+33.3)	33 (+ 4.0)	4 (−6.1)	5 (−4.9)	16 (+29.4)	2 (−9.7)
State	16 (+ 5.1)	16 (+13.2)	40 (+15.0)	5 (+0.5)	8 (−4.6)	13 (+29.1)	2 (−6.4)

Source: NESC (1980a).

insights into the extent to which government policies have achieved the professed aim of securing a more balanced regional socioeconomic system.

Despite evidence which points to a convergence between the most prosperous East region and the less developed Donegal/North-West region, variations in income levels remain considerable (Figure 2.6). This convergence, however, is essentially a feature of the 1970s since, during the preceding decade, divergence was more apparent as the benefits of industrial decentralization were only in their formative stages (NESC, 1980a). County level data provided by Attwood and Geary (1963) and Ross (1969, 1972) support these observations. While the East has remained the most prosperous region, the comparatively simple division between a medium-income belt of regions in the south (but extending to include the North-East) and a low-income group of regions in the Midlands, West, North-West and Donegal has been disrupted. By 1980, the poorer regions had gained strongly, while the North-East and South-East regions had declined in relative terms.

The differences in regional income levels and trends reflect, most importantly, changing population patterns, together with variations in the source of income (Table 2.8). Agriculture continued to have above-average importance for all regions, outside of the East, although the low or even negative growth in agricultural incomes did little to enhance incomes in the less prosperous regions. Some of the typical products of the western regions, such as oats, potatoes and sheep, were not covered by the CAP and prices within drystock farming were comparatively depressed. In contrast, dairying and cereal producers benefited and this is reflected in above-average gains for the North-East and South-West.

Probably the major factor in encouraging convergence of regional incomes has been the growth of manufacturing relative to agricultural incomes. The increase in manufacturing payrolls was especially high in the less prosperous regions, which illustrates that real progress was made in the IDA's programme of regional industrialization. The growing strength of the trade union movement in manufacturing, and the negotiation of national wage rates, ensured that workers in the west would not be at a disadvantage with respect to their counterparts in the more urbanized east. This contrasts with the situation for many families dependent on farming. Employment in factories therefore contributed strongly to the gains in the less developed regions. The importance of the availability of off-farm employment, with better income prospects, has also been stressed by Higgins (1986). There is an inverse relationship, especially in the western half of the country, between the percentage of income from farming and total income in farming households.

Real income growth in services was one of the fastest growing

Table 2.9   Regional variations in household incomes, 1980

Planning region	Average weekly income (IR£)	Percentage of household incomes	
		< IR£ 60	> IR£ 150
North-West/ Donegal	90	48.3	11.7
West	103	42.7	16.9
Mid-West	116	31.5	25.4
South-West	125	28.9	28.7
South-East	108	33.6	24.6
East	149	18.2	39.8
North-East	107	32.3	19.1
Midlands	116	34.4	24.4

Source: *Household Budget Survey* (1980).

components of total income and variations in the degree of dependency on this sector contributed in no small way to the regional inequality in overall incomes. One-half of income in the East derived from the service sector, and its contribution to regional prosperity increased sharply between 1973 and 1977. As much of the service employment in this region involves high-status and well-paid jobs, in 1980 the East possessed by far the highest proportion of weekly incomes in excess of IR£ 150, while in the more peripheral regions an abnormally high percentage of weekly incomes remained under IR£ 60 (Table 2.9). Although the service sector contributed approximately one-third of the incomes in most other regions, its poor growth performance reflected the generally lower quality jobs created. The need for a spatial policy for this sector clearly required a greater government commitment, especially if convergence in regional income levels was to be maintained. The greater availability of wealth in the East was further reflected in the degree of importance attached to interest and dividend payments.

Government transfers, especially via social security payments to maintain an acceptable minimum standard of living, clearly stand out as an important factor in the make-up of regional incomes. Dependency is particularly high in the West and North-West where state benefits, together with critical support for agricultural and industrial development, have made such regions increasingly reliant on state management policies. With no internal mechanism for growth, cutbacks in national expenditure have a disproportionate effect on standards of living. Foreign remittances also play an above-average role in the West and North-West/Donegal, reflecting the long tradition of emigration from these areas. This aspect is declining, although the movement of retired people to the western seaboard and the payment of government or foreign pensions to such individuals contributes to the region's income. The inflow of income brought about by retirees and other wealthy in-migrants to generally low-income regions, however, has the potential for a negative impact on local communities. Problems can occur due to inflated land and house prices, together with a clash of interest between 'outsiders' and 'insiders'.

By 1980, despite evidence of convergence, regional income disparities remained a central feature of the spatial economy. Moreover, during the difficult economic conditions of the 1980s, the forces of convergence undoubtedly have become more muted. Agricultural price changes continue to work against the poorer and more agriculturally dependent regions, while a less vigorous development of manufacturing will have removed the essential element that contributed to convergence in the 1970s. Against this, polarization of service employment on the East ensures the maintenance of the region's dominant income status. As national priorities orientate increasingly to wealth creation and the promotion of areas with potential rather than need, the less favoured regions could well see their dependency on central government support increase rather than decrease. For a country committed to public expenditure cuts in order to reduce pressing national debt problems, the immediate future for income growth in the depressed regions and for convergence with the core does not seem good. Financial support from the EC may partially redress the situation, but that again will depend on the government's perception of its 'regional problem'.

2.4   Regional variations in living conditions and lifestyles

In Sections 2.2 and 2.3 a strong relationship was established between regional trends in population, changes in economic structures and income levels. These economic and demographic variables, however, are insufficient to reflect adequately the spatial diversity in the well-being of regional populations. Other social indicators need to be considered to reflect more comprehensively the differences in lifestyles and living conditions within even a comparatively small country like Ireland. While the overall quality of life has undoubtedly improved and the degree of regional inequity has decreased over the past generation, important contrasts still exist.

This section reviews how variations in regional income levels are translated through household expenditure into different patterns of private consumption. State-sponsored collective consumption is considered finally in order to assess the extent to which this helps to offset regional inequalities based primarily on differential private purchasing power.

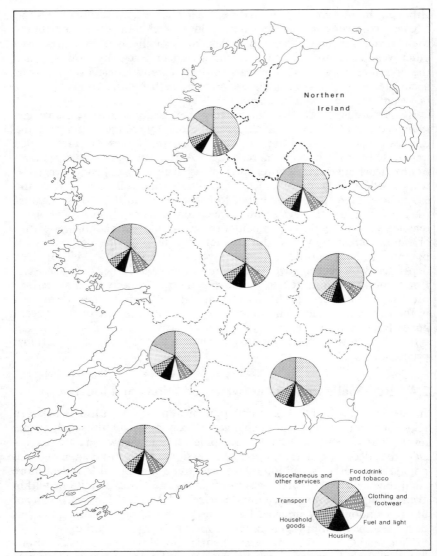

Figure 2.7   Regional patterns of weekly household expenditure, 1980 (*Household Budget Survey*, 1980).

2.4.1 Regional patterns of private consumption

The average level of household expenditure varies considerably from being highest in the East to its lowest point in the North-West/Donegal region, where outlay averaged only two-thirds of the more affluent core region. Consumption patterns reflect these differences in disposable incomes, but are also affected by differences in price levels, availability of goods and services and regional cultures (Figure 2.7).

Absolute and relative variations in the levels of expenditure on basic essentials such as food and drink, clothing and footwear, heat and light, are not great but, where they exist, they emphasize contrasts in the quality of life between core and peripheral regions. Expenditure on food dominates the household budget in all regions, but is most marked in the West and North-West/Donegal, where it accounts for approximately one-third of the weekly budget. In contrast, food absorbs only one-quarter of the household budget in the East, supporting the general observation that once basic requirements are satisfied, further increases in income levels generate a less than proportionate increase in food purchases. The higher-income levels, however, do encourage a change in food types; in the East and other larger urban-based areas dietary patterns contrast with those of the more rural communities, although the diffusion of national food outlets, such as Dunnes Stores and Quinnsworth, has made a greater variety of foods available throughout the country. The former areas tend to enjoy a greater diversity of foods, consuming a more varied and larger amount of vegetables, fresh fruits and meats, while in the western and rural areas a more 'wholesome' diet consists of familiar foods such as dairy products, eggs, cakes, bread and butter, bacon and chicken.

Similar observations can be made with respect to drink and tobacco although, in this case, relative and absolute expenditures tend to be highest in the more urbanized regions. Changing tastes and culture determine this pattern. In the West, culture tends to be male orientated, with visits to the pub and consumption of stout and tobacco an integral part of everyday life. While this is changing with rural industrialization, the influence of an older generation remains a vibrant force in shaping cultural expressions. In contrast, greater feminization of the workforce and a more cosmopolitan atmosphere in the more urbanized regions place less restraints on the role of, and opportunities for, women in society. This is reflected in higher personal expenditure on alcohol and tobacco, compounded by the fact that taste preference has shown a shift away from the more traditional stout or beer to more expensive lagers, cocktails and wines. While changes in many aspects of lifestyle spread throughout the country, not least prompted by industrialization, tourism and the role of television, the urban–rural/core–

periphery contrasts in food and drink preferences remain. Expenditure on clothing, footwear and energy supplies generally constitutes a higher proportion of the family budget in the poorer regions. The high price of electricity in Ireland, due in part to the paucity of indigenous fuel, contributes to the comparatively large outlay on fuel and light, although in the West and Midlands expenditure is less than might be expected, due to extensive peat deposits and the facility afforded to the local farmers to cut peat (turf) for domestic fuel use (see Section 3.3.1).

The housing market exhibits some interesting regional contrasts which, in turn, influence average expenditure on this basic necessity. Owner-occupancy is by far the dominant form of tenure in all regions, ranging from 61 per cent in the East to 80 per cent in the West. Local authority housing is most common in the South-East (27 per cent) and East (24 per cent), the rural areas showing a very low commitment to this type of tenure. In the West and North-West, only 9 and 12 per cent respectively of the total housing market was local authority housing. The general inverse relationship between regional household income levels and public sector housing is not borne out in the Irish case. This is undoubtedly due to the large number of small-scale, owner-occupied farms that are disproportionately represented in regions of comparatively low incomes. In addition, the more recent influx of migrants to such areas has almost exclusively involved owner-occupied or privately rented dwellings.

Quality of housing has improved throughout the country as housing codes have been strengthened and the provision of basic amenities has become a standardized feature of building practice. The rural electrification scheme of the Electricity Supply Board has made power available to all households, while home improvement grants have been made available to upgrade existing dwellings. Yet differences still exist, primarily related to older building stock in the more peripheral rural areas where owners have not been able to afford renovation or have opted to retain their homes in their existing form. Thus, although a convergence of housing quality has occurred, contrasts between Leitrim, the poorest county in Ireland, and Dublin are revealing. In 1981, the percentages of houses in Leitrim with a piped water supply and an indoor toilet were 77 and 64 respectively; for Co. Dublin the comparable figures were 99 and 95 per cent.

The housing stock increased markedly in all regions in the 1970s, primarily reflecting the general growth in population and improved income levels. Development was strongest in the East where population growth was greatest and where in-migration of young adults, allied to the youthful composition of the existing population, created a major demand for the supply of new housing units. This pressure of demand, together with high average income levels, inflated the price of housing and of building land and proved particularly attractive for private construction companies seeking profitable projects. New house building was also impressive in regions that traditionally had witnessed population decline and little new development, due primarily to the reversal of population decline as rural areas became attractive for both new industrial development and home ownership. This was a welcome boost for the local building trades. Demand was more dispersed, however, and the prices of new homes were generally lower than in the East. In addition, building land was much cheaper, especially for the many younger families who received gifts of building plots from parents or relatives who farmed land in the locality. In scenically attractive areas along the west coast, however, an additional element became increasingly important in the 1970s. In-migration, the purchase of second homes for summer vacations and retirees began to inflate land and housing prices in certain areas, causing growing concern for some communities (see Section 3.6.2). In aggregate, however, a marked gradient in house prices exists from the high levels demanded in Dublin and its immediate environs to lower levels in the west, although this latter zone is punctuated with areas of relatively high prices, especially around Galway, Limerick and Cork.

The net result of these regional differences in the housing market is that relative and absolute expenditure on housing is highest in the East. The above-average income levels within the region promote a greater supply of up-market housing and a desire, as well as an ability, of households to spend more of their income to achieve a prestigious living environment. The lowest expenditures on housing are generally found throughout the more rural communities, especially where pressures on land are not heightened by external forces.

Contrasts in the levels of expenditure on household durables and other goods and services are considerable. In general, they are highest, both relatively and absolutely, in high income regions where basic needs do not take up the majority of disposable income (Figure 2.8). The West and North-West/Donegal regions have particularly low outlays on these goods and services, and ownership rates of such labour-saving devices as vacuum cleaners and washing machines fall well below those in the East. For these regions, despite increasing family incomes, many households clearly are still unable to afford what many urban households regard as essential equipment rather than luxuries. In addition, the comparatively low rate of female involvement in the workforce and the more traditional family culture in these areas encourage the use of domestic labour rather than buying in goods and services to satisfy domestic needs. This, of course, is changing as more married females seek employment to augment household income, and the purchase of labour-saving goods and services becomes a key component in the redistribution of domestic duties

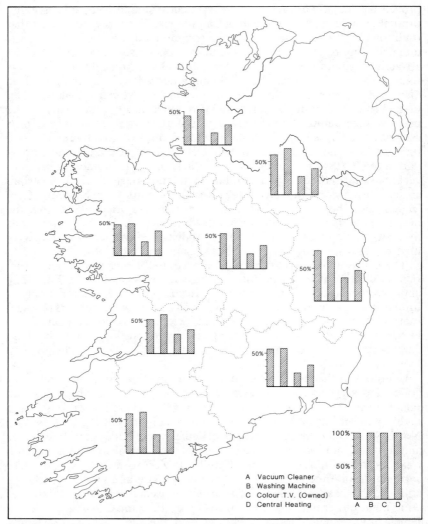

Figure 2.8   Regional variation in households with selected durable goods, 1980
(*Household Budget Survey*, 1980).

caused by such a change in lifestyles. In the more affluent and urban-based regions, the purchase of labour-saving domestic goods and services is more commonplace, and not only facilitates the entry of women into the labour force, but also enables them to benefit from the process of modernization.

Somewhat surprisingly perhaps, household expenditure on transportation is lowest in the East and highest in the West where disposable incomes are lower by one-quarter. While commuting to work is well developed in the East (centred on Dublin), the provision of a good public transport system helps to reduce dependence on the family car. In addition, the concentration of shopping facilities, schools and entertainment outlets reduces the necessity of long-distance journeys. In contrast, in the West and other regions of lower population densities, public transport facilities are poorly developed or non-existent, and there is often a considerable distance between the home and places of work, shopping, services, recreation and school. As a result, not only are the costs of public and private transport comparatively high, but the lower levels of car ownership and the use of the family car by the head of the household for commuting also relegate many family members to the ranks of the transport poor for much of the working week. This not only reduces the potential for social interaction, but also places constraints on the ability of some people to seek employment outside of severely prescribed labour market conditions. The enhanced mobility and flexibility of personal choice that are regarded as being an important accompaniment to modernization and improvement in quality of life are consequently less readily available to a large section of the population in the western regions.

2.4.2 Regional welfare and collective consumption

One of the central aims of government has been not only to build up an effective social infrastructure at the national level, but also to ensure that, in doing so, a greater degree of spatial equity would emerge, especially with regard to opportunity of access to health care and education. A great deal of capital has been directed to attain these objectives, although whether significant reduction in regional inequalities has resulted remains questionable.

The spatial distribution of hospital facilities is remarkably uneven and primarily reflects their development under a variety of organizational forms. Voluntary hospitals have their origin in the eighteenth and nineteenth centuries and are strongly focused on Dublin, although their presence is important in several other large cities (Figure 2.9). In contrast, state hospitals are far more dispersed, many having their origin in the workhouses and infirmaries of the nineteenth century, but even these tend to focus on the larger county towns. The net result is a generally well-developed pattern of hospital facilities in the East and South, while large

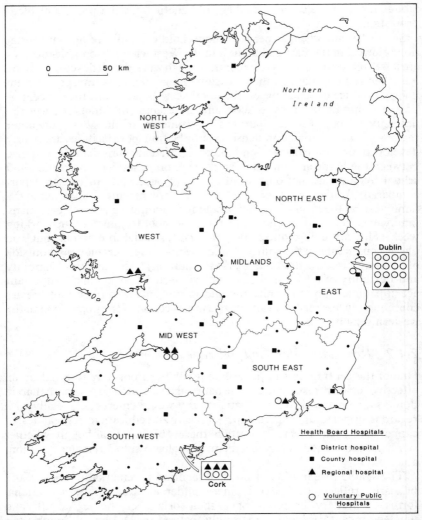

Figure 2.9   Health Board regions and location of general hospitals (after Gillmor, 1985a).

areas of the West and North-West have fewer and more dispersed facilities making access a problem for many rural communities.

Prior to 1971, the administration of the health system was vested in local health boards, based mainly on the 27 county councils of Ireland. With increasing state involvement in financing the service, and the need for larger and more efficient administrative units, the 1960s witnessed increasing demands to regionalize the health service. The 1970 Health Act led to the creation of eight new regional health boards (Paddison, 1970).

The regionalization of the health services and the recommendations of the Fitzgerald Report (1968) theoretically created the basis of a more efficient system, but the centralization process inherent within this development has often tended to work against the professed aim of improving accessibility to the service (NESC, 1977b). Reorganization has been heavily politicized and, while local and regional interests prevented closure or demotion of hospitals, especially in the more rural communities, the more prosperous regions benefited from a significant increase in new investment to promote high-quality regional hospitals and specialized staffing. Reallocation of resources has not worked in favour of those regions which had the poorest health-care facilities.

The regional health boards vary greatly in terms of their size and facilities, the East region serving a population of over 1.2 million compared with the 211,000 population base of the North Western Health Board. Despite a sizeable population in the East, the large number of hospitals in this compact region, together with a disproportionate number of consultant physicians, ensure good accessibility for the majority of potential patients. This contrasts with the more western areas where numbers of beds per capita are significantly lower and longer waiting lists are common for access to specialized facilities and consultation. The contrast is even more marked with respect to private hospital facilities. Thus, of 1522 private hospital beds available in the country in 1984, 706 were located in the Eastern Health Board region as against only 30 found in the North-West region. This is reflected in personal expenditure on private medical care by health board regions. While the national average in 1980 was some IR£ 118, the respective figures for the East and North-West were IR£ 161 and IR£ 71 (Tussing, 1985).

Inequity also exists at the general practitioner level. In the West and North Western Health Board areas, over one-half of the population are medical card holders, in contrast to only 28 per cent in the East region; this clearly reflects the income differential between the communities. Access to the choice of doctor scheme, however, is markedly better in the East where one doctor serves an estimated 656 medical card holders. For the West and North-West, the comparable figures are 1093 and 1176 (Department of Health, 1986). Similar variations also exist for per capita access to dentists, district nurses and pharmacies. For a population that displays an above-average number of low-income, elderly persons, inequities of this nature are a cause of serious concern.

The presence or absence of a well-developed and easily accessible medical service is inevitably linked to standards of health and life expectancy. Crude death rates are comparatively high in the North-West when compared with the South-East, but this differential is strongly influenced by the age and sex composition of the population. When allowance is made for these variables, a greater longevity of life occurs in the more peripheral regions (Pringle, 1982, 1986). This runs counter to the general pattern where death rates are expected to be higher in low income areas with a comparatively underdeveloped health service. The more relaxed lifestyle of communities in the West of Ireland may be one factor that is less than adequately appreciated in indexes of the quantity of life if not quality of life.

Spatial variation in the provision of, and participation in, education is generally considered to be less than that exhibited for health services. Differences at the primary and secondary levels reflect an urban–rural distinction rather than a broader regional dimension, although data inadequacies at the latter level make such conclusions somewhat tenuous. The increasing role of central government in the promotion of education and the drive to create larger school units (able to provide a greater range of facilities and teaching staff) undoubtedly helped the attainment of a more standardized system.

Rates of admission to the tertiary sector of education show a much greater degree of spatial variation, and this is borne out by a detailed study of participation in higher education in Ireland in 1980 (Clancy, 1982). While one in five of the 1980 relevant age-cohort was admitted into higher education, the range varied from 29 per cent in Carlow to 14.5 per cent in Laois. Perhaps of greater interest is the fact that seven of the nine counties with the lowest rates of admission are in Leinster, while three of the five counties with the highest rates are in Connaught. This seemed to conflict with the concept that movement into higher education would be greatest where income levels were also high. In seeking to explain this apparent anomaly, Clancy (1982) established that distance from a college was crucial in influencing the variation in admission rates. Thus three of the four counties with the highest rates of admission into university also possessed a University College (Galway, Cork and Dublin), and the leading six counties with highest admission to Technical Colleges possessed one of these institutions. It therefore appeared that the creation and dispersal of RTCs to centres such as Letterkenny, Sligo, Galway and Tralee significantly aided access to third-level institutions in many areas.

The modernization of the Irish economy encouraged state commitment to a welfare programme to improve the availability of state-sponsored services in deprived regions. Despite some success, the creation of a Welfare State was never as complete as in neighbouring Britain, and certainly did not achieve the anticipated degree of convergence in income levels, living standards and access to education and health services. Fundamental differences in the quality of life persist between the north-west and south-east. In a period of increasing fiscal rectitude, however, cutbacks in expenditure are likely to affect more adversely the western regions. In addition, as national policy orientates towards the development of high value added industry and international services, the maintenance if not enhancement of the urban core would seem logical. The geography of affluence and deprivation, as expressed between core and periphery, 'east' and 'west', is thus likely to be emphasized further. It remains to be seen to what extent politics will serve to deflect a resurgence of polarization.

2.5 Regional politics

The regional pattern of political support in Ireland is highly complex and exhibits few of the clear divisions within the British system (Hudson and Williams, 1986, pp. 101–10). In all 41 of the multi-seat national constituencies in the 1987 general election, at least one Dáil deputy was returned from each of the two dominant parties. This again points to the 'catch-all' nature of these parties in terms of electoral support, and makes recognition of a clear regional dimension to political expression difficult. Some generalizations can, however, be suggested. The Fianna Fáil heartland of support has traditionally rested in the west and north-west, and in the urban working-class areas, while Fine Gael is more represented in the well-developed farming areas of Munster and upper middle-class urban areas. For both parties, Leinster constituencies, especially those in the Dublin area, form the major battleground to gain support from a rapidly growing and more volatile electorate. Support for the Labour Party tends to be strongest in the south-east where rural constituencies traditionally contained a large farm labourer workforce although, as with The Workers' Party, some inroads are being made in large working-class urban areas.

The poorly developed structure and identity of regional politics are largely due to the pecularities of the Irish electoral system. Ireland operates a single transferable vote form of proportional representation (PR–STV). Under this system, voters are able to rank their preferences for all listed candidates and are furthermore able to vote for candidates of different political parties. Parker (1982a, 1986) has reviewed the elections of the 1980s and points out three main elements that determine the pattern of electoral success: constituency size change, and the number and domicile of the candidates selected by the parties.

In 1980, an independent commission was established to delimit constituencies and replaced an earlier system under which government itself was responsible for such reorganization. This had led to manipulation of the size of some constituencies to gain electoral support. The commission almost halved the number of three-seat constituencies and doubled the number of five-seat constituencies. The importance of this fact is that the quota of votes required for election to the Dáil within five-seat constituencies is much lower (17 per cent of the poll) than in three-seat constituencies (25 per cent) (Paddison, 1976). This not only allows a greater chance of election to the Dáil for independent and small-party candidates, but also requires careful management of electoral support by the larger parties. Should too many candidates be offered, party support many splinter and let in a rival party candidate.

Although Irish politics is essentially national in its orientation, the success of the parties at constituency level is ultimately dependent on local factors and the geographical spread and identity of candidates offered within the constituency. This is especially critical in the larger constituencies where, in order to maximize party support, voters need to be given the option of identifying with a local candidate. The belief that once a vote is captured it will transfer to other party members seems to be supported by Gallagher (1978), who pointed out that party solidarity for Fianna Fáil at the national level from 1922 to 1977 was as high as 82 per cent. A highly localized political system has consequently evolved within the country and, as Parker (1986) points out, 'arguably, the most basic geographic feature of the Irish electoral system and one which permeates throughout the rest of the system . . . is that known as localism' (p. 9). Successful politicians are forced to create, protect and become identified with particular territories (bailiwicks) within constituencies and these act as their personal power base. Examples abound of this practice, but particularly interesting cases have been documented in Donegal (Sacks, 1970, 1976) and West Galway (Parker, 1982b, 1983).

Constituency politics is often highly parochial and even the rise of left-wing deputies from urban areas is considered to reflect this aspect, rather than a more general belief in socialist ideology. The political machine of the dominant parties effectively utilizes localized strategies to ensure election of the preferred candidates, but ultimately these are dominated by national strategies. An extremely strong local identification with the national party results in even well-established local deputies performing a dual role. On the one hand they tend to function as national ombudsmen and a 'hawker of local interest' (Chubb, 1963, p. 285) while at the same time being expected to adhere rigidly to the party line. The quality of some deputies elected within this cult of localism and party political strategies is questionable, and, in the context of the critical decision making needed in a complex international trading economy, is hardly satisfactory. Also, within the national framework although local politicians perform an important function in mediating within a centralized decision-making structure, there are drawbacks to politicians being preoccupied with highly localized and personalized issues. Frequently, a political perspective which serves local and national issues means that a more coordinated and articulated political response to the problems of regional inequality is lacking. In such circumstances, dependency on the centre is exacerbated and any form of regional devolution is not even worth considering.

THREE

Rural Ireland

3.1 Introduction

Despite a comparatively recent surge in urban-industrial development associated with government attempts to modernize the national economy, the Irish landscape remains distinctly rural. Ireland is one of the most rural societies in Western Europe, and the countryside, more especially in the west, is dominated by a dispersed pattern of settlement forms focusing on small, compact family farms and small towns or villages. In 1981, 44.4 per cent of the national population resided in rural districts. Agriculture remains of principal importance in the social and economic life of large parts of the country, with 83 per cent of national space being utilized for farming. By the mid-1980s, approximately 11 per cent of GDP, 15 per cent of total employment and 23 per cent of the total value of exports related to agriculture. Only countries of the Mediterranean periphery — Greece, Portugal and Spain — showed a higher level of reliance.

Since 1960, however, the processes that shape the nature of the rural environment have undergone a significant change. Commercialization, diversification, centralization and specialization have combined to effect both a quantitative and qualitative transformation of rural Ireland. Against a background of general decline, the agricultural sector has become more commercialized, which in turn has encouraged greater specialization of production. At the same time, the loss of employment on farms was partially compensated for by a diversification of job opportunities within rural areas. This resulted in part from developments in other primary activities such as mining, forestry and fishing. Most notably, however, increased employment was related to the emergence of rural industrialization. Furthermore, the service sector became increasingly centralized on larger towns, as specialist services sought to benefit from economies of scale, and government policies for collective services favoured centralization. These new developments in the geography of production brought many opportunities and challenges for rural areas, not least because they tended to be more space-intensive and site-specific than those activities that preceded them.

Patterns of consumption also exhibited significant changes within the context of the modernization of rural Ireland. While these are partly conditioned by changes in patterns of production, of greater significance is the enhanced role given to rural areas as a place of domicile. An increasing number of people have opted to live in rural environments and commute to nearby urban centres of employment. The trend is compounded by the countryside proving an increasing attraction for retirement and second homes. Consumption is thereby significantly increased by a resident population that has little involvement in traditional means of production.

The complexity of rural life has been heightened by these new developments, especially since they include the potential for a conflict of interests between more established rural communities and newcomers recently opting to live in the countryside. The longer-established rural communities tend to perceive their needs as being based on the support and development of local employment and essential public services such as transport, education and health. In contrast, these matters have less priority with newer residents, whose middle-class status, greater affluence and personal mobility allow them consumption patterns based more commonly on personal and private services.

The juxtaposition of different social classes within the rural communities and a more dynamic economic system clearly demand careful planning. The 1963 Planning Act offers some guidelines, but these are not rigorously enforced and uncoordinated development seems to typify the contemporary landscape of rural Ireland. Transformation of the countryside has not benefited all communities to the same degree. The position of those living in more marginal areas, with poor access to urban centres and a lack of scenic qualities, has deteriorated relative to the position of those living near to an urban centre and/or a high-quality environment. After years of comparative stability, modernization has encroached on, and precipitated changes over, an increasing area of the country. If the benefits of such a process are to be maximized, a greater recognition of the complexities of rural areas must be incorporated within development planning.

3.2 Agriculture and the rural environment

The rural environment is strongly influenced by the nature of enterprise practised on farms. Traditionally, Irish agriculture included elements of a mixed farming system with some cereals, root crops and farmyard enterprises, involving a small number of pigs and free-range chickens, complementing the more primary activity of grass-based cattle rearing. This diversity has been substantially reduced, however, as the greater specialization of production at the national level, was replicated on individual farms (Gillmor, 1987). After 1960, a greater degree of uniformity of agricultural

Table 3.1   The structure of farm enterprises, 1960 and 1980

	National % change in number (or area)	% holdings with tillage or livestock type		Average herd size (or ha of tillage) per holding	
	1960–1980	1960	1980	1960	1980
Tillage (area)	(−18)	82	52	(2.8)	(4.0)
Cows	+59	80	63	5	13
All cattle	+46	88	79	19	33
Sheep	−24	30	17	49	75
Horses	−69	50	10	2	3
Pigs	+ 8	38	5	8	82
Poultry	−24	78	35	54	108

Source: Gillmor (1987).

practice was imposed on the landscape. By the mid-1980s, more than 90 per cent of agricultural land use was devoted to supporting livestock and 87 per cent of the value of gross agricultural output related to livestock and livestock products (Table 3.1).

The scale and intensity of farming operations also increased as farmers sought to raise productivity levels and benefit from internal economies of scale. An overt manifestation of this was the increasing appearance in the rural landscape of more machinery, a greater use of fertilizers, and new farm buildings such as modern milking facilities and renovated or new accommodation for the farmer and his family. However, not all sectors and areas were affected equally by the specialization of output based on the application of technology and economies of scale. Cattle- and sheep-rearing enterprises appear to be the least affected, and beef cattle-rearing remains common over large parts of the country. This is particularly apparent in the western regions, where the rural landscape continues to exhibit a less than vigorous response to the dictates of modern agricultural practices (NESC, 1978).

While it can be argued that a significant transformation of agricultural production occurred following 1960, the degree of change at other levels was less impressive and had a fundamental impact on the degree of prosperity and potential for agricultural development. Although the agricultural workforce was halved between 1960 and 1980, the total number of farm units declined by only 9 per cent. This clearly indicated that surplus labour, including farm labourers, family members and relatives, was

Table 3.2 Selected characteristics of farms where farm operator is aged 55–70 years, 1984

Characteristic	Ireland (%)	Less Favoured Areas (%)	East (%)
Proportion of total farms	33.1	37.0	26.4
Farm size less than 20 ha	59.5	61.6	54.0
Drystock system	59.6	62.4	55.4
'Full-time' farm	26.9	20.5	42.0
Farm with at least one man work unit (MWU)	17.3	11.2	32.9
Family farm income per labour unit less than IR£ 3800	72.2	78.7	55.2
Farm poorly developed	46.1	53.5	32.6
Farm operator has off-farm job	9.6	8.6	10.7
Single person household	18.9	17.0	24.1
Proportion of total gross output from farms	23.5	10.5	13.0
Estimated number of farms	64,000	44,000	20,000
Estimated number of hectares	1.4 million	773,000	581,000

Source: O'Hara (1986).

removed from the land. The individual small farmer, however, remained the basic unit of production. As a result, average farm size (20.7 ha in 1980) has shown little increase during the postwar period, and a proliferation of small- to medium-sized units continues to typify the rural landscape.

This stubborn persistence of a structural problem, and the potential to adjust to a modern form of agricultural activity, is strongly influenced by the demographic and sociocultural characteristics of the farmer (Scully, 1971). The successful farmer, especially if engaged in tillage or intensive dairying, is usually profiled as being generally well-educated, relatively young, married and with a family. In marked contrast, the less successful farmer is associated with small holdings, is involved with extensive rearing of cattle and is frequently elderly, widowed or unmarried, poorly educated and possesses no immediate heir (Frawley et al., 1974–75; O'Carroll et al., 1978). Kelleher and O'Hara (1978) show that many low-income farmers, even when possessing a somewhat better demographic profile, lack the personal capacity to adjust to the demands of a more business-like approach.

In many of the remote rural areas large numbers of farmers are only nominally engaged in agriculture, and yet an almost peasant-like attachment for the land makes significant structural change and modernization almost impossible to achieve in the short term. Table 3.2 shows the extent, and some of the dominant characteristics, of farm units operated by farmers aged between 55 and 70 years. For many such people, farming is a way of life and is not subject to the dictates of market forces. As a result, it provides a sense of continuity and tradition for much of the more extreme western areas, while the rural environments of the south and east are exhibiting greater signs of modernization.

Increased specialization of production and initial benefits derived from price increases under the CAP undoubtedly contributed to a general improvement in the well-being of the majority of Irish farmers. The sectoral and spatial duality of Irish agriculture, however, has ensured that the degree of prosperity and extent of rural transformation favours the more developed farming areas. Rural poverty is still a symptomatic feature of large areas, especially of those characterized by small farms geared to the raising of beef cattle (Duffy, 1980; Connolly et al., 1985). Thus, in 1984, farms of between 2 and 10 ha generated a family farm income of only 5 per cent that of farms in excess of 100 ha (Foras Taluntais, 1986). In addition, Riordan (1986) estimated that in 1985 45,000 farmers who were entirely dependent on raising cattle had herd sizes of less than 60 head. These farmers, the majority of whom reside in the Less Favoured Areas, had an average family farm income of only IR£ 1600.

Part-time farming now involves approximately one-quarter of all farmers (Higgins, 1983). A second income allows for the maintenance of living standards for many smallholders. At the same time, however, it encourages a shift to more extensive and less labour-demanding activities such as cattle rearing, while also reducing the possibilities of achieving a greater mobility in the land market. Rural depopulation is partially offset by rural industrialization, but it is somewhat ironic that modernization of the rural economy in one sector favours the conservation of traditional structures of land holding in another.

Government support of farming communities and agriculture is extremely strong and reflects the existence within the Irish political system of powerful agricultural and rural lobbies such as the Irish Farmers Association and the Irish Creamery Milk Suppliers Association. In addition, a sizeable number of Dáil deputies have either a direct or indirect interest in farming and land. The farming community in general has not yet been required to pay taxes, and even the introduction of a system of rateable valuation in 1974 proved ineffective. This was abolished in 1983 on constitutional grounds, the rateable values having been based on estimates made in the mid-nineteenth century. Another attempt is now being made to implement a more effective form of farm taxation, but in 1986 only IR£ 37 million was collected as against IR£ 2 billion from the pay-as-you-earn sector.

The operation of the EC's Less Favoured Areas scheme, the introduction of the Western Drainage Scheme (1979) and a special package of incentives to promote better infrastructural facilities for farming areas in the west (1981) have all directly contributed to supporting underdeveloped rural environments. And yet, much remains to be done to raise conditions in the west to levels comparable to those in the east and south. Reliance of rural communities in the LFAs on government income transfers is highlighted by Higgins (1986) who showed that, by 1980, 44 per cent of total household income was derived from such transfers. However, despite a consistent bias in the direct fiscal system which benefits rural households (Pratschke, 1984), their position relative to urban households has disimproved. Clearly, without significant government commitment to such areas, conditions in many rural communities would be extremely difficult. This poses the question of whether policies for, and the role of, agriculture in the promotion of rural well-being need to be reassessed.

If agriculture is at a turning point within the CAP, so also is its position with respect to the pivotal role it has traditionally played in rural societies. Two recent Green Papers on European agricultural policy options (Commission of the European Communities, 1985a, b) have clearly suggested that farmers in future will have to recognize greater efficiency in production, the dictates of the market-place and the desirability of promoting alternative or supplementary uses for their land. This will demand a greater flexibility of farm communities, especially for those in more marginal areas, than has been exhibited in the past. Forestry, farmhouse craft industries and tourist accommodation have to be further promoted as well as the contentious suggestion that farmers be recognized as custodians of the environment. In this sense, the farm should be operated in a manner to best preserve the quality and distinctiveness of the countryside for the benefit of non-farming communities. Unfortunately, there is little tradition within Irish farming communities of viewing the countryside as an amenity for urban dwellers. The land is, first, a family territory; second, the means of achieving social prestige; and, finally, a factor of production — irrespective of the level of efficiency attained. And yet the prosperity of rural areas has increasingly moved away from a principal dependency upon agricultural production. Farmers will have to try to adjust to the fact that rural economic and social progress in future will increasingly depend on a multisectoral approach. This will pose problems for both planners and farmers, especially in marginal areas where long-established cultural values are not easily changed. In the next three sections we review development patterns for some of the alternative sectors proposed as mainstays for rural economies.

3.3 An alternative primary base for rural areas

The process of modernization has influenced not only agriculture but also the development of other primary economic activities. To a large extent, developments within mining, forestry and fishing focus on rural environments and consequently have helped to diversify socioeconomic systems that have traditionally depended disproportionately on farming activities.

3.3.1 *Mineral resources*

Ireland possesses a long history of mineral exploitation, although its small-scale character did not encourage the emergence of any significant urban-industrial development. Increasing demands for base metals during the Second World War and active government support to foster an indigenous mining industry, however, led to a gathering momentum to exploit this resource (Holland, 1979). International investment in the exploration and exploitation of the mineral base in the 1960s increased, and major discoveries of lead, zinc and copper effectively discredited the myth that Ireland was minerally impoverished (Kearns, 1976a). Mines developed at Tynagh and Silvermines (Figure 3.1) became established as major European suppliers of metal ores, although these were quickly superseded by the discovery in 1970 of potentially one of the world's largest sources of lead and zinc at Navan (Walsh, F., 1977).

The national benefits of employment creation, enhanced capital investment and export performance were further emphasized by the spatial orientation of developments. The mines are predominantly located in rural areas, and they significantly aided the promotion of local economies. Capital injections improved physical and social infrastructures, while the availability of well-paid, male employment was highly beneficial to communities experiencing declining employment prospects. The almost boom conditions which affected mining communities in the 1960s and early 1970s, however, have unfortunately faded as all but Navan have closed. As a result, government has been pressurized to direct manufacturing enterprises into such areas to absorb displaced miners. The depressed state of the contemporary mining industry suggests, however, that apart from ongoing development associated with the Navan mine, it has reverted to a more traditional, neutral role in the development of rural Ireland.

The development of peat resources has played a more consistent role in the promotion of the rural economy. Peat is the most extensive mineral resource in Ireland and covers approximately one-seventh of the land

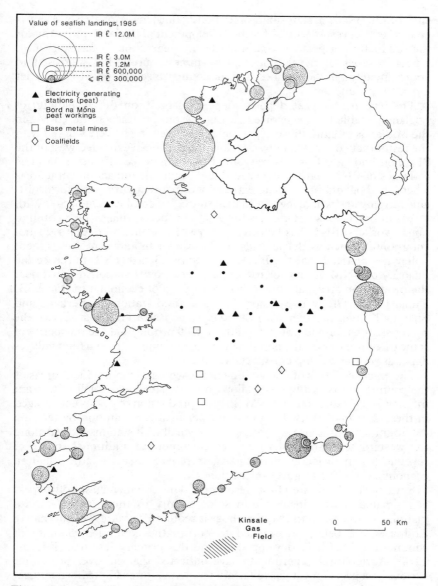

Figure 3.1 Location of major mineral workings and fishing ports.

surface. In 1946, a state-sponsored body, Bórd na Móna (BNM), was created to take responsibility for the development of bogland, primarily for the production of peat for use in electricity generation (Kearns, 1976b). Under a series of development programmes, output has increased to approximately 4 million tonnes, and the country is second only to the Soviet Union in production.

The working of peat deposits depends largely on the availability of bogland suitable for mechanized cutting. Extensive tracts of raised bog in the Midlands fall into this category and have been intensively worked with the result that commercial bog development has been extended west of the Shannon and into Cos. Galway and Roscommon (see Figure 3.1). The activities of BNM have a huge social and economic impact on rural areas where the bogland presents an extremely difficult environment for profitable farming and where few alternative sources of employment occur. With direct employment standing at some 6000 and special villages being built to house workers, BNM has helped to revive the fortunes of depressed rural communities such as Bellacorrick in Co. Mayo. In addition, government policy has dictated that the Electricity Supply Board (ESB) purchase the majority of BNM output for use in peat-fired power stations located near the production areas, although this priority is not economic for the ESB. Thus, in Co. Offaly two major ESB peat-fired stations at Ferbane and Shannonbridge, together with the two major BNM bogs that service the power stations, provide work for almost 2000 people, and the prosperity of some three-quarters of the population in the surrounding towns and villages depends on these complementary activities.

The extensive areas of blanket bog in the west and mountainous areas of the country are typically too shallow, remote, steep and small to warrant mechanized production by BNM. Private production of peat is encouraged in these areas and is used not only for personal consumption by farming communities, but is also sold to a series of small ESB stations located along the western seaboard. This provides an important additional source of revenue for small landowners and again reflects a social rather than an economic objective of government policy.

Since the boglands are a finite resource and the commercial supply of peat is estimated to terminate within some twenty to thirty years, careful planning of the use of the exposed bogs is required. A variety of alternative land uses are being investigated to ensure the continued viability of communities that have developed around this primary resource (Kearns, 1978). Agricultural experiments have indicated that cut-over bogs offer various prospects for intensive farming systems, for example horticulture, pasture and cereal cropping. In addition, the used bogs appear to be eminently suitable for reafforestation, if communities can be convinced of its potential. Finally, conservationists are increasingly pointing to the ecological importance of preserving large areas of bog and their potential as a tourist attraction. These contrasting claims need careful consideration if future communities living in such areas are to benefit.

3.3.2 *Forestry*

In order to counteract the declining role of agriculture in disadvantaged areas, the EC has advocated a much greater role for forestry, especially since market demand greatly exceeds the supply of wood.

Ireland has a particularly favourable environment for forestry, the mild maritime climate supporting a growth rate of some three to five times that experienced in mainland Europe (Dunstan, 1985). In spite of this, only 4.8 per cent of the country is forested and, with the exception of Iceland, this is the lowest level in Europe.

Since the extensive forestry clearances of the sixteenth and early seventeenth centuries, the country has had a very low level of tree culture, the rural population viewing woodland as a hindrance to land development for food production and the support of a high-density farming population. The almost negative attitude towards trees by individuals in rural areas resulted in the state being forced to take an active role in forest promotion (O'Carroll, 1984). Thus from the introduction of a major programme for forest development in 1948, when state forest amounted to 53,000 ha, the area has consistently increased to over 320,000 ha by 1984. However, until the 1980s the state did not recognize forestry as a major development option. Priority was afforded to improving the agricultural economy by increasing farm size, and this severely restricted tree plantings to areas largely unsuited for agriculture (Farrell, 1983). The pattern of woodlands that subsequently emerged was therefore one largely confined to the marginal uplands and bog areas of the country. This is likely to change, however, as greater emphasis is placed on forestry for national development and job creation.

Gardiner and Radford (1980) have estimated that almost one-half of Ireland can be classified as being marginal for agriculture. In spite of an apparent bias against forestry, evidence began to emerge of the positive developmental role this alternative land use could have for rural communities in such areas (Convery, 1973–74). This is highlighted by the opportunities in Co. Leitrim, where only 10 per cent of the land is regarded as being at least moderately suitable for agriculture and contributes to the poverty of this area. In contrast, the average yield on the heavy, wet soil is some 50 per cent above the national average for Sitka spruce. Additional employment can be created both directly and indirectly in spin-off industries. The clothing of the poorer environments with trees will also generate a new landscape with opportunities for multiple uses such as recreation, soil conservation, water control and nature reserves (Hickey and Killen, 1986). Coordinated planning is essential for such progress to occur but it also necessitates an acceptance of trees as a viable crop by the rural communities.

An impetus to private forestry development was finally provided in the Programme for Western Development which came into operation in 1981 and which offered grants to farmers of up to 85 per cent of the approved cost for planting trees on their land. However, between 1981 and 1986 only a little over 1000 applications were received for forestry grants within the Less Favoured Areas, and by July 1986 only 8 per cent of a ten-year target of 24,000 ha had been planted (Kelleher, 1986).

The almost innate conservatism of the farming communities, especially in marginal areas, together with the lack of tradition of forestry, and the comparatively high initial capital outlay with no immediate financial return all work against a rapid diffusion of this land use. In contrast, investment companies are taking an increasing and more active role in forestry development. Thus, in 1985, 25 per cent of state plantings were carried out by these institutions, although in a survey of four less favoured counties in 1986 (Leitrim, Cavan, Sligo and Monaghan), more than half of the total land planted to trees was accounted for by investment companies (Kelleher, 1986).

3.3.3. Fishing

The continental shelf around Ireland is an extremely rich fishing area, which remains remarkably underdeveloped (de Courcy Ireland, 1981). In order to improve this situation, the government established Bord Iascaigh Mhara (BIM) as a development agency to promote actively the industry both at sea and on land. Its efforts have been attended by some success, for the quantity and value of catch have increased dramatically, especially since the 1970s (Gillmor, 1985a). The creation of the Common Fisheries Policy for the EC, however, has caused concern for Ireland, since with some 25 per cent of the Community's waters Ireland's share of the total allowable catch is only 4.6 per cent. This quota restriction may well inhibit growth of an industry which has considerable potential for national and regional development.

Development of the fishing industry has important spatial consequences due to its increasing orientation to the west coast, where approximately three-quarters of the fish catch is now landed (see Figure 3.1). The western and southern coastline has a proliferation of natural harbours, and this formed the basis of a traditional fishing industry. It was small scale and involved a large proportion of part-time fisherman working out of small vessels in order to supplement farming incomes. The industry has now modernized and activity has increasingly focused on more commercial operations, working out of larger and better equipped ports (Went, 1979).

Killybegs, in Co. Donegal, has emerged as the nucleus of the industry with fish landings valued at some IR£ 12 million in 1985. This and other ports have helped significantly to support the depressed economy of this peripheral county. Spin-off industries include the development of modern fish-processing plants which bus in employees from the town's hinterland. They have complemented Killybeg's 'mackerel millionaires' and have succeeded in giving this small port one of the highest per capita incomes in Ireland (Siggins, 1987). Considerable scope exists for promoting the fishing industry and, with related multiplier effects, it could play an important role in transforming the lifestyle of coastal communities. Success is dependent, however, on more coordinated planning within both the various branches of the industry, for example supply, processing and marketing, and the broader economic system.

3.4 Rural industrialization: decentralization in practice

The promotion of an alternative primary base to agriculture has achieved some success, although its role in the transformation of rural communities has been spatially limited. Far more important in this respect is rural industrialization, which has played a particularly critical role in the poorly developed western counties (Breathnach, 1985).

The eleven western counties used in a definition of the West of Ireland cover approximately one-half of the country and are intensely rural. Some three-quarters of the population of almost 900,000 live in rural areas and only four of the region's thirty-five towns (classified as having a population of at least 1500) exceed 10,000 population. These areas traditionally held little attraction for industry and, prior to 1961, despite some growth in rural-based manufacturing, the proportion of all industrial employment located in the western counties declined sharply (Table 3.3).

This position was turned around in the 1960s, however, and is associated with the evolution of regional manufacturing patterns outlined in Chapter 2. Employment in manufacturing grew at three times the rate experienced in the rest of the country and signalled the enhanced attractiveness of rural communities for industrial development. O'hUiginn (1972), in a study of manufacturing firms in the 1960s, shows a clear preference for locating in smaller towns, and this is strongly supported by P.N. O'Farrell's (1975) survey of grant-aided establishments between 1960 and 1973. In this latter study, 56 per cent of such establishments opted to locate in urban centres of fewer than 5000 people.

Table 3.3   West of Ireland: industrial employment percentages, 1926–81

	1926	1961	1971	1981
Employment in manufacturing	4.8	7.9	12.9	19.2
Share of national manufacturing	19	13	16	21
Growth in Irish manufacturing		62.8	19.6	9.1
Growth in manufacturing in the West		8.9	44.5	44.9
Growth in the rest of Ireland		75.6	15.8	2.5

Source: after Breathnach (1985).

The ruralization of industry gathered further momentum in the 1970s, with the western counties accounting for almost 75 per cent of the national growth in manufacturing employment. Elsewhere in the country, rural industrialization also continued to develop, although much of this was associated with the positive performance of manufacturing within the hinterlands of the larger urban centres. Thus, in Cos. Kildare, Meath and Wicklow, employment continued to grow in contrast to the negative trend within the urban core of Dublin (O'Farrell, 1984). Similar developments occurred within the Greater Cork area (Brunt, 1980) and in the new town of Shannon, which deflected some growth from Limerick (see Section 3.7.2).

Several processes influenced the industrialization of the Irish country-side, although most notable were government policy, the restructuring practices of multinational investment and a new perception of rural areas and small towns. The latter were seen not only as practical sites for production, but also as pleasant environments in which to live and work. The differential operation of grants in favour of the west and the discretionary powers of the IDA in varying the allocation of the grants favoured rural areas. In addition, the site acquisition and advance factory building programme of the IDA was a most significant factor in promoting the establishment of new manufacturing enterprises in rural areas. Standardized and modern 'box-like' units have become a conspicuous new feature in rural Ireland and, between 1972 and 1981, approximately one-half of 600,000 m^2 of advance factory floorspace constructed in Ireland was sited at seventy-five locations in the eleven western counties.

Undoubtedly, the major factor in the promotion of rural industrialization has been the gravitation of foreign direct investment to such areas. Tarrant (1967) provides early evidence of this, pointing to the success of new ventures west of a line drawn from Galway to Cork. The reorganization of the structure of big business greatly aided the dispersal of manufacturing since the spatial separation of production from higher management and administrative functions made assembly-stage operations more footloose

(O'Farrell, 1980; Perrons, 1981). While the absolute cost and supply advantages of labour in rural communities may also have been prominent initially, these advantages are now marginal, especially given the high unemployment levels throughout the country. However, stronger traditions of trade unionism and greater social militancy in established urban centres contribute to deflecting industry from such areas, as agglomeration economies are seen to give way to diseconomies. In addition, the almost monopolistic position that can be achieved by large companies in small labour markets, together with the increasing involvement of part-time farmers and females in the rural workforce, all contribute to a higher level of labour adaptability and compliance with management decisions. A lack of industrial skills is not a problem since new production technologies have effectively deskilled many functions.

Indigenous industry has also contributed to the dispersal of development into rural areas, notably through the IDA's Small Industry programme. From 1973 to 1981, a net gain of 11,000 jobs was achieved in plants employing fewer than fifty people, and almost doubled its share of the Republic's manufacturing base to 10 per cent (O'Farrell, 1984). O'Farrell and Crouchley (1984) found a strong link between the degree of rurality and the establishment rate of small industries. As a result, the most impressive gains in this respect were to be found north of a line running from Galway to Drogheda, and centre on the least industrialized counties of Leitrim and Roscommon.

Apart from creating new employment, industrial dispersal has enhanced job opportunities in many areas, thus allowing higher female participation in the labour force. Higher wages have contributed to increased standards of living although the local multiplier effects have been less than satisfactory. Apart from food processing, O'Farrell and O'Loughlin (1980) report that industrial units purchase only 5 per cent of their material inputs within a 32-km radius of the plant and that 83 per cent of Irish service payments leak to the country's 10 largest urban centres.

Despite the enclave character of most rural factories, they have extended their labour catchment areas over extensive areas. A recent study of four large factories in Co. Mayo, which employ over 1000 workers, found that 44 per cent of the total workforce lived more than 8 km from their place of work (Lucey and Walker, 1987). This allowed agricultural workers to be attracted into industry, and has emphasised the role of part–time farming in the Less Favoured Areas. In an important earlier study by Lucey and Kaldor (1969), one-half of the employees in two plants located in Cos. Sligo and Clare lived on farms; in the Mayo study quoted above (Lucey and Walker, 1987) 39 per cent lived on a farm or were involved in farming.

Rural industrialization has further influenced the commercialization of agriculture through the increasing number of food-processing plants that locate in such areas to use local supplies of farm produce. Meat-processing plants and dairy cooperatives are particularly important given the nature of Ireland's pastoral farm economy. The development of the dairy cooperative creameries reflects the trend quite well. Essentially, this movement began in the rich dairy lands of Munster and south-west Leinster, but it has now diffused throughout much of the country. In recent times, however, the problems of milk quotas and costs have resulted in the amalgamation of some cooperatives and the rationalization of collection and production into larger and more centrally located plants. Many smaller milk collecting depots and creameries throughout the rural areas have closed, and a collection system via bulk tankers has been introduced. Not only has this taken employment from some areas, but it has also removed an important element in the social life of many small-scale dairy farmers who formerly congregated around such facilities after making their daily delivery of milk. Further aspects of the social and cultural impact of modernization on the rural environment are discussed in Section 3.6.

3.5   Service employment: centralization in practice

The increasing importance of the tertiary sector has brought additional employment opportunities to rural communities, although in general the service sector has remained more urban in orientation than manufacturing. Dineen (1985) points out that the five western regions gained only 30 per cent of a total of 130,000 new service jobs created in the 1970s, and their proportion of national service employment declined, albeit marginally. Nevertheless, these gains have been important in diversifying the employment base of rural communities.

The non-marketed public sector has come to play an increasingly dominant role in the development of service provision within rural areas, although the provision of marketed services has been more sluggish. The high profile of government-controlled service employment and the lack of any coherent planning for the private sector, however, have had important repercussions for rural areas, especially for the more marginal and less accessible communities. Interacting with this trend are two important processes which stress the difficulties and complexities of service provision in the countryside: demographic change and centralization.

Rural areas have traditionally experienced a below-average range and quality of services (NESC, 1978). The legacy of population decline and the increasing proportion of elderly persons left in rural communities effectively reduce the threshold levels of services, and facilities were withdrawn from areas unable to sustain a viable demand. Apart from a comparatively small number of remote and environmentally difficult rural areas, however, population decline has gradually been reversed over the past generation (see Section 3.6.1), and yet the transformation of many rural communities into centres of enhanced consumption has not brought about a commensurate dispersal of either private or public services. The reason for this lies partly in the changing social composition of the population but more especially in a movement to centralize and concentrate the provision of services (McCashin, 1982).

From the late 1960s onwards, all governments have favoured centralization of services in order to benefit from economies of scale and, theoretically, to provide more effective and higher-quality operations. Larger urban centres have benefited from this process to the detriment of smaller towns and rural communities. Market forces have also ensured that centralization characterizes private services. Some examples will highlight the contemporary position for rural service provision in Ireland.

Retail activity in rural areas has traditionally been provided by a relatively large number of quite small, unspecialized units. Many of these general stores also possess a licensed bar and thus also act as a social focus. The number of these rural shops has declined markedly throughout the postwar period (Dawson, 1972), and Cawley (1986) has recently shown that the category of 'country general shops' decreased by 86 per cent in Connaught between 1951 and 1977. Reorganization of the retail trade has contributed in no small way to this demise. The emergence of multiple outlet corporate chain companies such as Quinnsworth and Dunnes Stores, and voluntary trading group outlets, for example Spar and Centra/VG, has resulted in large-scale purchasing practice and self-service operations being used to reduce significantly their prices, to the detriment of the smaller shopkeeper (Parker, 1980b). Success of these larger retail outlets depends on a high turnover of goods, and thus they tend to locate within urban areas possessing good access to an extended rural hinterland. The enhanced personal mobility of a majority of the rural population further encourages centralization, and important market centres such as Tralee, Galway and Sligo have been major beneficiaries of this trend. For a disadvantaged minority in remoter rural districts, however, the erosion of local shops has served to compound their already marginalized position.

Centralization within the education system, especially at the primary level, is a particularly sensitive issue for rural families. The number of primary schools declined in most of rural Ireland following independence, as population decline led to a constant fall-off in school enrolment. Much of the decline was poorly coordinated, however, and a report by Hallak and McCabe in 1973 pointed to considerable spatial inequity in the education system in Co. Sligo, with the school network tending to reflect past demographic and socioeconomic patterns rather than contemporary realities (quoted in Gillmor, 1985a, p. 285). In a move to modernize the system and achieve economies of scale and greater efficiency of service provision, the government adopted the recommendations of *Investment in Education* (Department of Education, 1965). Some 1800 one- and two-teacher schools were phased out between 1965 and 1977, and an emphasis was placed on new and enlarged schools built at centrally located towns or villages (Curry, 1980). Children were bussed to these centres from the surrounding catchment areas. By the time the policy was revoked in 1977, it had had a dramatic effect on the school system. Almost one-half of the schools in Co. Leitrim, for example, were closed during this short time period, while in other western counties the proportion approached one-third (Cawley, 1986).

Primary health care and hospital services have also been subject to strong centralization with potentially far-reaching consequences for the quality of life in rural areas (see Sections 1.4.2 and 2.4.2). Sparsely populated rural areas are poorly served by doctors, and in 1979 one-fifth of medical card holders in the Western Health Board lived more than 11 km from the surgery of their general practitioner (Department of Health, 1981). Hospital facilities are even more spatially selective, and their concentration and centralization will be further exacerbated by the 1987 budget cuts.

Centralization and concentration increasingly typify the tertiary and quaternary sectors in Ireland. Remarkably little decentralization of services has occurred at the national level to support the ruralization of industry and, where evidence of this is to be found, it is invariably orientated to the larger urban centres within rural counties. Tourism, however, is characterized by dispersal and this has brought benefits as well as a potential for further development even to more peripheral rural areas.

Tourism has been a conspicuous growth industry in much of the postwar period and Ireland is similar to some Mediterranean countries in its degree of dependency on this activity (Seers, 1979). In more recent years, however, the industry has been less buoyant due largely to higher costs, resulting from inflation, and the need for more effective promotion in the overseas market. As a result, the real value of Irish tourism declined by 5 per cent between 1980 and 1984, while the average receipts from tourism in OECD countries rose in real terms by 21.3 per cent. A development plan for the industry envisages the possibility of doubling the real value of income from tourism and creating 40,000 additional jobs over a six- or seven-year period (Stokes Kennedy Crowley et al., 1987). The 1987 Programme for National Recovery, however, is less ambitious since its objective is to create an extra 25,000 jobs and attract an additional IR£ 500 million of foreign tourist receipts. Returns for 1987 indicate that tourism may have recaptured its

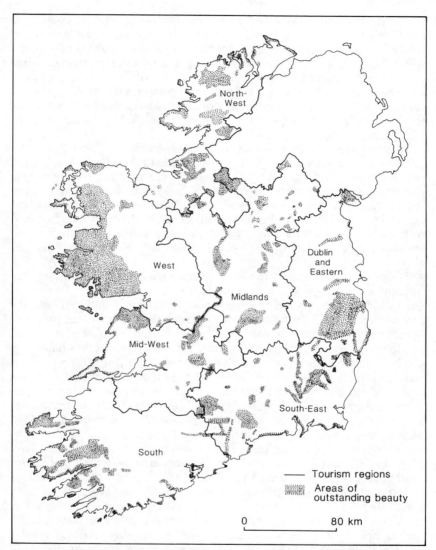

Figure 3.2 Tourist regions and areas of outstanding beauty (Foras Forbartha, 1977).

growth momentum, since revenue topped IR£ 1000 million for the first time and was ahead of the 1986 figure by some 40 per cent.

A statutory body, Bord Fáilte, was established in 1955 to coordinate effectively the promotion of tourism. While many tourists gravitate to the major urban centres, especially Dublin, it is the quality of Ireland's countryside and its diverse attractions (e.g. coastal and mountain scenery, cultural and historic landmarks and outdoor activities, especially golfing, fishing, sailing and horseback riding) which attract most overseas visitors (Mawhinney, 1979). Rural areas consequently possess many advantages for tourist development, notably in the more peripheral, pollution-free environments of the west.

This was clearly substantiated by a survey made by Foras Forbartha (1977) to evaluate landscape quality. Out of a total 1.2 million ha designated as being of outstanding quality (18 per cent of the country), the majority is predominantly in peripheral locations and in less developed areas (Figure 3.2). Apart from mountainous and upland areas, inland waterways and lakes, the coastal zone is particularly important for sightseeing and general recreation. The west has the greatest proportion of high-quality scenic coastline, especially in Cos. Donegal, Clare and Kerry (Brady et al., 1972–73).

Tourism clearly favours the four tourist regions of the West and has brought an important source of revenue to these communities (Table 3.4). In addition, central government support to maintain and promote the physical and social infrastructures of these regions for tourism has spill-over benefits for the local populace. Tourism has also brought some badly needed employment to these areas, ranging from dispersed farmhouse bed and breakfast activities to small craft enterprises supplying quality goods or souvenirs to tourists. Much of the employment is seasonal and/or part-time in nature and involves a predominance of female workers. It appears to be particularly beneficial for underemployed family members of small farm enterprises, providing them with an important additional source of income. Standards of living are consequently raised and some mechanization of farming practice is encouraged. Furthermore, some urban centres have come to rely almost exclusively on the servicing of tourist needs, for example Killarney, Lisdoonvarna, Bundoran.

Although tourism contributes positively to the development of rural areas, there are problems which have to be recognized. In addition to problems of seasonality, the potential and actual conflict between tourism and competing land uses requires careful monitoring (NESC, 1980b). Social and cultural conflicts have also become apparent, since an offshoot of the tourist industry has been the building of retirement and second homes. Some of theses impacts and repercussions are dealt with in the following section.

Developments in service provision within rural areas present something

Table 3.4   Patterns of regional tourism

Tourist region	Percentage share of all tourism accommodation, 1983	Percentage share of national tourism revenue, 1983	Estimated percentage of regional income derived from tourism
Dublin–Eastern	23.8	26.0	2
Dublin	15.3	18.6	2
East	8.5	7.5	3
Midlands	5.0	6.5	3
South-East	9.8	10.9	5
South	25.8	23.8	8
Mid-West	11.3	9.9	6
West	14.4	12.7	10
North-West	9.9	10.3	12

Source: Gillmor (1985a).

of a paradoxical situation. On the one hand, there is little doubt that the quality and range of services available to residents in rural areas have been improved. However, accessibility to those services has become increasingly conditioned by income level, socioeconomic status and location of domicile of the population. Modernization has therefore not had a uniform impact on rural communities. While voluntarism has some potential for meeting some of the more basic needs of these communities, there seems little doubt that their long-term viability will be dependent on government policy and the extent to which services can be subsidized from central funding.

3.6   The impacts of modernization on rural Ireland

Rural areas are under great pressures of change, induced primarily by the forces of modernization and the diffusion of urban-industrial influences over large parts of the country. Furthermore, the rapidity of change occurring within a single generation has added to the adjustment problems of conservative rural communities faced with the more dynamic, cosmopolitan values of an externally orientated urbanized system. Adjustment has been most complete in the hinterlands of the larger towns and cities, and especially in the eastern areas, since these act as the 'hinges' for the greater integration into the broader European and global cultural system.

Economic development has affected all aspects of Irish life, although some consequences are more subtle than others. The rural population have not been entirely passive agents within the process of change, however, and they have helped to shape the expression of modernization. As Smyth (1984, p. 221) points out: 'Obviously the distinctive structure and history of individual rural communities will influence patterns of rural–urban interaction; certainly it cannot be assumed that a simple distance equation from the urban centres will explain the complex mosaic of territorial and class structures that is now recrystallising across Ireland'.

3.6.1   Population change

Population trends within rural Ireland since the mid-nineteenth century have shown an almost continuous decline. This is most strongly seen in the west and north-west, where a combination of forces resulted in an inverse relationship between the density of population and the carrying capacity of the land. Since the end of the Second World War, however, there have been important modifications to the general spiral of population decline. A comparison of the situation in the 1950s, with that of the 1970s, highlights the major demographic adjustment that has occurred in most of the country (Horner and Daultry, 1980).

In the 1950s, national economic problems were expressed in a marked decline of population throughout most of rural Ireland (Figure 3.3); this was particularly acute in the north-western areas (Johnson, 1963). Fewer than 20 of 157 Rural Districts in the country experienced growth, and these were mostly located in the immediate hinterlands of the largest cities. The development of the peat deposits by Bord na Mona, however, did act as a stabilizing influence on population in some areas of the Midlands.

The ruralization of industry in the 1960s, together with the choice of the countryside as a place of domicile for an increasingly mobile and affluent population, had a major impact on rural demography. Table 4.1 (p. 139) highlights the transition from the 1960s to the 1970s and the performance of rural areas compared to urban centres. More than a century of population decline was turned around in the 1970s with fewer than thirty Rural Districts recording further reductions. The most impressive gains were recorded around the larger urban centres where growth was already well established prior to 1971. As a result, Horner and Daultry (1980, p. 133) suggest that a feature of the recent growth in Irish population has been its diffusion down through the urban hierarchy, and from east to west. The importance of proximity to an established urban base is therefore a major factor in shaping contemporary trends in rural population (Horner, 1986).

Changes in the patterns of population have been strongly influenced by significant modifications in net migration. Rural industrialization is the prime agent in significantly reducing emigration from many rural com-

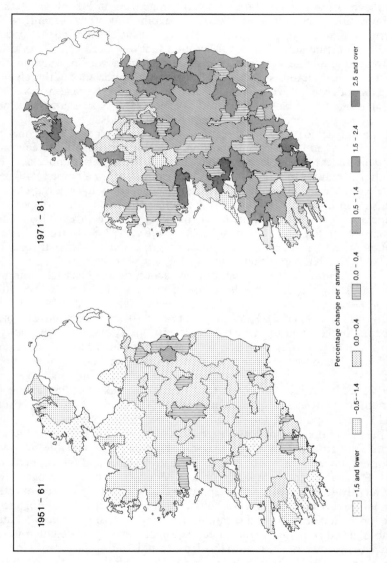

Figure 3.3   Population change 1951–61 and 1971–81 (after Horner and Daultrey, 1980 and Horner, 1986).

munities (Lucey and Kaldor, 1969; Lucey and Walker, 1987). Enhanced employment prospects have also encouraged an influx of workers to communities that were more used to the debilitating effects of emigration. Return migration forms a particularly significant element of this process and Ó Cinneide and Keane (1983) found that one-third of the workforce employed at a large synthetic fibre plant established in Co. Mayo in 1977 were returned migrants. Other studies show the importance of this element (e.g. Kupper, 1969; Hourihan, 1982b), and even in the weakly developed rural economy of South Leitrim, Foeken (1980) has found returnees occupying up to one-quarter of surveyed households.

The impact of new job creation, however, extends far beyond the workplace as an increasing proportion of people are prepared to commute long distances to their place of employment. Whether this is undertaken out of choice in order to satisfy middle-class aspirations for a home established in a picturesque environment, or through a necessity to seek out cheaper housing in less urbanized areas, the result is the same — the dispersal of population growth in rural areas surrounding urban centres. This is most extensive in the area around Dublin (Duffy, 1983; Hourihan, 1983), although the phenomenon is replicated on a smaller scale throughout Ireland (e.g. Kupper, 1969; Cawley, 1980).

The promotion of tourism and the attraction of small coastal communities and some inland towns for retirement migration have also helped to stabilize or even promote population growth in the countryside (McDermott and Horner, 1978). Relocation on retirement most frequently involves the middle class who are attracted by lower property costs and the quality of life. In the peninsulas along the West of Ireland, such as south-west Cork and Kerry and west Galway, retirement migration has an international dimension involving significant numbers of British, Dutch and German people. A beautiful environment, comparatively relaxed lifestyle and the benefits of a strong rate of exchange between the currency of their pensions and the Irish punt are important ingredients in this process.

In spite of these more positive trends, out-migration is still a characteristic of most rural communities, particularly in the less accessible areas with poor employment provision and inadequate services and recreational outlets. Even where local employment is provided, however, the range of jobs frequently fails to satisfy the aspirations of a generally more educated, school-leaving population. As a result, out-migration is a continuing fact of life for the majority of rural communities. Since it is the younger and more ambitious elements that tend to be disproportionately represented in this movement, concern exists as to the demographic and social balance in rural areas. In the 1980s, the national recession and the rationalization or closure of many rural branch plants have removed the basis of much of the growth that typified these areas in the 1970s. Rural population decline has again become a more common feature within Ireland.

3.6.2 *Settlement patterns and the environment*

One of the most notable consequences of the modernization of the Irish countryside and the reversal of a long history of population decline has been a change in the extent and form of rural settlement. Expansion of the housing market now characterizes large areas of the country, especially rural areas which possess good access to urban centres. In contrast, some of the remoter settlement areas still continue to illustrate the legacy of contraction.

The traditional form of rural settlement was highly dispersed, reflecting the primary role of the individual farmstead in a landscape dominated by small farms and villages. Agricultural decline and the inability of the environment to support such a large number of family farms, especially in the west, had a marked impact on the nature of settlement. Orme (1970, p. 191) vividly summarizes the legacy of decline for many farming communities: 'A melancholy assortment of ruins and redundancies, comprising abandoned cottages, derelict country houses and decaying farm clusters set amid weed-infested fields, still remains a distinguishing feature of the Irish rural scene'.

Since the 1960s, however, this image increasingly has less validity and is confined largely to the remoter and less hospitable physical environments of the west. In a study of two peninsulas in west Cork and south Kerry, Glebe (1978) pointed out the continuing tendency for farm abandonment, but desertion is much less common in the coastal areas where abandoned farmhouses are converted into second or retirement homes.

The increase in population and demand for housing in rural areas since the 1960s have to be seen against a new occupational and social structure in rural communities under the influence of urban-generated growth. An increasing proportion of rural residents are white-collar or skilled manual workers who commute to nearby urban centres for employment. This urbanization of the countryside has therefore created a demand for housing sites on or near principal roadways leading to urban centres. The net result is the emergence of extensive areas of ribbon development in place of dispersal. This is particularly well documented by Duffy (1983) for Cos. Meath and Kildare in the hinterland of Dublin.

Similar linear patterns are also recognized on the coastal roads of the west of Ireland, where additional pressures on the housing market are created by tourism and retirement migration. This inevitably raises the price and competition for housing sites and property in rural areas, although the adverse effects on local individuals seeking entry into the market are often reduced by building plots being made available through family connections. The importance of tourist development for the promotion of population growth and settlement form is illustrated in a study of two peninsulas in west Connemara (McDermott and Horner, 1978). Here, one-quarter of the housing stock was associated with tourism, and two-fifths of houses built after 1960 were either rented for tourism or were second homes.

The rapid and untidy spread of housing throughout the countryside suggests a less than effective system of planning controls. After generations of population decline, pressures to agree to new development are often intense, especially when taken in conjunction with a generally low appreciation of the need to preserve the rural landscape. Individual consumerism finds a strong expression in the emergence of one-off housing in Ireland, and roadside sites appear to be the cheapest and most satisfactory option for market demand.

The environmental impact of such uncoordinated development can often be extreme. Orme (1970) lamented the replacement of the picturesque thatched cottages by drab but better equipped modern bungalows. Duffy (1986) points to a bungalow-littered landscape, with building styles which often detract from the aesthetic quality of the environment that attracted their owners in the first place. A prime example of this occurs along the coastal roads in Connemara where McDonald (1987) calls attention to the 'bungalow blitz' that has blighted much of this traditional Gaeltacht area: 'The whole area has been destroyed. No matter what road you go down, there are monstrosities here, there and everywhere, and what's just as depressing is that you see all these signs advertising sites for sale to build more of the same.' Despite the fact that much of Connemara was designated as an area of 'outstanding natural beauty' in 1977, failure to curtail the rise in one-off bungalow development has resulted in a disharmony of landscape between the ostentatious new dwellings and the ruins of former cottages.

Fortunately, the introduction of factories into rural areas has generally been achieved relatively successfully in terms of impact on the landscape. The majority do not pollute the environment and are often well landscaped. Modernization of agriculture has, however, been a cause of concern for environmentalists. Agriculture is virtually exempt from planning controls, and removal of hedgerows or construction of farm buildings can often have a major impact on the landscape — as can the pollution effects of silage and slurry. Recent attempts by the EC to introduce elements of landscape planning for farm development schemes could be a welcome addition to the attempts to preserve the quality of the Irish countryside. Ultimately, however, as Duffy (1986, p. 64) indicates: 'Nobody — planners, politicians, and very few of the public — questions the fundamental right of the owners of the countryside to do with it almost as they will'. If rural areas are to be more effectively developed, while maintaining the reputation of a quality environment, this attitude has to be modified.

3.6.3   Social and cultural polarization

Ireland's location off the north-west coast of Europe, away from large-scale urban-industrial influences, has resulted in the preservation of a distinctive rural way of life, especially in the western regions (Arensberg and Kimball, 1940). The fundamental rural values of Irish society, however, have recently begun to be transformed as urban values and influences have extended into rural communities (Hannan, 1972). This has brought conflict between rural residents and a new non-rural population. The result has been a dual community structure in many areas of recent population in-migration, although a different form of duality was also emerging within farming communities themselves, based on their response to the modernization of agriculture.

Traditional Irish society is far from simple in structure or organization (Smyth, 1984). Taking a highly generalized view of the country, however, society in the south and east has tended to be more class-stratified than in the west. This latter region is the core of Ireland's 'traditional' culture, and the dominance of small-scale, owner-occupier farms gives rise to a more egalitarian social system than in areas where there is a strong heritage of landlordism. The Irish-speaking communities of the Gaeltacht add a further dimension to the regional character of the western seaboard. These relatively restricted areas are heavily subsidized by the state, since the survival of the Irish language is considered — by many — to be of vital importance to the cultural integrity of the country. However, although the Gaeltacht possess their own development agency, radio service and government ministry (see Section 3.7.3), their influence on the overall regional culture of the west is questionable. Improved communication systems and more diverse cultural contacts are placing increasing pressures on the Gaeltacht communities. In this way a defensive, rather than leadership, role in cultural development is more apparent within the broader context of the West of Ireland. It is interesting to note, however, that during the inter-censal period 1971–81 the population of the Gaeltacht areas rose for the first time since the Famine (from 73,521 to 79,502).

In spite of the traditional cultural strengths and class cohesiveness, western communities have been extremely sensitive to changes brought about by the extension of urban influences. Cawley (1979, 1980) has examined the repercussions of the gradual absorption of rural communities into the sphere of influence of Galway, largely through the increasing importance of commuting. Two dominant aspects of change are observed: a diversification of occupational structures and the frequent dilution of community cohesiveness. Elements of an urban-based occupational structure are extended into the countryside by the in-migration of professional and middle-class commuters, while the availability of work within Galway provides enhanced job opportunities for farmers and their families. This latter aspect not only promotes part-time farming, but also allows for the emergence of a new working-class population within the countryside. The middle-class commuters bring with them new values which can disrupt community solidarity and undermine the existing leadership system. The extent to which this occurs depends on the size of the in-migrant population, distance from the urban centre and the strength of the existing leadership structure. In the Gaeltacht, language differences also contribute to a polarization of social development, especially since in-migrants are far more likely to be monolingual English speakers than are local inhabitants. The net result of these trends has been an increasing tendency to accept urban lifestyles and a decrease in the importance of the countryside as a centre for social life.

Similar general conclusions apply to the south and east of the country; here, a more complex class division based on a traditional farm labour force and the coexistence of large and small farm enterprises, gave rise to elements of a paternalistic employee–employer relationship. This tended to be a well-integrated social system in which status was determined by skills as well as by occupation, for example priest, teacher and doctor. However, the non-rural commuting population often lack personal identification or kinship ties to their new domicile area. The majority appear to be at variance with established residents who, irrespective of their social status, work together within more established kinship systems and identify with local issues (Smyth, 1975; Hannan and Katsiaouni, 1977). This cleavage is most apparent within the commuting hinterland of Dublin where many small rural communities have been engulfed by the expanding urban system.

Rural communities are becoming increasingly open and are sometimes subjected to disintegrating forces, especially if the local leadership proves inadequate to deal effectively with the cleavage between newer and traditional interest groups (Commins, 1980). Many of the closed and integrated communities that once typified much of the West of Ireland are now less common (Brody, 1973). Yet there are many forces of reconstruction at work which are promoting a vigorous — albeit different — form of rural community life. Attempts are made to preserve the integrity of community life in more traditional areas, especially where local leadership is strong and housing programmes more carefully monitored. An example of this is the Mid-West region where the Rural Housing Organization has played an important role in community development (Bohan, 1979). Cooperative ventures in the Gaeltacht to stabilize Irish-speaking communities further illustrate a new sense of vitality for marginal areas. Meanwhile, in the commuting hinterlands of country towns, although traditional structures and values may change, a new form of community life often emerges under new leadership and class organizations. The sense of dynamism and growth in rural communities as a spin–off from modernization and reconstruction may not permeate all areas, but over an increasing area of the country it contrasts with the stagnation of previous generations.

3.6.4 Rural transport

Much of the recent development in rural areas has been intimately related to changes in transport and the growth of personal mobility. Many individuals now have greater choice when contemplating domiciles, employment or service provision. For a sizeable minority with reduced personal mobility, however, centralization of service provision has had an adverse effect on their quality of life.

Public transport has not emerged as a viable option to car ownership in many areas. Postwar public transport policy has generally brought about a decline in the provision of services, notably in rural areas. Rationalization of the rail service has continued since the 1950s and, today, is very much orientated to linking major urban centres and is focused on Dublin (McKinsey and Company, 1971; McKinsey International, 1980). By the 1980s, only 2000 km of track remain as opposed to some 4400 km at the time of independence.

In order to replace the branch lines closed in rural areas, CIE, the national public transport authority, introduced bus routes during the 1960s. For a while, these proved successful and the service not only operated at a profit but was also expanded (Killen, 1979a). Rising costs and increasing competition from private motorists, however, have caused a reduction in the route mileage and frequency of service provided. As a result, many village communities, especially in the west, are no longer served by a regular bus service. While this may not present a significant problem for middle-class or retired households with personal means of transport, it is yet another factor that emphasizes the replacement of collective by individual services.

Ireland possesses no coherent transport policy (Barrett, 1982), and although government subsidization of transport is recognized as an important social benefit, this focuses more especially on the larger urban centres and their suburban communities. In addition, further rationalization of transport services can be anticipated during a period of budget restraint and this will further aggravate the problems of disadvantaged groups. Many communities are now partially served by privately promoted local operations involving, for example, mini-vans. Some alternative strategies to improve the accessibility of marginal communities have also been implemented, such as the appearance of mobile banks, libraries and shops. While offering a valuable service, these need to be more effectively integrated within a broader policy programme which recognizes the complexities of the problem of accessibility as it affects diverse groups and areas.

3.6.5 Accessibility and social welfare

Modernization of the countryside has clearly had a differential impact on diverse rural communities, and this is especially apparent for a wide range of public and private services. The evolution of social structures within rural communities has further complicated the relationship between supply and demand in the countryside, and reflects social and income polarization. Social groups have different and frequently competing needs, and the ability to access those needs increasingly favours the affluent, more mobile sectors of the community. This disadvantages a sizeable number of rural residents, since they lack both the means to access easily more centralized services and the political clout to enforce the maintenance of well-developed public facilities. The plight of the rural disadvantaged is recognized as an important negative consequence of recent modernization, and requires immediate and more effective social planning (Curry, 1981).

In a principal components analysis of Ireland's Rural Districts, Cawley (1986) identified forty districts in which residents are generally exposed to a cycle of cumulative deprivation. Lack of employment encourages an out-migration of the younger, more able individuals. This not only results in a disproportionate number of elderly people remaining in the locality, but also causes a fall-off in the demand for essential services such as public transport, schools and retail outlets. This frequently causes closure or the severe curtailment of service provision, thus further aggravating the difficulty of residing in such areas.

The trend of declining and increasingly centralized service provision has not been reversed by the arrival of new, predominantly middle-class residents in many rural communities. While poorer families continue to rely on collective services and local public facilities, the non-rural commuters have access to private services. This frequently results in the erosion of support for local services, although Bohan (1979) cites one of the examples of migration turnaround in rural areas as being a marked increase in the number of children attending local primary schools. At the level of secondary school education, however, centralization is more pronounced and even the provision of free transport only partially addresses the problems of some children having to spend long periods of each day travelling to schools sited in centrally located towns. In areas of continuing population loss and those dominated by retirement in-migration, support for local school facilities continues to be eroded, to the detriment of local community development.

Cheaper prices and a greater range of goods in the larger retail outlets located in towns are major attractions for rural residents, especially those who are drawn to such centres by virtue of work and lifestyle. Thus in Galway, the non-farm commuters living in the hinterland of the city undertook 85 per cent of their grocery shopping at that centre. This contrasts with the shopping behaviour of the farm commuting population; 41 per cent of their expenditure was at local shops, as opposed to 32 per cent in Galway (Cawley, 1980). An overall decline in local shopping purchases also contributes to an increase in prices which disadvantages those families unable to shop where prices are lower. Where shops are forced to close due to inadequate local support, it represents an inconvenience and, sometimes, actual deprivation for those unable to use alternative outlets, such as the elderly and transport poor.

3.7 Rural development

3.7.1 The need for alternative approaches

Central government has increasingly tried to influence the scale and direction of regional development. While many rural communities have benefited both directly and indirectly from this involvement, others remain ill-equipped to function adequately within a national economy in modernization. This poses serious questions as to the type of policies and planning options which are appropriate to deal effectively with the diverse issues faced within rural areas.

Rural planning, as it has evolved in Ireland, has tended to be somewhat negative in that it has largely functioned as a reaction to problems as these have arisen. Comparatively little emphasis seems to have been placed on the more positive role of planning in guiding constructive and coordinated development. A multiplicity of centralized state agencies operate policy programmes on strictly functional lines, such as agriculture, transport, industry and environment. These are largely inadequate to deal effectively with area-based issues. In addition, centralized decision-making often views rural problems in an overly simplistic manner, far removed from the complexities of rural lifestyles and the sensitivity of such areas to externally induced pressures.

Traditionally, rural development has been viewed as being directly related to the promotion of agricultural prosperity, although in more recent years the positive role of rural industrialization has been appreciated. A far more flexible approach to rural development is required which stresses interaction between, rather than the independence of, policy programmes. Scully (1969, p. 8) recognized this, stressing that: 'survival of Western agriculture as a viable entity is largely dependent upon a comprehensive programme of regional development embracing many other activities apart from farming'.

The basic planning structures and organizations to foster such an approach are generally lacking. In an attempt to compensate partially for this lack of contact between government agencies at the local level, county development teams were set up in the 1960s initially for the western regions. Subsequently, these have been extended to most parts of the country. Basically, they attempt to promote and coordinate infrastructural development to service better the needs of economic development. Their role tends to be advisory, and they lack significant authority to influence the quality of development. Much the same can be said of the Regional Development Organizations (RDOs) set up to coordinate the development programmes for each planning region. A lack of executive power, inadequate financing and comparatively low status severely limit the potential of these organizations. In 1987 the RDOs were abolished, further emphasizing the national dimension to development strategy.

In spite of this, increasing interest has been expressed — if not implemented — in a more integrated approach to rural planning which incorporates social, economic and environmental considerations. At the level of the European Community, three Integrated Rural Development (IRD) programmes were implemented in 1979 to cover South-East Belgium, Lozere in France and the Western Isles of Scotland. The suitability of such an approach for Ireland has been stressed by Conway and O'Hara (1981). Whether the highly centralized political system, dominated by sectoral interests, can accommodate the changes needed to achieve a multisectoral, flexible and coordinated approach remains to be seen.

While a change in planning strategy is clearly required at government level, changes are also required at the local level. Traditionally, the majority of rural communities have expected central government intervention in response to local problems. There has been comparatively little tradition of community self-help, although Muintir na Tire (People of the Countryside) has a legacy since the 1930s of trying to promote a philosophy of self-help within which local initiative would be encouraged to develop better local resources. In the 1970s, however, community-based development became more common and found particular expression in the emergence of community cooperatives (Breathnach, 1984). Much of this movement gained impetus from the initially successful cooperative venture established at Glencolumbkille in the early 1960s by Father McDyer. This marshalled the local resources of a poor community in Donegal and provided the basis for some development in craft industries, tourism and agriculture.

The bottom–up approach to development, symbolized by community self-help, is an acceptable and necessary ingredient for IRD. To be successful, local views need to be effectively incorporated into decision-making. There are many difficulties in successfully sponsoring community-based development, but the benefits seem undeniable (Ó Cinneide, 1986). The state has a vital role in ensuring the success of these ventures, largely through financial aid, but whether or not it will accept the decentralization of authority implicit in this movement is uncertain.

Two examples now illustrate some of the possibilities for rural development based on a more integrated approach to development planning, and the enhanced role of community cooperatives in the Gaeltacht.

3.7.2 The development of Shannon

In 1959, the Shannon Free Airport Development Company (SFADCo) was created as a state-sponsored agency to promote increasing air traffic through the then declining Shannon Airport. As part of this promotion, the world's first airport duty-free industrial estate was created and the new town of Shannon was established to provide housing (Soulsby, 1965). SFADCo's role was primarily to integrate diverse responsibilities and this quickly became part of a coordinated package designed to develop more effectively the predominantly rural hinterland of this part of Co. Clare. Although initially focusing on Shannon, SFADCo's development mandate has extended throughout the Mid-West region where it has responsibility for tourism, housing and some aspects of industrial development. From 1968 to 1978, it administered all manufacturing promotion in the region, but was then restricted to dealing with the small industry scheme of the IDA. In 1987, however, it regained its responsibility for the overall development of industry in the Mid-West.

SFADCo's impact on development has been considerable, reflecting the strong executive powers and financial resource base of the agency, together with its multiplicity of functions; these facilitate comprehensive development, innovation and adaptability to changing conditions (Callanan, 1984). Employment increased strongly within Shannon and this stimulated a significant inflow of commuters to the estate and also encouraged in-migration to the new town (Kupper, 1969; Hutterman, 1978). A commuting hinterland of up to 65 km was established, and some 45 per cent of those working on the estate came from outside the (undefined) Shannon region. By the mid-1970s, Hutterman (1978, p. 182) found that more people born in Dublin than in Co. Clare resided in the new town. This illustrated the pull effect of this successful venture. In 1985, the population of the town had reached 8800, while employment provided on the industrial estate (4400) and related airport complex numbered 7750.

SFADCo has successfully cooperated with local authorities and other parties who have an interest in promoting the development of the Mid-West. As the driving force within the Mid-West RDO, it provides an organizational lead that appears to be lacking in many other bodies. It is particularly conscious of the role of small industries in rural development, but also recognizes the growth potential of air traffic-related tourism and the need to ensure that housing, agricultural and industrial land use must be carefully coordinated.

3.7.3   The Gaeltacht and community development

Scattered along the western and southern coastline from Donegal to Waterford are a series of residual pockets of Irish-speaking populations that are collectively referred to as the Gaeltacht. Today, approximately 80,000 people occupy these comparatively restricted areas, in contrast to some 1.5 million in the mid-nineteenth century when the Gaeltacht would have extended over much of western Ireland (Kearns, 1974b). Although confined to some of the more difficult physical environments, with poorly developed infrastructures and a recent tradition of economic and demographic decline, these areas have acquired a disproportionate importance in Irish society. They form the heartland of the national culture and language, and consequently a variety of special organizations and structures have been created to ensure their continued survival. These reflect both centralized, state-sponsored development programmes as well as a more recent attempt to induce 'development from below' through community-based initiatives (Breathnach, 1983).

Direct intervention to promote development did not really emerge until 1956 when a separate department for the Gaeltacht (Roinn na Gaeltachta) was created. Its brief was to encourage economic, social and cultural development and promote the use of the Irish language, while a state-sponsored body, Gaeltarra Éireann, was established specifically to promote industrial development. In 1980, these development functions were taken over by a newly created body, Údarás na Gaeltachta.

Central government support has involved a variety of incentives to upgrade social and economic conditions in the Gaeltacht. Grants have been paid to subsidize agricultural improvements and house construction and to improve both social and physical infrastructure. However, the main emphasis was on job creation, especially in the industrial sector, as a means of reducing out-migration and of improving the standards of living of the local population. Generous incentives succeeded in attracting some new investment, although a study of Gaeltacht factories in the late 1960s (Kane, 1977) suggested that the creation of new jobs did not check the emigration of young people. Drudy and Drudy (1979) found similar evidence in a survey of schoolchildren in the Galway Gaeltacht, where 65 per cent of male and 73 per cent of female school leavers indicated an intention to migrate. Continued efforts during the 1970s to promote jobs were more successful, however, since enhanced employment prospects undoubtedly contributed to an overall net gain in the Gaeltacht population from 1971 to 1981 after generations of decline. The successful promotion of jobs has continued and, between 1981 and 1986, employment in Údarás-assisted firms rose from 4011 to 4695.

While this centralized planning had some successes, concern mounted as to the cultural ramifications of such a 'centre–down' strategy, especially with respect to language preservation. As a consequence, an alternative approach — which had largely begun in the 1960s — gathered momentum. In contrast to the reliance on externally promoted industry, it involved multi-purpose community cooperatives based on the principle of self-help (Johnson, 1979; Breathnach, 1984). State finance and support have been a crucial factor in their establishment, but they fundamentally involve local communities in promoting economic and social development to suit local needs. In this way, it was hoped that external influences could be reduced, or at least be more effectively controlled, thereby minimizing the risk of diluting cultural and linguistic values.

The wide variety of community projects undertaken includes such diverse schemes as establishing piped water supplies for rural communities, providing an electricity supply on island Gaeltachts, and organizing Irish colleges for teaching the language to children from outside the Gaeltacht but who stay at the homes of local residents. One of the most successful schemes has occurred in the West Kerry Gaeltacht, where community action has involved deep ploughing techniques to reclaim bogland, construction of community centres, development of greenhouse market gardening and arrangement of Irish language summer schools. Another interesting prospect for development lies in aquaculture. In 1987, it was estimated that there were 200 full-time and 600 part-time jobs in fish farming of all types in the Gaeltacht, and that the region produced some 70 per cent of all farmed salmon in Ireland. By the early 1990s Údarás estimates that this should have increased to 500 full-time and 1000 part-time jobs, with another 1000 jobs in ancillary industries (Douthwaite, 1987).

The non-economic aspects of these schemes are often more important for the longer-term future of these communities. Development of the local resource base and the fostering of positive attitudes after generations of decline and despair may be less tangible than a new factory, but are vital ingredients for development. Unfortunately, local financial resources are rarely sufficient to initiate and maintain local development projects and dependency on outside financial support is an ongoing difficulty for many community cooperatives. Government policy therefore needs to combine more effectively community projects within an overall strategy for coherent development (Breathnach, 1983). Development has to be seen to improve the sociocultural and environmental conditions of life as well as generate a new economic base. For rural areas, and especially those that have failed to benefit significantly from recent modernization, IRD, which incorporates community self-help, may be an approach leading to greater conditions of equity. Even in the Gaeltacht communities, however, the concept is far from universally accepted.

FOUR

Urban Ireland

4.1 Introduction

In Ireland, the definition of an urban centre involves a population cluster of at least 1500 people. On this basis, the 1971 Census of Ireland indicated that for the first time a majority of the national population resided in officially defined urban centres. The degree of urbanization increased to 55.6 per cent in 1981, but this still makes Ireland one of the least urbanized societies in Western Europe. In addition to this comparatively late urbanization, Ireland's urban structure is characterized by a very high level of primacy. In 1981, the Greater Dublin area had a population of 915,115, 26.6 per cent of the national total, while a little more than one million people (31.7 per cent) resided within the Dublin metropolitan region. Cork, the second city of the Republic, was the only other urban area with a population over 100,000 (149,792). These two centres, together with the three county boroughs of Limerick (75,520), Waterford (39,636) and Galway (41,861) (the latter only attained this status in 1986), account for over 40 per cent of Ireland's total population. The ten largest towns are all ports, and inland centres are comparatively small. They are most strongly represented in the east and south of the country, and Kilkenny (16,886) is the largest inland town. The west remains the least urbanized part of the country (Figure 4.1).

The role of urban centres has undergone a significant change within the past quarter-century. Traditionally, towns functioned as service or market centres for their dominantly rural hinterlands and, given the underdeveloped state of agriculture, slow growth or even decline typified them. From the 1960s, however, the national commitment to modernization brought new functions and growth to many of these centres. The location of manufacturing within rural towns became a key element in the spatial rearrangement of the settlement hierarchy. In addition, the centralization of services, together with the enhanced perception of country towns as a place of domicile, boosted the growth of those settlements that benefited especially from good transport linkages.

The largest cities shared in this general growth, although during the 1970s restructuring of the economy and government policy options had a

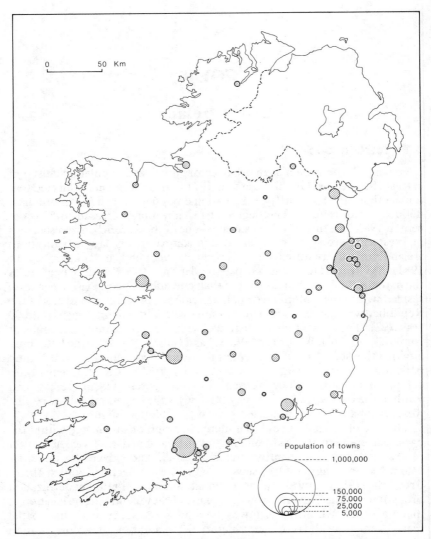

Figure 4.1 Urbanization in Ireland, 1981 (Census of Population, 1981).

less favourable impact on major centres of population, particularly their inner cities. A principal factor was the decentralization of manufacturing which removed basic employment from within the cities to suburban areas or smaller towns. Population redistribution also occurred within the cities and there was a significant reversal in the fortunes of the inner cities. Higher- and middle-income groups moved out from the inner cities resulting in a disproportionate residual of lower socioeconomic groups remaining within the cities. Social polarization has been the outcome of these differential movements.

These contemporary trends in urban development have largely occurred in the absence of any coherent policy to address effectively the urban dynamics of modernization. This has merely served to aggravate the differential growth performance of urban centres and has facilitated the increasing primacy of Dublin to the detriment of other major regional centres such as Cork and Limerick. The demise of the inner cities, and the economic deprivation and low social status of their residents, have also been largely ignored by central government. It was not until 1986, however, that central government finally introduced a policy specifically designed to meet some of the urgent problems of these areas. This belated attempt may achieve some benefits for designated areas, but the continued absence of an overall policy programme for the country's towns and cities remains a serious impediment to successful socioeconomic development.

The degree of primacy exhibited by Dublin has resulted in much of the literature relating to urban development in Ireland focusing attention on the capital city region to the comparative neglect of other areas. This reflects, furthermore, the influence that Dublin exerts over all aspects of national life. We begin this chapter with a brief description of the evolution of the Irish urban system and the contemporary pattern revolving around the primacy of Dublin. This is followed by an outline of the processes which are currently shaping urban development.

4.2 Evolution of the urban system

4.2.1 The urban pattern prior to 1961

The historical evolution of the urban landscape has played a major role in shaping the contemporary spatial pattern and functional status of many Irish towns. Urban settlement, as this evolved, could be considered an intrusive element in an otherwise dominantly rural society. Historically, therefore, town development became strongly associated with expansive epochs of colonization which significantly changed the human landscape (Jones-Hughes, 1959; Butlin, 1977). Vikings, Normans and the colonial plantation system all extended the urban base of the country, and by the end of the seventeenth century only Connaught could still be recognized as an under-urbanized province (Andrews, 1976).

In the eighteenth century, towns and cities flourished, with Dublin more than any other centre reflecting the elegance and prosperity of neo-classical Georgian town planning. Political and economic developments emphasized the site and situation advantages of this east coast port, which controlled a natural routeway into the rich agricultural hinterland of Leinster. As the chosen political and administrative centre for the British in Ireland, Dublin emerged by 1800 as a thriving city of some 200,000 people with its dominance of the Irish urban system clearly established (Haughton, 1949).

The prosperity of the eighteenth century quickly gave way to agricultural depression in the following century, epitomized by the major famines of the 1840s. The Act of Union (1800) and the loss of the parliament to London proved particularly disastrous for Dublin's prosperity. In addition, most towns, failing to attract any specialist new functions associated with the industrial revolution, stagnated or declined. As a result, large-scale surburban expansion and the creation of working-class housing areas, so typical of most major cities in nineteenth-century Europe, did not emerge in Ireland's dominant urban centres. Much of the fabric and morphology of the eighteenth-century town was therefore brought through into the current century. While the major urban centres experienced a loss of prosperity and status, migration from the countryside greatly added to their populations. With comparatively little new building to accommodate the influx of rural poor, a housing crisis emerged especially in the cores of the cities. The elegance of many inner-city buildings, such as the Georgian terraces in Dublin, was lost as they were converted into high-density tenements. The inner-city problems which emerged as early as the nineteenth century have yet to be resolved satisfactorily.

Ireland's urban system prior to independence reflects many of the classical influences of colonial rule. The urban hierarchy was primate, while the dominant cities were all ports and were located especially along the east and south coasts for trade to Britain. Few towns of significance were located inland, although the more commercial agriculture of the eastern half of the country was able to support a considerable density of market centres. Economic and political subservience to Britain, together with the absence of commercially exploitable indigenous resources, ensured that the dominant settlement form would be small-scale service centres meeting the needs of a relatively limited agricultural hinterland. The major south-east–north-west contrast in urban development and the comparatively limited functional status of the majority of towns would have far reaching implications for post-independence Ireland.

Following independence, urban patterns continued to exhibit the characteristics that had become well established under colonial dominance. Three factors contributed to this trend: the continued dominance of Britain in

Irish trade and economic development, the size distribution of the urban system, and the primacy of Dublin.

The Irish trading system remained strongly orientated to the British market, and internal development reflected this dependency. As such, Huff and Lutz (1979) suggest that the Irish urban system is perhaps unique in Europe in that it was 'one of the few countries of the continent whose urban network was closely tied to the needs of a single outside state over such a long period of time' (p. 198). Another indirect British influence can be recognized along the border counties, where the consequences of partition have been adverse for urban development. This has been emphasized since the emergence of 'the troubles' in the 1970s and the 'break' with sterling in 1979. Partly as a result of the latter, significant retail price differentials have emerged on either side of the border, and a recent survey (Fitzgerald, 1987) indicates that supermarket prices in the Republic are 10–40 per cent higher than those in Northern Ireland. This encourages cross-border shopping which reduces considerably retail activity within the border towns of the Republic.

A second factor in the development of the modern Irish urban system was the existing size distribution of cities and towns. During the period of economic nationalism and protectionism, the larger urban centres emerged as the logical centres for internal development. Not only were the major port cities the largest centres of purchasing power and possessing some industrial traditions, but also their infrastructures were better able to support infant import-substitution industries.

Proximity to the expanding urban centre of Dublin was the final influence shaping urban developments within this period. Its political status and administrative functions as the capital of the new state merely reinforced its historic role as the dominant urban centre and acted as a catalyst for even further growth. Urban centres in the hinterland of Dublin were able to benefit from some spill-over effects and, together with the rich agricultural base of the region, this provided many towns with a degree of prosperity that allowed for the retention or growth of their population. Throughout much of the rest of Ireland, however, many smaller towns and villages, especially in the west and north-west, continued to experience population decline (Bannon, 1975).

The new nation state had declared itself committed to a policy of decentralization and the support of small towns and rural communities, but this approach was seen to fail as the degree of centralization increased. While the urban population rose from approximately one-third in 1926 to 46 per cent in 1961, some 60 per cent of that was due to the growth of Dublin (Figure 4.2). On the eve of the adoption of the policy of modernization, the pattern and the structure of the urban base still reflected that of a pre-

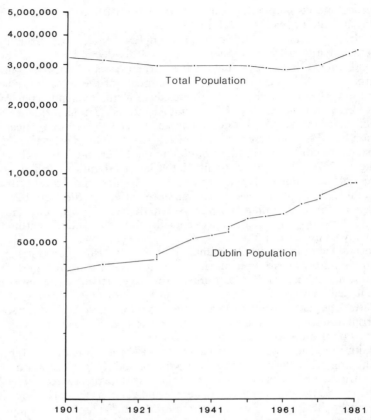

Figure 4.2 Population trends of Ireland and Dublin, 1901–81 (Census of Population).

industrial economy. Clearly, to support the drive to modernization, significant changes could be expected in the pattern of Ireland's towns and cities.

4.2.2 Urban development in an era of modernization

Coinciding with the new state policy for economic development, significant changes occurred in the extent of urbanization. The linkage between urbanization and industrialization became increasingly apparent, and urbanization accelerated to an annual growth rate in excess of 2 per cent in the 1970s. Table 4.1 outlines the trends for the period 1961–81.

In the 1960s, urban development dictated the spatial expression of the

Table 4.1 Population by size of urban place, 1961–81

Size of centre	1961 Number of towns	1961 Population	1971 Number of towns	1971 Population	% change 1961–71	1981 Number of towns	1981 Population	% change 1971–81
Rural areas	—	1,309,363	—	1,193,357	− 8.9	—	1,260,957	+ 5.6
200–499	255	78,709	199	63,988	−18.7	252	79,503	+24.2
500–1499	156	131,122	152	129,348	− 1.4	177	162,191	+25.3
1500–2999	46	104,333	41	89,460	−14.3	38	83,062	− 7.2
3000–4999	21	84,139	24	91,122	+ 8.3	26	96,362	+ 5.7
5000–9999	17	106,311	22	139,060	+30.8	31	217,369	+56.3
10,000–150,000	14	336,741	16	419,694	+24.5	18	540,797	+28.9
Dublin area*	1	663,389	1	852,219	+28.5	1	1,003,164	+17.7
Cork†	1	115,102	1	135,456	+16.8	1	149,792	+10.6
Limerick†	1	51,967	1	63,436	+21.2	1	75,520	+19.0
Waterford†	1	28,303	1	34,837	+19.0	1	39,636	+13.8

* For 1961, Dublin is inclusive of suburbs and Dun Laoghaire. The totals for subsequent years are for the subregion including Dublin City, Dun Laoghaire and County Dublin which includes all places with at least 50 inhabited houses.
† Includes the county borough and suburbs. Totals included in size group 10–150,000.
Source: Bannon (1984) and Census of Population (1961, 1971, 1981).

country's first decade of sustained population increase for over a century. Growth was almost entirely confined to the larger urban centres and settlements located within their spheres of influence (Johnson, 1968; Parker, 1972). Medium (over 5000 population) and larger centres (over 10,000) increased in number and in the proportion of national population they housed. Smaller towns fared less well and there was a sharp decrease in the number of settlements with fewer than 1500 residents. These smaller centres are more representative of the urban structure in the western areas, and this indicates the continued erosion of this disadvantaged area's urban system. Dublin and the three County Boroughs all performed favourably and the increased concentration of population in these centres continued.

During the 1970s, growth was widespread throughout the urban system (Downey, 1980). Towns with a population of 5000–9999 performed particularly well and had clearly benefited from the policy of industrial dispersal enacted by the IDA. The county towns generally increased their resident populations, as did settlements within commuting distance of Dublin, Cork and Limerick. The better performance of the smaller towns also reflects the fact that the country was experiencing population dispersal down through the urban hierarchy (Horner and Daultrey, 1980). Settlements of fewer than 1500 residents exhibited significant growth, in contrast with their dismal record in earlier decades. The smaller towns and rural districts appeared to be reasserting themselves within the Irish settlement system, although their fortunes were no doubt conditioned by proximity to expanding urban centres. The major urban settlements continued to grow, but at a generally reduced rate compared with the 1960s.

Ireland has clearly followed general European trends in the growing relative and absolute importance of smaller urban centres during the 1970s. In marked contrast, however, to the absolute and relative decline in the major metropolitan region(s) of other urban-industrialized countries, Ireland's premier urban agglomeration has continued to grow (see Figure 4.2). Despite efforts to curtail its growth, not only has Dublin grown faster than was anticipated, but it has also rapidly diffused over much of the adjoining rural areas. Between 1971 and 1981 the Dublin region accommodated over one-third of the net increase in national population.

Extension of urban land use into the surrounding rural collar has become a notable feature of contemporary Ireland. In 1970, Orme suggested that 'the physical distinction between town and country is easily recognized because most town limits are quite abrupt, and only around Dublin and Belfast is there any kind of urban–rural continuum' (p. 206). However, this generalization was already breaking down in the 1960s, and by the 1970s the interface between town and country was becoming more blurred and the conversion of rural land for urban use was estimated at some 1200 ha per year, with a further 26,500 ha required to accommodate possible urban expansion to 1991 (Bannon, 1979).

The distribution of urban centres is unevenly balanced in favour of the east and south (see Figure 4.1). This is especially the case for major centres in excess of 10,000 population, which house 45 per cent of the national total. The primate character of the structure is easily identifiable, with Dublin being described as 'an extraordinarily isolated giant', standing in the East region (Forbes, 1970, p. 308). A zone of rich agricultural land stretching from Leinster to north Munster, however, has provided the opportunity for development of a more favourable hierarchy. The more western and northern areas, on the other hand, do not possess a well-defined hierarchy of towns, and they remain overly dependent on lower-order market centres. The planning regions of the North-West, Donegal and West all have less than 30 per cent of their populations residing in towns of greater than 1500 residents (Table 4.2). This is in marked contrast to the East, where the level of urbanization in 1981 reached 85 per cent. Geographical variations of this magnitude suggest considerable differences in regional accessibility to services and job opportunities.

4.3   The process of urban change

4.3.1   *Demographic trends and the mobility of the population*

Rural–urban migration has played a fundamental role in the development of European towns and cities. This process also operated within Ireland, although the rate of residential mobility and internal migration has been quite low by international standards (Hughes and Walsh, 1980). A high proportion of people living on farms, as well as a strong emphasis on owner-occupancy rather than tenancy in the housing market, have restricted mobility within the country. In addition, much of Ireland's population has moved to urban destinations outside the country. By the 1960s, four out of every five people leaving the provinces within Ireland emigrated, the remaining proportion moving primarily to Dublin. This pattern was substantially modified, however, as the British economy stagnated and better employment opportunities became available in Ireland's urban centres.

Migration has contributed both directly and indirectly to the growing extent of urbanization, and the net inflow of people from rural to urban areas accounts for approximately one-quarter of the recent growth of urban populations. The East region, and Dublin in particular, has consistently benefited from this process. Hourihan (1982b) stressed the increased importance of urban centres in shaping the direction as well as the amount

Table 4.2   Urban population by region, 1981

Region	Percentage of total population in				
	Towns 100,000 and over	Towns 10,000– 100,000	Towns 1500– 10,000	Towns 200– 1500	Rural areas
Donegal	—	—	19.7	16.2	64.1
North-West	—	21.7	2.0	13.8	62.5
West	—	14.6	12.7	8.5	64.1
Mid-West	—	29.3	11.9	11.3	47.6
South-West	28.5	3.2	17.7	7.8	42.8
South-East	—	26.5	14.1	8.7	50.6
East	70.9	5.3	8.9	2.8	12.0
North-East	—	27.1	13.1	9.5	50.3
Midlands	—	10.3	19.6	10.8	59.3
State	30.9	12.0	12.7	7.2	37.2

Source: Census of Population (1981).

of internal migration. In a detailed study of migration for 1970–71, he found that almost three-quarters of all those who moved residence during the previous year located in an urban centre of at least 1500 people. Return migration has also played a role, since many returnees favour urban centres. Dublin has been especially attractive for such people, and a disproportionate number of younger, more educated and professional people have returned to the metropolitan area (Walsh, J.A., 1979).

Comparatively low rates of in-migration are recorded for the largest cities, while a high inflow has typified the settlements which surround the County Boroughs. In addition, outflows from the inner cities have benefited adjacent towns. This is particularly apparent for Dublin, where the County Borough experienced a net loss of over 94,000 people during the 1970s, while towns within its hinterland grew extremely rapidly (e.g. Portmarnock +373 per cent; Lucan +171 per cent; Leixlip +285 per cent). Similar characteristics are found in the newer towns around Cork (Ballincollig + 242 per cent; Carrigaline +283 per cent) and Limerick (Shannon +117 per cent). Migration into the medium-sized towns generally appears to be greatest where there is a conjunction of spread-effects from one of the major cities and/or the availability of local employment associated with the dispersal of manufacturing (Curtin *et al.*, 1976; Hughes and Walsh, 1980). The changed fortunes of many middle-sized Irish county towns have depended heavily on this latter factor, together with their enhanced role as centres for service provision (see Chapter 4.4.4).

Migration also has indirect effects as the age-selective aspect of personal mobility gives a further impetus to population growth, through higher rates of natural increase. Dublin, for instance, has one of the most youthful populations in Europe with 49 per cent of its population being less than 25 years old. This will almost certainly ensure a continuing high natural rate of increase for the future. Improved job opportunities in medium-sized towns within the more rural counties have allowed them to retain a higher proportion of their youth, who hitherto would have emigrated. In addition, these towns have emerged as centres of intervening opportunity for young people opting to leave more peripheral communities. The consequences of a more youthful population structure have been significant in turning around the stagnation and sense of despair that formerly typified many county towns. However, the current recession and the increased rate of emigration have diluted the encouragement for further development that was widespread in the 1970s.

4.3.2   *Reassessment of the urban base for manufacturing*

The majority of Ireland's manufacturing activities have traditionally focused on the major port cities, with inland towns being effectively bypassed as a suitable location for industrial production. In 1961, almost 53 per cent of the nation's manufacturing workforce were resident in the four County Boroughs (Table 4.3). Changes in national economic policy, however, were to modify significantly the conditions for urban-industrial development.

Between 1961 and 1981, the growth performance of the County Boroughs deteriorated, and by the latter date only 29 per cent of total manufacturing employment remained within these centres. While the national commitment to modernization initially boosted the industrial fortunes of Cork, Limerick and Waterford, greater difficulties were experienced in the 1970s with the net result that the industrial employment base declined in Cork and Limerick, and achieved only a marginal gain for Waterford. Dublin's position was far more critical, however, with decline in both decades; the 1970s were especially traumatic with a loss of almost one-third in the city's manufacturing labour force. In marked contrast, many of the smaller and medium-sized urban centres were increasingly seen as successful locations for contemporary manufacturing enterprise (O'Farrell, 1975, 1978).

The government policy of industrial decentralization contributed to this differential performance of manufacturing. In effect, Dublin has been discriminated against throughout the postwar period as a location for new industrial investment. Government and IDA officials appeared to be

Table 4.3   Manufacturing employment in Ireland's county boroughs, 1961–81

	1961	1971	1981	% change 1961–81
Dublin*	75,376	69,899	47,715	−36.7
Cork	9905	13,096	11,797	+19.1
Limerick	4341	5323	5264	+21.3
Waterford	3655	4581	5004	+36.9
% State total	52.5	43.5	29.3	

* Includes Dun Laoghaire Metropolitan Borough.
Source: Census of Population (1961, 1971, 1981).

working on the assumption that the city's well-established manufacturing base was self-sustaining and that non-grant aided development would be sufficient to meet the employment needs of local blue-collar workers. Events in the 1970s have proved this to be a false premise, and from 1977 the IDA has begun to promote the city as a location for new industry. The most recent element of this new concern to promote Dublin's economic base was the 1986 decision to redevelop the Customs House Dock area as an International Financial Services Centre (see Section 4.6). While this is to be welcomed, the large number of office jobs created will not address the continued problem of high unemployment and poor job prospects experienced by poorly educated and blue-collar workers.

The deflection of manufacturing from the Dublin region initially held the promise that the larger regional centres would benefit through development as growth centres (Buchanan and Partners, 1968). The political ramifications of focusing too much attention on a limited number of larger towns and cities (see Section 4.3.4), together with a successful dispersal of manufacturing to smaller centres in the 1960s, ensured that this approach would be ignored. Instead of focusing on a few major growth centres, a policy of dispersing industry widely over rural areas was adopted and appeared to complement the preferences of international investment for production sites in smaller towns (see Section 3.4). Many smaller towns gained a new functional identity based on the acquisition of IDA-sponsored industrial investment, for example Clonmel, Kilkenny and Nenagh (Curtin et al., 1976). In comparison, the comparative failure of the larger regional centres to generate new industrial employment has caused government to redirect efforts in their favour. Thus in the IDA *Industrial Plan*, 1978–82 (1979), 'rapid growth in manufacturing employment is scheduled for the main urban centres but, in addition, the nucleus of industrial employment will be further encouraged in the smaller centres' (p. 45). In spite of this apparent commitment, the declining status of the large urban manufacturing centres has yet to show major improvement.

The decline in larger urban centres illustrates the apparent failure to compensate for job losses through closure and contraction of pre-existing plants. Although the size of towns within which a plant is located appears to be unrelated to the probability of closure (Dublin excluded) (O'Farrell and Crouchley, 1984), larger urban centres have experienced a significant erosion of their employment base through this process. In Co. Dublin closures and contractions in the period 1973–81 amounted to 40 per cent of base year employment (O'Farrell, 1984). A disproportionate presence of small and inefficient industries, many having been established under conditions of protectionism prior to 1960, partially accounts for this adverse trend, coupled with a concentration on more traditional and declining sectors of activity, such as textiles and clothing. Against this, new openings and expansions amounted to only 53 per cent of total losses. The trends within Dublin city were thus regarded as being 'worse than all other areas with respect to every component of change' (O'Farrell, 1984, p. 173).

Similar, albeit later, trends can be observed in Cork. The advantages of Cork Harbour and the availability of industrial land adjacent to sheltered, deep water have proved particularly attractive for port-related industrial development. One consequence of this had been the emergence around the harbour of the largest concentration of heavy industry within the Republic and this was regarded as a basis for continued growth. The optimism of the 1960s, however, was gradually replaced by a greater sense of pessimism as the area's industrial economy faltered (Brunt, 1980, 1984). The more competitive trade conditions of the 1980s caused severe problems for the city's long-established port-related industries, and the majority have closed or been subjected to large-scale redundancies. The foundations of the local economy have been largely removed, and the newer — but smaller — plant start-ups have been inadequate to replace the large-scale, labour-intensive operations that have been lost.

The positive association between urbanization and industrialization appears to have weakened — if not been broken — for the larger urban centres. The divergence between manufacturing employment and population trends is exemplified in the case of Dublin. While its primacy within the urban hierarchy has increased, the city's dominant role as a centre for industry has declined. At the lower level of the urban hierarchy, however, the multiplier effects associated with manufacturing developments continue to influence strongly their status and growth potential (NESC, 1977a).

4.3.3   Developments in service employment

The rate of growth in services and white-collar employment has been comparatively slow compared to that of other OECD countries, and the percentage of total employment allocated to the service sector remains one of the lowest in the EC. In spite of this, service employment and knowledge-based occupations have played an increasingly important role in national and regional development (see Chapters 1 and 2). While their relative and absolute role has increased, Bannon (1985) suggests that there appears to be little understanding of the role of services in promoting development. As a result, three assumptions have become subsumed within economic policy as it applies to service activities. First, any expansion of service employment was considered dependent on growth in the productive sector. Second, the multiplier effects of such a development would occur in the same general location as the basic source of activity. Finally, the service sector would be able to make a full and balanced contribution to national development in the absence of both a policy for services and an infrastructure within which development could be promoted.

These assumptions have proved to be fundamentally incorrect, and instead of a more equal distribution of service activities throughout the country, there has been further concentration on the East region and on Dublin in particular. This has contributed significantly to local job creation in the capital city and has more than compensated for the decline in manufacturing. By 1985, two-thirds of Dublin's employment were in services compared to only 22 per cent in manufacturing. In addition to these absolute gains, the capital has continued to attract a disproportionate amount of high-quality office functions and has strengthened its position as the dominant-centre of decision-making within the state. The growth momentum and polarization of such occupations contribute in no small way to the restriction of growth in other regional centres and thereby emphasize the most fundamental fact of the Irish urban system — the primacy of Dublin (NESC, 1977a, 1979).

Ireland is an exceptionally centralized state by European standards, and Lee (1985) has strongly argued that it has been political rather than economic forces that have contributed to the predominance of Dublin. Only five of more than eighty government departments and state agencies have headquarters outside the capital. This degree of centralization of administration has promoted many direct and indirect multipliers; one calculation suggests that one-quarter of the city's population and more than one-third of its purchasing power can be traced to this fact (Lee, 1985, p. 86). Decentralization of public employment has been extremely limited, and dispersal of the Civil Service from Dublin has met with remarkably little success. By 1983, existing and proposed dispersals were the equivalent of only 6 per cent of all Civil Service posts. As a result, almost two-thirds of all non-industrial civil servants were located in Dublin at the start of the 1980s. This compares with a figure of only 25 per cent for similar public servants in the United Kingdom who are based in London (Humphreys, 1985).

A high degree of concentration of executive power also occurs in the private sector since the headquarters of most insurance companies, banks, industrial and other trading or professional organizations are located in Dublin. In addition to the clear advantages to be gained from proximity to a centre of decision-making, rationalization and reorganization within the service sector have emphasized the attractions of the capital. It stands at the focal point of the country's internal and international transport network, and its hinterland covers the entire country for first-order services (Huff and Lutz, 1979; see also O'Sullivan, 1968).

A process of cumulative causation is operating based on the inherent advantages displayed by the capital and the failure of government to implement an effective decentralization programme. From 1960 to 1975, while office space in Dublin increased by some 464,500 m², the additional floorspace for the rest of the country amounted to less than 10 per cent of that figure (Bannon, 1979). 'The absence of any effective or realistic urban-regional policy with regard to white-collar jobs and information activities in this small, centralized and open economy has left such activities no viable alternative to a Dublin location' (NESC, 1981a, pp. 259–60).

Contact potential, which measures the attractiveness of an urban place for business, rapidly declines with distance from Dublin and is a further cause and effect of the centralization of decision-making. In a recent study, Bannon and Blair (1985) (ranked Ireland's top fifteen urban centres, together with Letterkenny, on the basis of indicators of their role as service centres. Their results clearly illustrate the extraordinary advantages of Dublin in terms of its contact potential, whereas neither Cork nor Limerick possess an adequate business environment for effective interface at higher levels of management. For the smaller urban centres, there is a general absence of higher-order business facilities, emphasizing their production role within a corporate system dominated by the capital.

The low degree of contact potential available outside of Dublin results in a significant leakage of employment and capital from regional centres. This results in a loss of internal multiplier effects, especially for the producer services (O'Farrell and O'Laughlin, 1980). An input–output study of Cork confirms the high level of leakage from city to Dublin (Blackwell, 1976). Offices located in provincial centres tend to serve a restricted regional hinterland. They are, however, usually controlled from Dublin, and many of their office supplies and key personnel are made available from the national headquarters. In marked contrast, the Dublin office system appears to be largely self-sufficient. Out of a total network of services utilized by Dublin offices in 1971, less than 1 per cent originated outside the city region. Furthermore, this low proportion had declined during the ten-year period from 1961 (Bannon, 1973, 1979).

In spite of this centralization of decision-making and higher-order service functions, other cities and county towns have benefited from the improved range and quality of services. Reorganization of public services has focused on the larger and more accessible towns, while marketed services have also shown a preference for such localities. This has improved their employment base and contributed to a greater sense of prosperity and vitality. Developments in the retail trade illustrate this point.

Although relative stability exists in the upper levels of the retail hierarchy, some significant changes have occurred in many smaller and medium-sized urban centres. In a study of the changing retail structure of 49 towns in the Midlands and Border area between 1951 and 1971, O'Farrell (quoted in NESC, 1979) recorded increases in the centrality values for all categories of town size. Dillusion of new and higher order functions, changed the relative performance of the towns. In general, newer functions focused primarily on towns in excess of 5000 population and emphasized their prospects for further growth by extending their effective hinterlands. Smaller centres failed to diversify upwards and continued to rely on the provision of low-order goods and services.

Similar conclusions appear to be the result of a recent survey (Hourihan and Lyons, forthcoming) which updated a 1966 study of central places in Co. Tipperary (O'Farrell, 1969). Over the twenty-year period, the five major towns (Clonmel, Thurles, Nenagh, Tipperary and Carrick-on-Suir) have gained substantially in their number and range of functional units. This is most noticeable for higher-order functions such as building societies, credit unions, handicraft and hobby shops and more specialized food outlets. In contrast, more traditional services such as grocery and drapery outlets have declined markedly as larger retail stores have taken their place.

The medium and larger country towns of Ireland have benefited from elements of centralization and specialization of service functions. Many are thriving communities and have dynamic retail and service cores. While shopping centres have become quite common in these towns, they are not too far removed from the existing cores, and the main streets still maintain a central importance for trade. Although the new prosperity and enhanced functional base initially appeared to threaten the traditional appearance of the towns, greater consideration is now taken of aesthetic qualities. Increased use is made of traditional sign-writing and building façades are restored to harmonize more effectively with the traditional architecture of these old centres. Kilkenny provides an outstanding example of this contemporary movement.

4.3.4 An urban policy gap

In a 1965 statement on regional policy, the government indicated its intention to promote urban centres which 'are likely to become the commercial, financial, educational, health, social and administrative centres of each region'. A commitment to physical planning had apparently emerged which prompted government to seek advice on an optimum strategy for urban development, one which would be consistent with their longer-term social and economic objectives. Consultants were commissioned to prepare advisory plans for Dublin (Wright, 1967), Limerick (Lichfield and Associates, 1967) and the country as a whole (Buchanan and Partners, 1969), while a detailed physical planning study of the Cork subregion was later published by Gillie (1971).

The Buchanan Report (1969) proposed a national strategy for physical development based on a hierarchy of growth centres (see Figure 2.1). Dublin's growth was to be limited to its natural increase, and to counteract the primacy of the capital two national growth centres were proposed for Cork and Limerick. These would deflect internal migration from Dublin and be bases for major industrial expansion. Six other regional centres were suggested, together with four local centres; the latter were located in areas considered too remote to benefit from spread effects from higher-order growth centres.

To achieve the population totals projected in the Buchanan Report, 75 per cent of new manufacturing employment was to be targeted for these growth centres. This level of discrimination received a largely negative response, and in its place a compromise appeared which held within itself a paradox. In 1972 the government accepted the Buchanan population targets as a basis for regional development, yet rejected the means by which these could realistically be attained. The IDA's policy of job dispersal included 177 towns and villages throughout the country, which meant that less than 50 per cent of manufacturing jobs were allocated to the original growth centres. In addition, the continued absence of any policy programme to curtail the concentration of the tertiary and quaternary sectors on Dublin failed to encourage a significant dispersal in service employment. Table 4.4 illustrates the failure of the centres to achieve their projected population targets.

By 1981, Dublin had achieved almost two-thirds of the 1986 population target. Apart from Galway, which benefited significantly from the dispersal of manufacturing to the West region, and some positive multipliers spinning off into services, all other centres performed poorly, particularly Cork and Limerick. While the smaller and medium-sized towns benefited from a decentralization of production, the larger urban centres designated as growth poles for the national economy have benefited least. The poor performance of the urban centres should be a source of concern for a country wishing to offer a choice of location for modern growth industries, and which are attracted to developed infrastructures best found in urban environments.

Although population trends were less positive than projected, the advantages of urban centres for economic activities ensured that total employment increased within all suggested growth centres (Table 4.4). The rates of increase, moreover, were significantly greater than the national average (6.7 per cent), which was adversely influenced by the decline of agriculture. By 1981, the nine urban areas accounted for 40 per cent of national employment compared with 36 per cent in 1966. Gains were most impressive within the western centres and Athlone, while the larger towns and cities along the east and south coasts experienced losses or slow growth in the productive sector, reducing the effect of net gains in services.

The differential performance of manufacturing and service sectors in the context of a growing and youthful population base in the cities and towns, contributed to a significant rise in unemployment. An erosion of the traditional industries effectively reduced the opportunities for blue-collar employment, and newly created jobs were frequently white-collar occupations or demanded skills and attributes that were not possessed by the redundant workforce. The new job opportunities favoured the younger and more educated people from within the cities' traditional labour shed, and further stimulated in-migration. This increased the total labour force and, within this more competitive environment, less educated youths and displaced workers (especially male) found increasing difficulties of access to the job market.

This mismatch between the supply and demand characteristics of workers within urban areas was accentuated by the economic recession which had a severe impact on established manufacturing. By 1981, national unemployment approached 10 per cent, but this figure was higher in most of the major urban centres. As the recession worsened, so did the severity of unemployment within urban centres (Table 4.5). The unemployment crisis, while of national proportions — with a 1986 level of 18 per cent — had focused increasingly on the formerly buoyant urban centres. Cork in particular has emerged as an unemployment blackspot (Brunt, 1984), and in 1986 an unemployment rate of 22 per cent attested to the city's plight.

Hoselitz's (1955) review of the charges against primate cities — swallow-

Table 4.4 Growth of proposed 'development centres', 1966–81

Centre	Population 1966	Recommended 1986 population	Actual 1981 population	1981 population as % of target	Total employment change, 1966–81
Dublin subregion	795,047	1,125,000	1,003,164	63.1	+18.9
Cork	122,146	250,000	149,792	21.6	+12.8
Limerick	57,570	175,000	75,520	15.3	+21.6
Waterford	29,842	55,000	39,636	38.9	+18.7
Galway	26,295	47,000	41,861	75.2	+47.1
Dundalk	21,678	44,000	29,135	33.5	+15.2
Drogheda	17,908	35,000	23,615	33.4	+10.9
Sligo	13,424	25–30,000	18,002	39.6 or 27.6	+36.3
Athlone	10,987	18,000	14,426	49.2	+28.6
Total	1,094,897	1,774,000– 1,779,000	1,395,151	44.2	+19.1

Source: Buchanan (1969) and Census of Population (1981).

Table 4.5   Growth of unemployment in the major urban centres, 1981–86 (June)

	1981	1986	% increase 1981–86
Dublin*	35,814	74,780	108.8
Cork	6399	13,054	104.0
Limerick	4241	8217	93.8
Waterford	2746	5287	92.5
Galway	3182	5341	67.9
National rate of unemployment	9.7%	17.9%	

* Includes Dun Laoghaire.
Source: Central Statistics Office.

ing investment, absorbing manpower, achieving a cultural dominance, retarding the development of other cities and generally consuming more than they produce — appears to have great validity with respect to Dublin. Despite the fact that both public and political sentiment seems to support the contention that Dublin's degree of dominance is too high, very little has emerged by way of policy to control development. Several reports have, however, advocated a more relevant urban policy, particularly with respect to the growing service sector of the economy. Relocation of services, and especially decision-making functions, to a limited number of cities was a central argument of a 1977 NESC report (see also Bannon, 1978). Two years later, O'Farrell proposed the development of one or two counter-magnet cities as the only realistic chance of stabilizing the East region's share of national population (NESC, 1979, pp. 97–8). This strategy was similar to the French planning strategy of establishing *métropoles d'équilibre* to counterbalance the dominance of Paris.

Whether Dublin is indeed too large is a controversial issue. By international standards, the Irish capital is not unduly large, and it can be argued that the country needs a metropolitan area like Dublin to integrate effectively with the international economy. Of greater relevance, however, is the fact that the conurbation may be growing too quickly in relation to development elsewhere in Ireland. 'The crucial issue is not whether Dublin is too big or smaller towns in the provinces too small, but whether the changes in the spatial structure of the Irish urban system and, in particular, the increasing concentration of population in the Greater Dublin area, are in harmony with the goals of the community' (NESC, 1979, p. 49). Given that the goals of the 1972 government *Review of Regional Policy* included significant development of the country's major regional and county towns, it would appear that the degree of centralization that has unfolded is counterproductive.

The economic recession of the 1980s has created a new environment within which urban centres have to function (Couniffe and Kennedy, 1984). Emphasis on international traded services and higher-order business functions within the productive sector (e.g. research and development, marketing) has revived interest in a growth-centre strategy. Larger urban centres usually possess the critical infrastructural facilities deemed vital for successful modern developments. In these circumstances, it seems realistic to anticipate that Dublin will benefit disproportionately from these new developments by virtue of its pre-existing infrastructure and contact potential. Development of business parks in Cork and Limerick, allied to their existing centres of higher education, should see some trickle-down of high technology enterprise to these major centres.

Modern growth industries tend to exhibit greater centripetal tendencies than do more traditional production units and routine service functions. A more discriminating policy of development is required based on the potential of urban centres for growth rather than as a response to localized need. Dispersal of basic production units into many towns may have facilitated growth in the 1970s, but the current recession has removed much of this positive impulse through plant closure or contraction. Unfortunately for such centres, infrastructural deficiencies have not been addressed, and their potential for development is thereby circumscribed. A NESC report (1981b) has strongly argued that a policy of decentralized centralization is required to allocate capital resources effectively for major infrastructure improvements. This drive for a more balanced approach to urban development has met — and will continue to meet — with strong opposition from bodies based on local rather than national interests.

There has been an increase in functional specialization in Ireland's urban centres since the 1960s, with the emergence of commuter towns, industrial towns and trading centres. Initial evidence from the first half of the 1980s indicates that the current reorganization of towns is based on differential rates of decline rather than the growth which typified the previous twenty years. Restructuring of the urban system has occurred within the context of a *laissez-faire* approach from government. If the towns are to recapture their earlier growth momentum to effect significant economic development while minimizing social dislocation, government must finally embrace a coherent and coordinated urban policy. Economic recession will make this politically difficult, but decisions have to be made regarding the form of the urban system which is most suitable for Ireland's long-term development. Uppermost in this debate have to be the primacy of Dublin and its relationship with its subordinate centres.

4.4   Changing patterns within the major cities

As urban centres have grown, the composition of their population, economy and society has evolved and has influenced their internal structure. These factors have been both cause and effect of the underlying perceptions of, and attitude toward, the city while continued decline of the central city has resulted in an environment that discourages investment, the basically negative attitude towards the inner city has directed investment to the suburbs. This vicious circle is most notably expressed in the largest metropolitan centres.

4.4.1   *Dispersal of population within the city regions*

During the twentieth century, the major urban centres have evolved from relatively compact and dense forms of settlement to more mature types. In the process, these cities have come to exhibit the twin characteristics associated with most contemporary large urban centres: decline in the central city and a major growth of population in a sprawling suburban and commuting hinterland. Hourihan (1982a, 1983) detailed the evolving patterns and processes as they affect the cities of Dublin, Cork and Limerick.

Between 1901 and 1981, the built-up areas surrounding all three cities increased fivefold and, by the latter date, the contiguous built-up area of Dublin exceeded 250 square kilometres. Each census has shown a progressive outward surge of population into the newer suburbs and adjacent exurban areas. Much of Dublin's growth has recently been channelled into the new towns of Blanchardstown, Lucan-Clondalkin and Tallaght, located to the west of the city but which now form part of the contiguous built-up area. By 1981, these three towns collectively had a population in excess of 100,000, which compares with 26,000 a decade earlier and only 1300 in 1946 when Haughton (1949) referred to them as 'small rural villages' (p. 270).

While the newer suburbs grew, the inner city experienced a continuous decline, and by the 1980s central Dublin had a population density of only one-fifth that of 1901. With a centre-city population of some 85,000, this area accounts for 10 per cent of the total population of the sub-region as opposed to 50 per cent at the time of independence. The net result has been a flattening-out of the density profile of the city in line with developments elsewhere in Europe. However, as Hourihan (1982a) comments, 'the speed with which Dublin has been transformed into a sprawling low-density city has been very rapid compared to developments elsewhere (in the world)' (p. 143).

Similar trends are observable in both Cork and Limerick, although the degree of urban sprawl has been more effectively contained than in Dublin. Central city populations within both regional cities have declined significantly, but the resulting overspill has been directed into satellite settlements. In spite of this, ribbon development and one-off housing are all too apparent within the commuting hinterlands of the cities.

4.4.2 Urban planning and housing

The 1963 Local Government (Planning and Development) Act, subsequently updated in 1976 and 1982, provides the basis for contemporary urban planning. Objectives and policy programmes for development are established and reviewed every five years. While these plans take note of essential social and economic changes and requirements within the urban areas, these elements appear to be a secondary consideration. Instead, local authority planning has tended to be largely physical and has had a less than positive impact on the problems of the contemporary urban environment. This problem is accentuated by the fact that urban planning has to function within a localized context, due to the absence of any coherent regional and national planning. Conflicts of interests between urban areas and surrounding county planning authorities can militate against a satisfactory solution to problems which have a common base — urban sprawl.

An increase in the populations of the major urban centres has placed additional strain on the housing markets in these localities. Underfinanced local authorities, faced with the dual task of renovating existing dwellings as well as constructing new housing, have shown a willingness to allow private developers to shape the property market to a greater extent than may seem desirable. The housing policies of city corporations are therefore of great significance in terms of both the scale and direction of housing development, either because of their direct intervention in house building and land-use planning or due to a *laissez-faire* attitude to private home developments. On both counts, the outward surge of housing was aided by the changing land values ascribed to the city by private individuals. Transport changes have further facilitated the flexibility of population and land-use relocation, resulting in the suburbanization of housing, especially for the middle and higher-income groups.

In Dublin, the corporation has been faced with a major problem of substandard housing and slum conditions in the inner city — a legacy of developments in the nineteenth century (NESC, 1981a, pp. 62–68). In a survey conducted in 1938 the corporation found that 70 per cent of 33,411 families lived in single room dwellings. An extensive rehousing programme was therefore initiated as part of a slum clearance scheme. This involved some refurbishment of existing dwellings, together with rebuilding of new houses and flats to accommodate displaced families. By far the most common solution to overcrowding, however, was the removal of inner-city residents to large, new local authority housing estates on the outskirts of the city (e.g. Cabra and Crumlin) (Horner, 1985).

Following the Second World War, the increasing competition for land within the core area caused public housing development to be pushed further away from the city centre (Haughton, 1970). Within the core area, corporation flats became a dominant dwelling type in order to maximize the rehousing of family units. One-class communities were being created in the inner city and over large areas of the expanding suburbs. Rehabilitation of buildings appears to have been abandoned as a cost-effective mechanism of meeting housing demands in the city, and between 1945 and 1979 Dublin Corporation reconditioned only 188 dwellings. It was cheaper and more efficient to raze buildings and communities irrespective of the resulting social dislocation. A further consequence of the destruction of tenements and of the absence of grants effectively to refurbish existing buildings has been a decline in the already small private rental property market. Rent controls have also worked against this type of tenure and have put further pressure on local authority housing. Municipal housing has increasingly come to dominate residential land-use within inner Dublin. By 1971, 51.5 per cent of housing units in the inner city were rented from the local authority in contrast to 20 per cent for the Dublin subregion.

The preference of the corporation for greenfield estate development has been largely maintained through to the present, although some notable policy modifications emerged in the 1970s. The social inadequacies of high-rise flats as a solution to inner-city housing needs became increasingly apparent, and in 1973 a Ministerial embargo from the Department of the Environment discontinued this policy option. In their place, the corporation has opted for low-rise town houses built at relatively high densities (McNulty and MacLaran, 1985). Although at least 50 per cent more expensive than greenfield housing estates, this option affords an opportunity for inner-city residents to remain within identifiable communities, while the corporation can meet its stated objective of maintaining a sizeable resident population in inner-city Dublin. Long waiting lists and economies of scale to be derived from large-scale, purpose-built housing on greenfield sites, however, are likely to ensure that the balance of municipal housing development remains on the periphery, rather than in the centre.

The disproportionate presence of local authority housing in the inner city and a concentration of large municipal estates north of the Liffey have influenced the pattern of private housing development. The 'repellent' effects of proximity to local authority housing, together with the high costs of inner-city land and a less than satisfactory environment related to problems of traffic congestion, derelict land and social problems of higher crime rates, have all combined to induce the more mobile and higher-income families to opt for suburban living. The buoyant market created by this group has encouraged a large amount of private building on the periphery of the city.

Building societies and other financial institutions readily advance capital to support home ownership in these expanding private housing areas. In addition, public policy encourages the process through providing tax relief on mortgages and generous incentives for first-time purchasers of new homes. This effectively means loans for houses in the outer suburbs. The availability after 1985 of home improvement grants of IR£ 5000 for pre-1940 houses, however, has encouraged many inner-city dwellers to upgrade their premises. This scheme was discontinued in 1987 due to escalating costs, which reflected the number of take-ups. Ranged against this are the penalties imposed in the form of stamp duty and the absence of grant aid for the purchase of old houses in the existing built-up areas. While this has undoubtedly favoured the building industry, the financial advantages for new home construction have resulted in a leap-frogging of urban development in an unrestricted manner around the capital city. Between 1971 and 1981, smaller towns within 16 km of the suburbs more than doubled their population to 93,618 (Hourihan, 1983). The occupational and social composition of these suburban zones contrast markedly with the residual populations in the still declining centres (Brady and Parker, 1975, 1986; Hourihan, 1978). These social polarities are further discussed in Section 4.5.

The Wright Report (1967), although never formally accepted by government, has apparently been the basis for much of the physical planning in Dublin, and more especially for Co. Dublin. While growth has therefore tended to follow the suggested policy of focusing predominantly on four self-contained new towns, much of the urban development has spilled over into the green wedges that were to separate the new towns. Clearly, there is no containment policy for population growth around the capital. Furthermore, the extension of the built-up area well beyond the administrative boundaries of the city involves different planning authorities trying to organize locally the expansion of the metropolitan area. In these circumstances, a comprehensive plan for the Greater Dublin area is urgently required.

The availability and price of land in the urban fringe have been a key problem for all planning authorities trying to control development. The Kenny Report (Committee on the Price of Building Land, 1975) proposed that local authorities should be able to acquire land designated for development through compulsory purchase at its existing value plus 25 per cent. Possessing such a land bank would greatly facilitate a more effective use of land in the public interest. This has not been acceptable to government. Partly as a consequence of this, development of land around Dublin has been more intensive and a greater infill of the suggested open-spaces has occurred. Although planning authorities have indeed acquired some land through compulsory purchase, development has been primarily of a *laissez-faire* nature (Zimmerman, 1978). The problem of having to pay heavy compensation to the owners of private property through loss of value under restrictive land-use zoning has also tended to make planning authorities less than willing to control development in the urban fringe.

The Eastern Regional Development Organization (ERDO) (1985) illustrates a possible future scenario for Dublin and the surrounding counties in the year 2011. In the absence of a comprehensive settlement policy, this region's population base would increase by 560,000, two-thirds of this occurring in the metropolitan region. Each of the new towns to the west of the city was expected to grow to greater than 100,000 in population, while the city centre was not considered suitable for rehousing even 10,000 people! Fortunately, all political parties have rejected this policy in the interests of both the regional cities and the communities within Dublin itself. It does, however, highlight the need for a comprehensive plan for this complex urban region.

4.4.3   Suburbanization of manufacturing

Industrial activity within the largest urban areas has traditionally centred on the inner city, which provided access to the large resident labour force, and proximity to port facilities and to an internal transport network. The advantages of these localized external economies of scale have been significantly reduced, however, as the age of factory buildings and plant equipment, traffic congestion and high land costs (which largely check the opportunities for site expansion) have led to plant closures and rationalizations. The inevitable redundancies and negative multipliers affect all aspects of the local economy.

Suburbs have become the preferential location for production within the cities. Here, the more open environment offers cheaper land for more effective plant layout and easy access to modern transport systems, while maintaining proximity to the service facilities of the central business district. Decentralization of population to the urban fringe is both a cause and an effect of this relocation.

Surveys conducted by the Dublin City Planning Department in 1975 indicated that between 1966 and 1974, the inner city experienced a 30 per cent reduction in industrial land use, while more than one-quarter of the establishments located on suburban industrial estates had relocated from the inner city (quoted in NESC, 1981a and MacLaran and Beamish, 1985). The erosion of the production base has continued, and the IDA has estimated that the inner city was losing 2000 manufacturing jobs annually during the late 1970s (NESC, 1981a, p. 181).

In addition to the changed demand for industrial land, MacLaran and Beamish (1985) suggest that the limited supply of industrial space within the inner city has contributed to suburbanization. In an investigation of speculative industrial property within Dublin, it is apparent that the inner city lost out heavily in the creation of new industrial space. Between 1960 and 1982, the inner city could account for only 9 per cent of new factories and warehouses and 6 per cent of all industrial floorspace made available.

Heavy manufacturing employment losses within the capital prompted the IDA to promote Dublin more actively as an industrial location. In addition to the extension of the Small Industry Programme to Dublin, the IDA established an Inner-City Unit to promote further the disadvantaged area. The preferred strategy involved the acquisition and provision of suitably serviced industrial land for development. Almost 40 per cent of all factory units established by the IDA in Dublin were in the inner city, which contrasts markedly with only 3.8 per cent of all privately financed factory space. By 1982, the dependency of the inner city on state promotion of industrial production can be gauged by the fact that the IDA was responsible for over four-fifths of factory floorspace constructed since 1960 (MacLaran and Beamish, 1985, p. 46).

Ireland's other major cities also exhibited similar patterns of differential development. In Cork, the long-established industrial core, centred around the quays of the inner-city port, has collapsed. The once thriving industrial zone is now characterized by empty factories, run-down buildings and former warehouses occupied by transitory enterprises. Modern development has largely bypassed this area in preference for newer suburban areas and satellite towns. While the remaining larger port-cities possessed some traditional manufacturing activities, they were less strongly orientated to industry than either Dublin or Cork. As a result, cities such as Waterford and Limerick exhibit a less marked differential in terms of industrial land-use changes between their central areas and suburbs. Peripheral development typifies such centres, however, and large industrial estates can be found on the major routeways leading into them.

4.4.4 Reorganization of retail and office activities

As the focus of population growth and consumer purchasing power has gravitated to the suburbs, so too has a significant degree of retailing activity. Following the opening of the first planned shopping centre at Stillorgan, Co. Dublin, in 1966, out-of-town shopping centres have become increasingly important in urban areas. Lower land values in the surburban fringe allow for the convenient layout of shopping units and provide ample car parking for a shopping public anxious to avoid the congestion of the city centre (Parker, 1980a, 1981). Residents of the newer suburban areas have found these arrangements particularly suitable for their more flexible lifestyles and reliance on the automobile. The initial success of these surburban centres, however, was often bought at the expense of older shopping areas within the urban core. Many smaller and general merchandise stores were forced to close, and retail activity increasingly concentrated on higher-order functions. While this attracted shoppers from an extensive hinterland, they offered fewer advantages for local residents more interested in purchasing general items for everyday needs.

Since the 1970s, there has been a partial reversal of the suburbanization of retail activities as attempts have been made to revive the city centres. In 1977 the first in-town shopping centres appeared in Cork, Limerick and Dun Laoghaire. Government directives in 1981–82 further strengthened the move to invigorate declining central business districts: planning authorities were required to assess the impact any new, large-scale retail development would have on the existing system. This has led to several refusals to grant planning approval for suburban centres, which have benefited urban renewal. Conflict of interests between planning authorities, however, can obstruct this rational approach. The city of Cork, for instance, has succeeded in sponsoring four major new shopping developments within its core area, but the county planning authority has sanctioned a large new development at Douglas, a dormitory village some 6 km from the city centre. This will inevitably deflect customers from the revived city centre. The city has appealed against this and is awaiting a government decision. However, for Cork as for other cities, the success of in-town shopping will ultimately depend on an effective resolution of the traffic problems, together with an upgrading of the urban environment.

While the private market has effectively zoned out much residential, industrial and retail land uses from the inner city, due largely to inflated land values, the general advantages of a central location for office functions are still considerable. Office development has been prepared to meet the high costs of land — for which it is largely responsible due to the pressures of demand it has placed on a limited land market — in order to benefit from centrality. The tradition and esteem of a city-centre location, access to a multiplicity of back-up services, a well-developed communication system and the cultural and social outlets of the inner city, all prove attractive for high-order office functions.

The provincial cities all tend to possess a relatively small and compact area of office activity. In Dublin, however, the concentration and growth of office development within the city centre are remarkable. By 1971, 43 per cent of the country's office employment was in central Dublin (Bannon, 1979). Centralization of decision-making in the capital has merely served to increase the pressure for office space and, from 1960 to 1980, office floorspace almost doubled with the construction of an additional 743,000 m² (Malone, 1981, 1983). Growth in new office development has not, however, been uniform but exhibits a cyclical pattern with peaks of office building completions occurring in 1972–73 and 1981–83. These correspond to particularly buoyant conditions for investment during the years immediately prior to accession to the EC and to the inflated economic conditions of the late 1970s. The recession of the 1980s and oversupply of office space have subsequently curtailed the rate of new development. Little of this development has occurred north of the Liffey — apart from local government offices — as this low-income area with a disproportionate presence of local authority housing has proved commercially unattractive for private developers.

Office development has strongly concentrated in the south-eastern sector of Dublin (Bannon, 1972). New purpose-built office blocks have been constructed, while the large Georgian and Victorian residences of this area have been readily converted into office accommodation. These developments also stimulated the appearance of a comparatively new element into the housing market. Private apartment buildings have emerged to cater for the needs of the younger, and often single, professionals who are employed in these offices. This intensive form of residential land-use allows it to compete effectively with office development (Holdship and Gillmor, 1976).

The forces of centrality are extremely strong with respect to office developments in Dublin, and very little suburbanization has occurred (Fernie, 1977). An important contributory factor is the apparent tolerance of city planners to the scale of office construction in the inner city and the conversion of Dublin's Georgian and Victorian heritage to accommodate private office development. The major increase of labour-intensive office activities within the inner city has provided jobs for a labour force largely resident in the outer suburbs. Large-scale commuting and a severe mismatch in the local labour market have been the result.

4.5 Social areas in Dublin

Dublin has a long tradition of social polarization for, as a recent report clearly indicated, 'to speak of Dublin as a single social entity is to ignore the existence of two separate Dublins — that of the rich and the poor — the Dublin of the ascendency and the Dublin of the poor and of the tenements' (NESC, 1981a, p. 62). Recent demographic trends have emphasized the degree of social polarization and social deprivation within the city by interacting in a cause–effect relationship with changing land-use patterns. While Haughton (1949, 1970) identified some basic functional divisions within the city, more recent studies into the factorial ecology of Dublin have allowed for a much better appreciation of the underlying sociodemographic structure (Brady and Parker, 1975, 1986; Hourihan, 1978). Three factors in particular appear to help explain the complex social mosaic of the city: socioeconomic status, stage of lifecycle and housing type. On the basis of these factors, plus other critical indicators, social areas of the city have been delimited (Hourihan, 1978; NESC, 1981a).

The built-up area of Dublin involves a complex web of interlocking social structures. Recent and rapid growth of the urban system, however, focuses attention on the degree of polarization that has emerged between two fundamentally contrasting areas of the city. Within the inner city and extensive tracts of local authority housing, problems of social deprivation and economic decline are manifest. In contrast, the expanding suburban fringe illustrates the growth and prosperity associated with modern urban lifestyles.

The inner city has experienced significant population decline, due partly to lower rates of natural increase but more importantly to net out-migration. The operation of the housing market has played a critical role in shaping out-migration, especially since it has only partly functioned within the context of a planned decentralization. Both private developers and the corporation have preferred developing new housing areas to refurbishment or infilling with existing communities. Access to new housing, however, has been socially selective and reflects the stage reached in the lifecycle, together with the means to acquire a new home to accommodate either a newly formed or growing household. For inner-city residents having the means as well as the desire for owner occupancy, this almost inevitably means a relocation to the suburban fringe, since private developers have not found inner-city areas attractive for investment. This has tended to remove higher socioeconomic groups from the core of the city, especially those with relatively young and growing families. In contrast, lower socioeconomic groups, lacking the basic means to purchase housing, have become trapped within the local authority housing section. Opportunities for such families to move out of this sector are limited, and this type of tenure increasingly conforms to areas of concentration of the more socially disadvantaged groups. Major concentrations of single-class housing consequently emerge and are a recipe for polarization.

A major report (NESC, 1981a) highlights some of the characteristics of the more deprived communities living within the larger local authority housing zones, especially those in the inner city. In this latter area, multi-dwelling units and local authority housing provide more than one-half of the building stock. For some localities, more than 90 per cent of housing is provided by the corporation. By 1979, an estimated one-third of housing required modern bathing facilities, and 30 per cent were overcrowded. Over half the housing was pre-1919, and many structures needed renovation.

The high rates of unemployment and the dominance of lower socioeconomic groups within the inner city are further associated with restructuring of the area's economic base. Jobs lost within manufacturing and through the reorganization of the labour force at the docks have not been replaced in either sufficient number or type by the local expansion of office employment. The information-based sector is selective in terms of entry requirements and excludes many of the inner-city blue-collar workforce.

Two elements in particular work against the traditional inner-city workforce and compound the problem of social deprivation. First, many blue-collar workers have to reverse commute to suburban industrial estates. This can be both expensive and time consuming, especially since public transport offers the only practical solution for those who lack private transportation. Moving house is not a realistic option for many displaced workers, other than within the spatially restricted local authority housing system.

Second, access to well-paid office employment largely depends on educational qualifications, but enormous differences exist with respect to educational achievement levels for residents within Dublin. Breathnach (1976) has shown that one-sixth of the city's 192 electoral wards exhibit education deprivation, and this strongly correlates with the areas of poverty and low socioeconomic status typical of the inner-city and public housing areas. Polarization of achievement rates can be self-perpetuating, since a poor school environment is often exaggerated by a home environment in which parents and other peer groups downplay the significance of education. This suggests that a greater degree of intervention is required to promote better educational opportunities if inner-city youths are to have a better chance of employment within their immediate area, and achieve some degree of upward social mobility.

In the inner-city and the large municipal housing estates, poor access to better housing, employment and education results in a predominance of low socioeconomic groups · and high levels of unemployment, particularly among the youth and elderly male workers. This frequently results in recourse to the more informal economy to supplement social security payments and also can spill over into higher rates of crime and general antisocial behaviour. Unfortunately, a stereotyped image has been created of the conditions and types of residents in these areas. This is generally of a negative nature and further limits the potential mobility of people anxious to gain access to better employment and living conditions.

The expanding suburban fringe contrasts markedly with the inner-city areas. Private housing development has favoured the emergence of relatively homogeneous areas of middle and higher socioeconomic groups, although the timing of the development has resulted in communities differentiated by stages of the lifecycle. Thus, while Brady and Parker

(1986) note that the socioeconomic status of most communities did not change much in the decade to 1981, family status is more dynamic. In some of the more established suburban housing zones, the communities are showing signs of 'growing old together', which creates new demands on the infrastructures of these areas. In addition, the concentration of young families in the rapidly growing new towns has introduced a major new structural component into the built-up area. While this latter area seems underserviced in the provision of schools, the older suburban zones are now probably oversupplied. A more effective mix of both age and class groupings would help to resolve this problem. The social rather than the physical requirements of housing developments have not, however, been a strong point of planning policy in Ireland.

Since the publication of the *Dublin Transportation Study* (Heanue et al., 1971–72), which was designed to assess the city's transport needs, the scale of the traffic problem has increased. And yet Dublin still awaits a coordinated policy to deal effectively with the pressures placed on both private and public transport (Killen, 1979b). Improvements within the public sector include the introduction of bus lanes and the beginnings of a modern commuter rail system (DART), but planners remain inordinately committed to development of a transport infrastructure based on new roads for private cars. Although scaled down from the early 1970s, due to escalating costs and increasing public concern as to the effects on the city's morphology, elaborate plans for road development persistently appear. Many of these schemes for road widening or new arterial routes directly affect the inner city. Destruction of a large number of buildings, the break-up of community cohesiveness, increased dereliction in the face of uncertainty and land speculation, all contribute to a further and marked deterioration of the inner-city environment. As a result, in Dublin and other major urban areas, pressure has mounted to check the decline of the city centre and to introduce more socially responsive policies which stress renewal rather than redevelopment as the basic premise of planning.

4.6   Urban renewal

Modernization of the economy based on urban-industrial development has had a largely negative effect on the inner areas of Ireland's major cities. For more than twenty years, these core areas have been largely ignored as the dictates of capital accumulation clearly failed to correspond with the social needs of inner-city communities. A largely anti-urban bias found expression in decentralization policies for employment and population. As a consequence, large areas of the inner cities were allowed to run down in a spiral of decline. Decaying buildings and derelict sites combined with speculative office and road development projects to reduce severely the environmental conditions and morale of residents in these areas.

During the 1980s, however, there was a reaction against this partial abandonment of inner-city communities. Rising levels of unemployment within these areas, together with other obvious manifestations of social and economic deprivation, such as high rates of crime and poverty, focused attention on the need for more positive planning for the inner city. Community action groups emerged to press and publicize the case for urban renewal rather than redevelopment and relocation. Despite difficult environmental conditions, inner-city communities have exhibited great attachment to their neighbourhoods and oppose relocation to other housing areas. In a survey of Dublin inner-city residents, 70 per cent of respondents indicated that they did not want to move house. Furthermore, almost 60 per cent had lived in the area for at least twenty years and one-third in the same dwelling (NESC, 1981a). The election of independent politicians from such areas who were sympathetic to these ideals furthered the pressure for a change in policy. Meanwhile, conservationists, anxious to protect the fabric of the older parts of the cities, became increasingly outspoken in their objections to redevelopment.

Somewhat belatedly perhaps, the government recognized urban decay as a problem and in 1986 passed the Urban Renewal Bill. This is designed to encourage urban renewal in the worst areas of the centres of five cities — Dublin, Cork, Limerick, Waterford and Galway. Significant financial incentives are offered in these designated areas and include 100 per cent capital allowance on commercial buildings, tax allowances for construction or conversion costs on dwellings, and full remission on rates for ten years on new buildings or on any increase in the valuation of enlarged or improved buildings. The central aim is to attract private enterprise back into the city centres, but in a more coordinated and planned fashion. As Fergus O'Brien, former Minister of State at the Department of the Environment, has stated, 'The package of urban renewal measures . . . includes a range of incentives which are intended to create a suitable financial climate for large-scale investment by the private sector and generate a self-sustaining urban renewal process in the years ahead' (*The Irish Times*, 1986).

Although generally welcomed, this policy has raised two principal concerns. First, some observers feel that the package is spread over too wide an area and should be more focused. Thus, Dublin has three designated areas (65 ha) and a special site at the Custom Docks (11 ha), while Cork has two areas (40 ha). By international standards, these are not large areas, but financial resources are limited. Second, the package of incentives is to run for three years, terminating in May 1989. Developers consider that this may be too short a time period for successful take-off of renewal. The process tends to be comparatively slow at first and only gathers momentum after the approach has shown signs of success for private investment.

Concern with Dublin's inner-city problems undoubtedly lies at the heart of the new policy direction. Designated areas now cover 6.5 per cent of its inner city, and although this zone has experienced some attempt at urban renewal, it has generally been fragmented in nature. Employment creation schemes under the IDA's Inner-City Unit have achieved some success with the promotion of small industries, while local enterprise centres and community workshops have been established under self-help programmes, for example the Liffey Trust (Cottuli, 1986). Local authority housing has also been upgraded, with greater attention being given to preserving neighbourhoods. The offer of the IR£ 5000 home improvement grant for pre-1940 houses was also useful for inner-Dublin as 75 per cent of the area's housing were of this vintage in 1981. Upgrading of the housing stock would be a clear benefit, but the measure was discontinued in 1987. The establishment of the Metropolitan Streets Commission in 1986 to try to reverse the decline in the city centre through beautifying the main streets and thereby providing a more attractive environment for retail and business functions was another positive development.

Perhaps the most interesting aspect of the new approach, however, is the development proposed for the Custom House Docks area. This is seen as the key to the redevelopment of the redundant dockland area of Dublin port and will act as a catalyst for inner-city revival. A heavy bias within the urban renewal programme favours this scheme over the three other designated areas of Dublin. Thus 100 per cent — as opposed to 50 per cent — capital allowances on construction costs and a more favourable tax relief on rented apartments are available, while the incentives will be offered over a five-year period, rather than three years elsewhere. A Custom House Development Authority has been created, with an initial budget of IR£ 10 million, to oversee the planned development of the area. The contract to develop the site was awarded in October 1987, and involves a mix of land uses, including a hotel and trade centre, offices, residential and retailing. The centrepiece of the entire development, which will cost an estimated IR£ 250 million, will be an International Financial Services Centre to cater for offshore banking and internationally traded services. This reflects the importance being attached by government to these increasingly mobile international growth industries and their potential for both wealth and high-quality employment creation. Advantageous financial incentives (e.g. no exchange control for dealings in foreign currencies to overseas clients, no Capital Gain Taxes on gains from financial dealings within the Centre and application of 10 per cent rate of Corporation Tax to the year 2001) and the established infrastructure of Dublin have resulted in a great deal of interest from business organizations. At the start of 1988, 18 companies had pledged to take up space at the Centre, with a potential workforce of 1000. Over the next 3–4 years, however, it is confidently estimated that the International Financial Services Centre will generate some 7500 jobs.

In spite of these more positive prospects for inner-city renewal, difficulties and conflicts of interest persist. Unfortunately, the Metropolitan Streets Commission has been abolished, and road-widening schemes continue to be advocated as a solution to traffic problems within the centre of the city. In trying to accommodate traffic, rather than adjusting traffic flows to the existing structures, streets and buildings are being destroyed. Ultimately, this removes the sense of place that is so vital for inner-city communities and is the basis for the recent urban renewal programme.

Inner-city renewal has also gathered momentum in the other cities scheduled to benefit from the Urban Renewal Act. In Galway, the Spanish Arch area has been transformed from one of dereliction to a fashionable centrepiece of city life, while in Limerick, the Granary, once the largest derelict building in the city, has been converted into a visually attractive historical building comprising offices, tourism and retail activities. Both cities have further plans for revivifying their central areas, and the incentives available through the new legislation will accelerate the process. Waterford also has committed itself firmly to a policy of urban rather than suburban development.

Cork, however, possibly provides the best illustration of urban renewal occurring within the context of a broader-based policy for the city region. By the late 1970s, extreme problems of traffic congestion aggravated the depopulation and dereliction within the inner city. Vacant sites in the centre were increasing at a rate of 5 per cent a year, and great uncertainty existed regarding future land-use development. The Cork Land Use and Transportation Study (Skidmore et al., 1978) was commissioned to address these issues and produced a comprehensive plan for the 850 km² region (Hourihan, 1979; Brunt, 1980). While recognizing the need to promote major industrial and residential zones outside of the city, the study stressed the central role of the inner city in future development. Labour-intensive industries were proposed for areas adjacent to large residential districts to minimize the need for journey to work, and a reorganized transport system was established to ease traffic flows through the city without adversely affecting inner-city communities.

The city's development plans have been based on the study and have brought immediate benefits to the central area. Planning controls limit decentralization, and progress is being made on improving the city-centre environment. A vigorous policy of infill housing schemes is pursued, which avoids large-scale site clearances and thereby maintains the integrity of old residential areas near the centre. To facilitate this, the corporation operates a revolving fund of IR£ 300,000 to buy old houses, rehabilitate them and sell them, the sale price being used to make further purchases. Cork still has severe problems of unemployment, but at least a renewed sense of community spirit and a more buoyant business atmosphere exist within the inner city.

Many of the developments in Ireland's cities and towns, however, have occurred within the context of *laissez-faire* planning and an anti-urban sentiment. The net result has been the maintenance of a poorly balanced urban hierarchy and a high degree of suburban and ex-urban development at the expense of the urban cores. This has proved inefficient in terms of social, economic and environmental considerations, both for the country as a whole as well as for communities living within the cities. A much greater priority needs to be given to developing a more comprehensive policy to control the complex spatial and sectoral relationships that revolve around modern urban systems. While Ireland appears to be strongly committed to a rural tradition and lifestyle, the country has to recognize that it is now a dominantly urban-based society. If the very real social and economic benefits that can be derived from urban development are to be achieved, then the country has to address the question of the role it foresees for its urban centres. To date, this has not been done, but the answer to the question will fundamentally shape national and regional development as Ireland prepares to enter the twenty-first century.

FIVE

Summary and Conclusions

For many of the generation born during the twenty-year period prior to 1980, Ireland was a nation that had undergone a major transformation from a traditional and depressed rural economy to a far more dynamic socioeconomic system in which problems — both potential and real — were usually submerged beneath an optimism that typified the country. However, just as the hopes of a rural utopia of the 1930s gave way to the depression of the 1950s, so too did the belief in an industrial utopia of the 1970s recede in the face of an international business crisis in the 1980s. Ireland is still very much a country in transition as it seeks to adjust, in a comparatively short space of time, to the dictates of international capitalism and a new technological revolution. But many of the benefits gained in the 1970s have been diluted, and government and people are faced with the need to make difficult choices if national growth is to be promoted to a level which meets the expectations of present and future generations.

Ireland's decision to opt for development based on principles of modernization and free trade significantly enhanced its position within the international economy. Both its role and image as a centre of production for global trade have improved, as has its political profile, consequent on its greater involvement in international affairs. Membership in the European Community has been critical in all these changes.

Agriculture, for long the basis of the national economy, has been subjected to considerable change, largely under the influence of CAP. Higher prices and improved market opportunities induced greater intensity and specialization of production but especially favoured the larger-scale farm enterprises working more productive land. On the other hand, many small-scale farm operators, involving a disproportionate number of elderly, conservative and poorly educated individuals who work land of poor carrying capacity, have failed to benefit significantly from, or respond to, the incentives offered by CAP. A system geared to reward production to the comparative neglect of the producer, and which failed to recognize the difficulties as well as the urgency of inducing structural reform, was inappropriate for the majority of Ireland's farmers. The extraordinary rights and symbolism of property have militated against a more flexible market for land. This immobilization of the periphery's principal asset and the inefficiency with which it is worked, marginalizes many rural communities to a greater degree than is necessary. In aggregate, agriculture in Ireland remains underdeveloped by European standards, but limitations on its growth forcibly suggest that alternative land uses must be accepted and developed if the benefits of improved standards of living are to permeate all sectors of the farming populace. Duality within agriculture is now a well-established feature in Ireland. A comparatively small number of wealthy farmers are benefiting disproportionately from the current farm policy while as many as one-fifth of the country's small farmers may be living beneath the poverty line, as illustrated by the depressed farming communities found in large areas of the West of Ireland. The easy option of using price increases to boost farm incomes in the 1970s provided some temporary sense of prosperity, but it clearly failed to address more central issues of structural reform.

The government's policy of industrialization by invitation, achieved through proffering generous incentives to international companies, appeared to herald a new age of prosperity. Manufactured goods quickly replaced agricultural commodities as the dominant element of trade as the country acquired the status of a production platform for companies seeking access to the European Community, as well as serving a more global market. The international division of production and labour associated with large-scale business reorganization favoured the establishment of a branch plant economy in Ireland. Furthermore, the ability to separate spatially production and decision-making facilitated the dispersion of manufacturing into the more rural areas. This was the major factor in the convergence of regional socioeconomic indicators in the 1970s, and gave a new sense of optimism for residents living in rural areas long exposed to decline. In addition, broadening of the economic base encouraged the emergence of a much larger working-class element within rural society as comparatively well-paid factory employment proved especially attractive for a population more accustomed to poor returns from farming. Feminization of the workforce was another result of rural industrialization which had important social consequences, modifying family lifestyles and adding to general family prosperity.

The commitment to the branch plant economy, however, failed to create an environment for self-sustaining industrial growth at the national level, least of all for the many communities that had come to rely disproportionately on a single factory unit. Increased rates of plant closures and redundancies were widespread in the more difficult trading environment of the 1980s. The failure to generate sufficient replacement industries in terms of both the quantity and quality of employment, as well as the extremely difficult task of matching the locational preferences of new development with the needs of redundant workers, have resulted in a high rate of unemployment and a reappearance of uncertainty for many communities. While these problems have affected all parts of the country, the issue has become acute within the inner-city areas, where the scale and localization of unemployment have created high levels of deprivation. Added to an existing problem of poverty, this has created a potentially explosive social and political atmosphere.

The enhanced role of production was the principal cause of a reversal in the long-established pattern of high rates of emigration and overall population decline. This, perhaps more than any other single factor, came to symbolize the apparent success of the policy of modernization and the sense of optimism about the ability to support an extremely youthful demographic profile. Population growth was widespread, although the preference for town life resulted in Ireland finally achieving (officially) the status of an urbanized society by 1971. Urbanization of the countryside, however, brought new pressures to bear on rural areas. The absence of effective physical planning has resulted in an overly dispersed pattern of housing developments which frequently infringe adversely on the environmental qualities of the countryside. In addition, the growing presence of a middle-class commuter population, with lifestyles based on privatized home-based consumption and values which are urban rather than rural, has created a conflict of interests with established rural communities. A new form of rural society is emerging, which expresses outward signs of growth and prosperity but frequently conceals a substantial number of poorer people who have failed to adjust to the dictates of a more privatized system of consumption based on personalized mobility and high incomes. Failure to maintain the momentum of economic growth into the 1980s, however, has witnessed a reappearance of rural depopulation and questions the ability of many rural settlements to continue to grow. Settlement restructuring appears likely, but it will depend more on an ability to offset the differentiated impacts of decline rather than constituting a response to the generalized growth impulses of the 1970s.

The overwhelming primacy of Dublin has remained untouched by the process of modernization. If anything, its dominance as a centre of control has been further emphasized by its new responsibilities as an international capital within the European Community. Failure to decentralize services and decision-making has not provided the few other major cities (and the country) with a sufficiently well-developed functional base to offer an effective balance to Dublin. The increasing specialist role of the capital and its sprawling physical expression have, however, created several internal problems for the city's planners. While a growing professional and middle-class population enjoy the benefits of well-paid employment and suburban lifestyles, the collapse of traditional industries and the concentration of lower-income, working-class residents in the inner city and on large public housing estates highlight marked divides in the social and economic system. Unemployment, deprivation and poverty are all too frequently visually manifest in large areas of the capital. The lack of an urban or social policy certainly contributed to the problem, and its present scale makes effective remedial action difficult to envisage.

Economic development has succeeded in raising general standards of living and in reducing the degree of income inequality that characterized the broader regional divisions. Large-scale expenditure on the promotion of a social welfare system and the greater availability of, and access to, housing, education and health services have benefited most social classes. Yet, the benefits have been less than evenly distributed either by social class or spatially, and these differentials have been aggravated by the recession of the 1980s and the resultant cutbacks in government expenditure.

Ireland has become an increasingly divided society when compared to the period immediately following the Second World War. Small-scale farm operators and unskilled or semi-skilled workers have tended to benefit less from the development process than larger-scale farmers and the more skilled manual or professional workers. Above all, however, the massive growth in unemployment levels, resulting from a growing labour supply competing within a narrowing job market, has had a selective impact on the population, and this has emphasized contemporary divisions within society. In general, unskilled or semi-skilled blue-collar workers, younger but less-educated individuals, and older and less-adaptable workers have all suffered disproportionately from displacement from existing employment and/or find it difficult to enter a more restrictive and new job market. Apart from Spain, Ireland now has the highest unemployment rate in the European Community. The position is further aggravated by the fact that two out of every five unemployed people have languished in that state for more than one year. A society of 'haves' and 'have-nots' has to be recognized, and poverty in Ireland has been rediscovered on a scale not even contemplated in the previous generation.

Contrasting levels of consumption highlight the divisions. Some 40 per cent of the population depend on some form of weekly welfare payment, and severe restraints limit their access to a diverse range of convenient consumer durables, owner-occupancy of housing or a private car which would facilitate greater flexibility in the job market and in shopping. Attention in this section of society is directed more to securing the basic essentials of food, shelter, clothing and electricity supply. This contrasts with the conspicuously high levels of consumption that typify the middle class who benefit from stable and well-paid employment. State support of public housing, education and health care reduces partially the impact of free market forces, but even in this sphere there is a bias in the quality and degree of provision which favours the wealthier and more politically powerful middle class. Recent budget pronouncements on the urgent need for public sector expenditure cuts, already affecting the education and health sectors, seem likely to downgrade further the principle of equity.

Ireland has not only become socially more divided, but the spatial contrasts have also become more complex and, in some cases, more acute. Spatial policy remains markedly underdeveloped and reflects the traditional preoccupation with national problems of poor economic performance and population decline. Apart from a brief interlude in the 1970s, when a buoyant national economy allowed for a stronger commitment to regional planning, national and sectoral interests have been stressed. An almost logical outcome of this has been the translation of sectoral and societal inequities into the spatial framework in a manner which frequently exacerbates division and conflict. Thus, although the essential east–west divide may have become somewhat attenuated, the majority of indicators utilized to measure socioeconomic well-being still favour the eastern half of the country. The core–periphery concept remains fundamental in the spatial arrangements of human activities. A newer dimension of the spatial question has emerged, however, at the urban–rural level. Depressed and declining standards of living for many residents in the cores of the major cities contrast with the prosperity and quality of environment that are to be found in the suburbs and commuter towns or villages of the urban fringe. This inversion of the more traditional centre–periphery relationship has placed the larger urban centres at the forefront of contemporary planning problems. And in rural areas, duality has become more evident, as seen in the conflict between newer middle-class commuters and longer-established rural residents of a lower socioeconomic status, and between a richer and poorer farmer class.

The country faces severe problems, but these are no different from those confronting many other small, open economies. Of particular concern for Ireland, however, has been the less than effective response by government, first to the opportunities of growth generated in the 1970s and, more recently, to the problems and pressures associated with recession. Furthermore, the potential effectiveness and flexibility with which the present government can act are now severely restrained by a massive debt problem. The open-door policy of modernization held out the prospect of immediate economic gains, but it equally exposed the country to risks based on the loss of effective control over economic decision-making. Although acquiring a neo-colonial status, Ireland was not immediately exposed to the problems frequently associated with this position. The political stability of the country and the critical advantages gained on entry to the European Community served as a basis for a major inflow of foreign investment to boost national production and employment. Transference of capital under various European Community policies also minimized concern over the levels of dependency that were built up. Significant cutbacks in the degree of foreign investment and rationalization of existing production facilities exposed the negative side of dependency and the inability to develop adequately a domestic economy with some prospect for self-sustaining growth.

While Ireland's high level of dependency on external capital offers some clues for the present crisis, of even greater importance has been the internal political response to the development process. Planning has tended to follow a sectoral approach in which compromises have been made to satisfy sectoral — and sometimes local — interests. This has allowed for policies to avoid the need for coordinated planning programmes which inevitably would have involved a greater commitment to establishing priorities and making difficult investment choices. Consensus politics operating in the buoyant conditions of the 1970s furthered this approach and led to a general increase in expenditure programmes. Thus, the CAP sheltered government from having to make a difficult choice between structural reform and price support. A high-price support system satisfied farming interests and consequently deflected attention from the far more difficult task of reorganizing Ireland's highly traditional farming system. This was a lost opportunity for, while change would have been difficult at any time, the greater availability of funds and alternative employment prospects outside the primary sector might have allowed some success. The situation is now more difficult. Reliance on multinational branch plants also brought immediate benefits without forcing government to evaluate the infrastructural requirements and support systems necessary to build up indigenous industries. Urbanization of the countryside and decentralization of manufacturing appeared to exempt government from any attempt to introduce an urban policy to check the primacy of Dublin. And, paradoxically, the only sector of the economy which did not have any sort of policy to it, and which clearly encouraged polarization of economic activity, was the service sector.

A long history of political compromise exists as far as policies designed to promote social and economic development are concerned. The political consensus has favoured spending money to resolve potential problems and a form of crisis management has been built up, which became increasingly apparent in the recession of the 1980s. Some attempts at a more coordinated development policy did appear, but the political will to implement it was not forthcoming. Expenditure on public services and social welfare amply illustrates the point. Despite inflated costs, it was politically more expedient to maintain a high rate of borrowing to support the services rather than sanction cutbacks and attempt to achieve greater levels of efficiency through a carefully planned programme of rationalization. It was small wonder that problems have emerged.

What are the prospects for the country? In the short term they do not appear optimistic for the large numbers already unemployed, on low incomes or experiencing poverty. Ireland is now one of the world's major debtor countries and was ranked fourth in 1985 in terms of its per capita foreign debt and eighth on the basis of its ratio of foreign debt to GNP (72 per cent). To attempt to control this problem, major cutbacks in government expenditure were a central element in the Fianna Fáil budget of 1987 — a policy supported by the main opposition party, Fine Gael. Expenditure now appears to be under more effective control, which has allowed a reduced level of commitment to foreign borrowing as a mechanism to find national development. An important consequence of this has been the emergence of greater optimism within business and finance. This has been further supported by the recent strong performance of Irish industry and the balance of trade surplus achieved by rapid export growth. Unemployment shows little sign of declining in spite of an increasing rate of emigration. In addition, restraints imposed on public expenditure are having an adverse effect on the weaker members of society, despite protestations to the contrary. If anything, the immediate prospect is for the numbers of poor and disadvantaged to increase rather than decrease.

The severity of the current crisis may, however, hold the key to improving the longer-term position for the social and economic system. Much will depend on a change being achieved within the civic and political culture. Ireland's civic culture has been extremely conservative and has adapted less well to change than might have been hoped. Government policies did not help in this respect, but the new policies which stress a greater role for higher technology and promotion of entrepreneurial skills demand a more adaptable culture. Ireland's youthful demographic profile and more cosmopolitan value system may provide a cultural environment better able to respond to the dictates of change. Education will be a key ingredient in this development.

Of greater implication for Ireland's future development are some signs of potentially far-reaching changes in the country's political culture. Consensus politics have characterized many of the developmental strategies undertaken by governments since independence, and short-term rather than long-term solutions have frequently negated the need for making strategic choices. The current crisis has introduced a different dimension for the major parties since hard choices now have to be made as to the areas of expenditure which are to be reduced. Forward planning has become more critical in this context, as has the recognition of coordinated planning strategies. While political consensus holds for the present, this may fragment to reflect fundamentally different philosophies of the Right and Left. Already, there is some evidence of this with the emergence of the Progressive Democrats as a party of the Right, while Labour has been pushed more effectively to a position on the Left of the political divide instead of maintaining a less-than-satisfactory coalition arrangement with Fine Gael. In many ways, Ireland is having to face choices made by Britain almost a decade earlier and which gave rise in that context to Thatcherism. Already, there are signs that this approach is being adopted with attempts to privatize some state bodies and reduce social expenditure. Whether this is the correct policy for Ireland, however, is far more debatable, especially given the magnitude of existing spatial and societal divides. But at least strategies are now likely to be debated more actively and will reflect a political division based more strongly on economic and social class rather than on constitutional matters reflecting the early period of independence. It will be interesting to see to what extent political expediency re-emerges to dilute this scenario. Whether or not the buoyancy that highlighted Ireland's socioeconomic system in the period 1960–1980 was a temporary deviation from more typically depressed conditions, or whether it provided initial indications that the country was ready to undertake a more sustained level of development, may well find an answer in the evolution of the political system in the remaining years of this century.

BIBLIOGRAPHY

Andrews, J. (1976) 'Land and People c. 1685'. In Moody, T.W. et al. (eds) *A New History of Ireland*, Vol. III. Oxford: Clarendon Press.

Arensberg, C.M. and Kimball, S.T. (1940) *Family and Community in Ireland.* Cambridge, Mass.: Harvard University Press.

Attwood, E.A. (1983) 'Financing and investment in Irish agriculture'. *The Irish Banking Review*, December, 13–26.

Attwood, E.A. and Bateman, W.M. (1981) 'Temporal and spatial change in Irish agricultural output and incomes, 1960–1977'. *Agricultural Economics Society of Ireland Proceedings*, 75–113.

Attwood, E.A. and Geary, R.C. (1963) *Irish County Incomes in 1960.* Paper 16. Dublin: Economic and Social Research Institute.

Baker, T.J. and O'Brien, L.M. (1979) *The Irish Housing System: A Critical Overview.* Broadsheet Series, 17. Dublin: Economic and Social Research Institute.

Bannon, M.J. (1972) 'The changing centre of gravity of office establishments within Central Dublin, 1940–1970'. *Irish Geography*, **6**, 480–484.

Bannon, M.J. (1973) *Office Location in Ireland: The Role of Central Dublin.* Dublin: Foras Forbartha.

Bannon, M.J. (1975) 'The Republic of Ireland'. In Jones, R. (ed.) *Essays on World Urbanization.* London: George Philip.

Bannon, M.J. (1978) 'Service employment, occupational change and regional development'. *Administration*, **26**, 180–196.

Bannon, M.J. (1979) 'Office concentration in Dublin and its consequences for regional development in Ireland'. In Daniels, P.W. (ed.) *Spatial Patterns of Office Growth and Location.* New York: John Wiley & Sons.

Bannon, M.J. (1984) 'The Irish national settlement system'. In Bourne, L.S., Sinclair, R. and Dziewonski, K. (eds) *Urbanization and Settlement Systems: International Perspectives.* Oxford: Oxford University Press.

Bannon, M.J. (1985) 'Service activities in national and regional development: trends and prospects for Ireland'. In Bannon, M.J. and Ward, S. (eds) *Services and the New Economy: Implications for National and Regional Development.* Dublin: Regional Studies Association (Irish Branch).

Bannon, M.J. and Blair, S. (1985) *Service Activities: The Information Economy and the Role of Regional Centres.* Dublin: National Board of Science and Technology.

Barrett, S.D. (1982) *Transport Policy in Ireland.* Dublin: Irish Management Institute.

Blackbourn, A. (1972) 'The location of foreign-owned manufacturing plants in the Republic of Ireland'. *Tijdschrift voor Economische en Sociale Geografie*, **63**, 438–443.

Blackwell, J. (1976) *An Input-Output Model of the Greater Cork Area*. Cork: Cork Corporation.

Bohan, H. (1979) *Ireland Green: Social Planning and Rural Development*. Dublin: Veritas.

Boylan, T.A. and Cuddy, P. (1984) 'Regional industrial policy: performance and challenge'. *Administration*, **32**, 255–270.

Boyle, G.E. and Kearney, B. (1983) 'Intensification in agriculture—trends and prospects'. In Blackwell, J. and Convery, F.J. (eds) *Promise and Performance: Irish Environmental Policies Analyzed*. Dublin: Resource and Environmental Policy Centre, University College, Dublin.

Brady, Shipman, Martin and Hyde, N. (1972–73) *National Coastline Study*. Dublin: Bord Fáilte Eireann and Foras Forbartha.

Brady, J. and Parker, A.J. (1975) 'The factorial ecology of Dublin: a preliminary investigation'. *Economic and Social Review*, **7**, 35–54.

Brady, J.E. and Parker, A.J. (1986) 'The socio-demographic spatial structure of Dublin in 1981'. *Economic and Social Review*, **17**, 229–252.

Breathnach, A. (1976) 'Towards the identification of educational priority areas in Dublin'. *Economic and Social Review*, **7**, 367–382.

Breathnach, P. (1982) 'The demise of growth centre policy: the case of the Republic of Ireland'. In Hudson, R. and Lewis, J.R. (eds) *Regional Planning in Europe*. London: Pion.

Breathnach, P. (ed.) (1983) *Rural Development in the West of Ireland: Observations from the Gaeltacht Experience*. Occasional Paper 3. Maynooth: Geography Department, St Patrick's College, Maynooth.

Breathnach, P. (1984) 'Co-operation and community development in the West of Ireland'. In Jess, P.M. et al. (eds) *Planning and Development in Rural Areas*. Belfast: Queens University.

Breathnach, P. (1985) 'Rural industrialisation in the West of Ireland'. In Healey, M.J. and Ilbery, B.W. (eds) *Industrialisation of the Countryside*. Norwich: Geo Books.

Breen, R. (1984) *Education and the Labour Market: Work and Unemployment among Recent Cohorts of Irish School Leavers*. Paper 119. Dublin: Economic and Social Research Institute.

Breen, R. (1986) *Subject Availability and Student Performance in the Senior Cycle of Irish Post-Primary Schools*. Paper 129. Dublin: Economic and Social Research Institute.

Brody, H. (1973) *Inishkillane: Change and Development in the West of Ireland*. London: Allen Lane.

Brunt, B.M. (1980) 'Industrial and harbour development in Cork'. *Irish Geography*, **13**, 88–94.

Brunt, B.M. (1984) 'Manufacturing change in the Greater Cork area, 1980–1984'. *Irish Geography*, **17**, 101–108.

Brunt, B.M. (1988) 'The new industrialisation of Ireland'. In Carter, R.W.G. and

Parker, A.J. (eds) *Ireland: A Contemporary Geographic Perspective*. London: Croom Helm.

Buchanan, C. and Partners (1968) *Regional Studies in Ireland*. Dublin: Foras Forbartha.

Busteed, M.A. (1974) *Northern Ireland*. Oxford: Oxford University Press.

Butlin, R.A. (ed.) (1977) *The Development of the Irish Town*. London: Croom Helm.

Cahillane, G. and Lucey, D.I.F. (1983) 'An examination of the operation and scope of the farm modernisation scheme up to 1981'. *Irish Journal of Agricultural Economics and Rural Sociology*, 9, 107–120.

Callanan, B. (1984) 'The work of Shannon Free Airport Development Company'. *Administration*, 32, 342–350.

Cawley, M.E. (1979) 'Rural industrialisation and social change in Western Ireland'. *Sociologica Ruralis*, 19, 43–57.

Cawley, M.E. (1980) 'Aspects of rural–urban migration in Western Ireland'. *Irish Geography*, 13, 20–32.

Cawley, M.E. (1986) 'Disadvantaged groups and areas: problems of rural service provision'. In Breathnach, P. and Cawley, M.E. (eds) *Change and Development in Rural Ireland*. Dublin: Geographical Society of Ireland, Special Publications, 1.

Chubb, B. (1963) 'Going about persecuting civil servants: the role of the Irish parliamentary representative'. *Political Studies*, 11, 272–286.

Clancy, P. (1982) *Participation in Higher Education: A National Survey*. Dublin: Higher Education Authority.

Clark, C., Wilson, F. and Bradley, J. (1969) 'Industrial location and economic potential in Western Europe'. *Regional Studies*, 3, 197–212.

Commins, P. (1980) 'Agriculture and rural life'. In *Ireland in the Year 2000*. Dublin: Foras Forbartha.

Commission of the European Communities (1985a) *Perspectives for the Common Agricultural Policy*. Brussels.

Commission of the European Communities (1985b) *A Future for European Agriculture*. Brussels.

Commission on Social Welfare (1986) *Report of the Commission on Social Welfare*. Dublin: Stationery Office.

Committee on the Price of Building Land (1975) *Report to the Minister for Local Government* (Kenny Report). Dublin: Stationery Office.

Connolly, L. Hickey, B. and Kavanagh, A. (1985) 'Cattle production — investment for development. In *The Challenge Facing Agriculture in Difficult Times*. Economics and Rural Welfare Research Centre, 12th Annual Conference. Dublin: Foras Taluntais.

Convery, F.J. (1973–74) 'Some regional impacts of alternative rural land uses'. *Irish Journal of Agricultural Economics and Rural Sociology*, 4, 29–49.

Conway, A.G. (1986) 'Prospects for the CAP and its modifications'. In *The Changing CAP and its Implications*. Economics and Rural Welfare Research Centre, 13th Annual Conference. Dublin: Foras Taluntais.

Conway, A.G. and O'Hara, M.P. (1981) *Irish Case Study to Identify Strategies for Integrated Rural Development — Proposed Framework for Study*. Dublin: Foras Taluntais.

Conway, A.G. and O'Hara, P. (1985) *Living and Working in the West: Prospects and Challenges for the Future*. Dublin: Foras Taluntais.

Corcoran, T. (1985) 'Irish youth unemployment policies in the 1980s'. *Administration*, **33**, 258–268.

Cottuli, T. (1986) 'The Liffey Trust: an urban enterprise initiative'. In Davis, J.P. and Byrne, S. (eds) *New Directions in Development Policy*. Dublin: Regional Studies Association (Irish Branch).

Coughlan, A. (1984) 'Ireland's Welfare State in time of crisis'. *Administration*, **32**, 37–54.

Couniffe, D. and Kennedy, K. (eds) (1984) *Employment and Unemployment: Policy for Ireland*. Dublin: Economic and Social Research Institute.

Crotty, R. (1987) *Ireland in Crisis: A Study in Capitalist Colonial Underdevelopment*. Dingle: Brandon Books.

Curry, J. (1980) *The Irish Social Services*. Dublin: Institute of Public Administration.

Curry, J. (1981) 'Rural poverty'. In Kennedy, S. (ed.) *One Million Poor*. Dublin: Turoe Press.

Curtin, D., Geary, R.C., Grimes, T.A. and Menton, B. (1976) *Population Growth and Other Statistics of Middle-Sized Irish Towns*. Dublin: Economic and Social Research Institute.

Davy Kelleher McCarthy Ltd (1987) *Ireland's Changing Population Structure*. Dublin.

Dawson, J.A. (1972) 'Retail sales of towns in the Republic of Ireland in 1966'. *Irish Geography*, **6**, 487–492.

de Courcy Ireland, J. (1981) *Ireland's Sea Fisheries: A History*. Dublin: Glendale.

Department of Education (1965) *Investment in Education*. Dublin: Stationery Office.

Department of Finance (1958) *Economic Development*. Dublin: Stationery Office.

Department of Health (1981) *Information Relevant to the Health Services*. Dublin: Central Statistics Office.

Department of Health (1986) *Health Statistics*. Dublin: Stationery Office.

Dineen, D.A. (1985) 'The western regions and the development of services'. In Bannon, M.J. and Ward, S. (eds) *Services and the New Economy: Implications for National and Regional Development*. Dublin: Regional Studies Association.

Donaldson, L. (1966) *Development Planning in Ireland*. New York: Praeger.

Douthwaite, R. (1987) 'The Gaeltacht'. *The Irish Times*, Special Feature, 13 August 1987.

Dowling, B.R. (1978) 'Budget deficits and fiscal policy'. In Dowling, B.R. and Durkan, J. (eds) *Irish Economic Policy: A Review of Major Issues*. Dublin: Economic and Social Research Institute.

Downey, W.K. (1980) 'The physical environment and implications for the year 2000'. In Foras Forbartha, *Ireland in the Year 2000*. Dublin: Foras Forbartha.

Drudy, P.J. and Drudy, S.M. (1979) 'Population mobility and labour supply in rural regions'. *Regional Studies*, **13**, 91–101.

Drudy, P.J. and McAleese, D. (eds) (1984) *Ireland and the European Community*. Irish Studies, 3. Cambridge: Cambridge University Press.

Duffy, P.J. (1980) 'Cooperative agriculture and rural development in Ireland'. *Antipode*, 12, 97–107.

Duffy, P.J. (1983) 'Rural settlement change in the Republic of Ireland – a preliminary discussion'. *Geoforum*, 14, 185–191.

Duffy, P.J. (1986) 'Planning problems in the countryside'. In Breathnach, P. and Cawley, M.E. (eds) *Change and Development in Rural Ireland*. Special Publications, 1. Dublin: Geographical Society of Ireland.

Dunstan, J. (1985) 'Forests in the landscape'. In Aalen, F. (ed.) *The Future of the Irish Rural Landscape*. Dublin: Trinity College.

Eastern Regional Development Organization (1985) *Eastern Region Settlement Strategy 2011*. Dublin: ERDO.

Farrell, E.P. (1983) 'Land acquisition for forestry'. In Blackwell, J. and Convery, F.J. (eds) *Promise and Performance: Irish Environmental Policies Analysed*. Dublin: Resource and Environmental Policy Centre, University College, Dublin.

Fernie, J. (1977) 'Office linkages and location: an evaluation of patterns in three cities'. *Town Planning Review*, 48, 78–89.

Fitzgerald, G. (1968) *Planning in Ireland*. Dublin: Institute of Public Administration.

Fitzgerald, J. (1987) 'Consequences for cross-border trade between Southern Ireland and Northern Ireland'. Dublin: Economic and Social Research Institute (unpublished).

Foeken, D. (1980) 'Return migration to a marginal rural area in N.W. Ireland'. *Tijdschrift voor Economische en Sociale Geografie*, 71, 114–120.

Foley, A. (1986) 'The Irish response in a time of change'. In Davis, J.P. and Byrne, S. (eds) *New Directions in Development Policy*. Dublin: Regional Studies Association (Irish Branch).

Foras Forbartha (1977) *Inventory of Outstanding Landscapes in Ireland*. Dublin: Foras Forbartha.

Foras Taluntais (1986) *Irish Agriculture in Figures, 1986*. Dublin: Foras Taluntais.

Forbes, J. (1970) 'Towns and planning in Ireland'. In Stephens, N. and Glasscock, R. (eds) *Irish Geographical Studies*. Belfast: Queens University.

Frawley, J., Bohlen, J.M. and Breathnach, T. (1974–75) 'Personal and social factors related to farming performance in Ireland'. *Irish Journal of Agricultural Economics and Rural Sociology*, 5, 157–181.

Freeman, T.W. (1945) 'The agricultural regions and rural population of Ireland'. *Irish Geography*, 1, 21–30.

Freeman, T.W. (1965) *Ireland: A General and Regional Geography*, 3rd ed. London: Methuen.

Gallagher, M. (1978) 'Party solidarity, exclusivity and inter-party relationships in Ireland, 1922–77: the evidence of transfers'. *Economic and Social Review*, 10, 1–22.

Gardiner, M.J. and Radford, T. (1980) *Soil Associations of Ireland and their Land Use Potential*. Soil Survey Bulletin 36. Dublin: Foras Taluntais.

Gillie, F.B. (1971) *The Cork Sub-Regional Planning Study*. Dublin: Foras Forbartha.

Gillmor, D.A. (1972) 'Aspects of agricultural change in the Republic of Ireland during the 1960s'. *Irish Geography*, 6, 492–498.

Gillmor, D.A. (1977a) *Agriculture in the Republic of Ireland*. Budapest: Akademiai Kiado.

Gillmor, D.A. (1977b) 'The spatial structure of agricultural output in the Republic of Ireland'. *Economic and Social Review*, 8, 127–142.

Gillmor, D.A. (1977c) 'EEC scheme for farming in Less Favoured Areas'. *Irish Geography*, 10, 101–108.

Gillmor, D.A. (1982) *Manufacturing Industry in the Republic of Ireland: its Development and Distribution*. Dublin: Bank of Ireland.

Gillmor, D.A. (1985a) *Economic Activities in the Republic of Ireland: A Geographical Perspective*. Dublin: Gill and Macmillan.

Gillmor, D.A. (1985b) 'Recent changes in the employment of women in the Republic of Ireland'. *Irish Geography*, 18, 69–73.

Gillmor, D.A. (1987) 'Concentration of enterprises and spatial change in agriculture of the Republic of Ireland'. *Transactions of the Institute of British Geographers*, New Series 12, 204–216.

Glebe, G. (1978) 'Recent settlement desertion on the Beara and Iveragh peninsulas: a methodological approach'. *Irish Geography*, 11, 171–176.

Gould, F. (1981) 'The growth of public expenditure in Ireland, 1947–1977'. *Administration*, 29, 115–135.

Hannan, D.F. (1972) 'Kinship, neighbourhood and social change in Irish rural communities'. *Economic and Social Review*, 3, 163–189.

Hannan, D.F. and Katsiaouni, L. (1977) *Traditional Families? From Culturally Prescribed to Negotiated Roles in Farm Families*. Paper 87. Dublin: Economic and Social Research Institute.

Haughton, J.P. (1949) 'The social geography of Dublin'. *Geographical Review*, 39, 257–277.

Haughton, J.P. (1970) 'The urban–rural fringe of Dublin'. In Stephens, N. and Glassock, R.E. (eds) *Irish Geographical Studies*. Belfast: Queens University.

Heanue, K. et al. (1971–72) *Dublin Transportation Study*, 2 Vols. Dublin: Foras Forbartha.

Heavey, J.F., Harkin, M.J., Connolly, L. and Roche, M. (1984) *Farm Management Survey 1983*. Dublin: Foras Taluntais.

Hensey, B. (1980) 'The health services and their administration'. *Administration*, 30, 147–164.

Hickey, B. and Killen, L. (1986) 'Farm forestry in Ireland — economic aspects'. In *The Changing CAP and its Implications*. Economics and Rural Welfare Research Centre, 13th Annual Conference. Dublin: Foras Taluntais.

Higgins, J. (1983) *A Study of Part-Time Farmers in the Republic of Ireland*. Socio-Economic Research Series 3. Dublin: Foras Taluntais.

Higgins, J. (1986) 'The distribution of income on Irish farms'. *Irish Journal of Agricultural Economics and Rural Sociology*, 11, 73–91.

Holdship, J.A. and Gillmor, D.A. (1976) 'Private apartment development in Dublin'. *Irish Geography*, 9, 123–128.

Holland, C.H. (1979) 'Minerals'. In Gillmor, D.A. (ed.) *Irish Resources and Land Use*. Dublin: Institute of Public Administration.

Horner, A. (1985) 'The Dublin Region, 1880–1982: an overview on its development and planning'. In Bannon, M.J. (ed.) *The Emergence of Irish Planning 1880–1920*. Dublin: Turoe Press.

Horner, A.A. (1986) 'Rural population change in Ireland'. In Breathnach, P. and Cawley, M.E. (eds) *Change and Development in Rural Ireland*. Special Publication, 1. Dublin: Geographical Society of Ireland.

Horner, A.A. and Daultrey, S.G. (1980) 'Recent population changes in the Republic of Ireland'. *Area*, **12**, 129–135.

Horner, A.A. and Taylor, A. (1979) 'Grasping the nettle — locational strategies for Irish hospitals'. *Administration*, **27**, 348–370.

Horner, A.A., Walsh, J.A. and Williams, J.A. (1984) *Agriculture in Ireland: A Census Atlas*. Dublin: Department of Geography, University College, Dublin.

Hoselitz, B.F. (1955) 'Generative and parasitic cities'. *Economic Development and Cultural Change*, **3**, 278–294.

Hourihan, J.K. and Lyons, D. (forthcoming) 'Service changes in County Tipperary towns, 1966–86'.

Hourihan, K. (1978) 'Social areas in Dublin'. *Economic and Social Review*, **9**, 301–318.

Hourihan, K. (1979) 'The Cork Land Use and Transportation Study'. *Irish Geography*, **12**, 99–104.

Hourihan, K. (1982a) 'Urban population density patterns and change in Ireland, 1901–1979'. *Economic and Social Review*, **13**, 125–147.

Hourihan, K. (1982b) 'In-migration to Irish cities and towns 1970–71'. *Economic and Social Review*, **14**, 29–40.

Hourihan, K. (1983) 'Population redistribution in Irish cities: Dublin, Cork and Limerick'. *Irish Geography*, **16**, 113–120.

Hudson, R. and Williams, A. (1986) *The United Kingdom*. London: Harper & Row.

Huff, D.L. and Lutz, J.M. (1979) 'Ireland's urban system'. *Economic Geography*, **55**, 196–212.

Hughes, J.G. and Walsh, B.M. (1980) *Internal Migration Flows in Ireland and their Determinants*. Paper 98. Dublin: Economic and Social Research Institute.

Humphreys, P.C. (1985) 'The role of public sector employment in the service economy'. In Bannon, M.J. and Ward, S. (eds) *Services and the New Economy: Implications for National and Regional Development*. Dublin: Regional Studies Association (Irish Branch).

Hutterman, A. (1978) 'Shannon 1976: the industrial estate and its regional implications'. *Irish Geography*, **11**, 179–183.

Ilbery, B.W. (1984) 'Core–periphery contrasts in European social well-being'. *Geography*, **69**, 289–302.

Industrial Development Authority (1972) *Regional Industrial Plans, 1973–77*. Dublin: IDA.

Industrial Development Authority (1979) *IDA Industrial Plan 1978–82*. Dublin: IDA.

Johnson, J.H. (1963) 'Population changes in Ireland, 1951–1961'. *Geographical Journal*, **129**, 167–174.

Johnson, J.H. (1968) 'Population change in Ireland 1961–1966'. *Irish Geography*, **5**, 470–477.

184   *Ireland*

Johnson, J.H. (1987) 'Republic of Ireland'. In Clout, H.D. (ed.) *Regional Development in Western Europe*, 3rd ed. London: David Fulton.

Johnson, M. (1979) 'The cooperative movement in the Gaeltacht'. *Irish Geography*, 12, 68–81.

Jones-Hughes, T. (1959) 'The origin and growth of towns in Ireland'. *University Review*, 11, 11–27.

Joyce, L. and McCashin, A. (1982) *Poverty and Social Policy*. Dublin: Institute of Public Administration.

Kane, E. (1977) *The Last Place God Made: Traditional Economy and New Industry in Rural Ireland*. New Haven, Connecticut: Human Relations Area Files.

Kearns, K.C. (1974a) 'Industrialisation and regional development in Ireland, 1958–1972'. *American Journal of Economics and Sociology*, 33, 299–316.

Kearns, K.C. (1974b) 'Resuscitation of the Irish Gaeltacht'. *Geographical Review*, 64, 82–110.

Kearns, K.C. (1976a) 'Ireland's mining boom: development and input'. *American Journal of Economics and Sociology*, 35, 279–292.

Kearns, K.C. (1976b) 'The role of peat fuel in Ireland's changing energy balance'. *Irish Geography*, 9, 104–108.

Kearns, K.C. (1978) 'Bogland utilization: an impending Irish land use dilemma'. *Scottish Geographical Magazine*, 94, 103–112.

Keeble, D., Owens, P.L. and Thompson, C. (1982) 'Regional accessibility and economic potential in the European Community'. *Regional Studies*, 16, 419–431.

Kelleher, C. (1986) 'Forestry and farmers'. In *The Changing CAP and its Implications*. Economics and Rural Welfare Research Centre, 13th Annual Conference, Dublin: Foras Taluntais.

Kelleher, C. and O'Hara, P. (1978) *Adjustment Problems of Low Income Farmers*. Dublin: Foras Taluntais.

Kelleher, C. and O'Mahony, A. (1984) *Marginalisation in Irish Agriculture*. Dublin: Foras Taluntais.

Kelly, P.W. (1983) 'Farmland transfer in the Republic of Ireland'. *Irish Journal of Agricultural Economics and Rural Sociology*, 9, 161–172.

Kennedy, K.A. and Dowling, B.R. (1975) *Economic Growth in Ireland: The Experience since 1947*. Dublin: Gill and Macmillan.

Kennedy, K.A. and Giblin, T. (1987) 'Employment'. In O'Hagan, J.W. (ed.) *The Economy of Ireland: Policy and Performance*, 5th ed. Dublin: Irish Management Institute.

Kennedy, S. (ed.) (1981) *One Million Poor*. Dublin: Turoe Press.

Killen, J.E. (1979a) 'Transport'. In Gillmor, D.A. (ed.) *Irish Resources and Land Use*. Dublin: Institute of Public Administration.

Killen, J.E. (1979b) 'Urban transportation problems and issues in Dublin'. *Administration*, 27, 151–166.

Kupper, U.I. (1969) 'Socio-geographical aspects of industrial growth at Shannon'. *Irish Geography*, 6, 14–29.

Lee, J. (1984) *Reflections on Ireland in the EEC*. Dublin: Irish Council of the European Movement.

Lee, J. (1985) 'Centralisation and community'. In Lee, J. (ed.) *Ireland: Towards a Sense of Place*. Cork: Cork University Press.

Lichfield, N. and Associates (1967) *Report and Advisory Outline Plan for the Limerick Region*. Dublin: Stationery Office.

Lucey, D.I.F. and Kaldor, D.R. (1969) *Rural Industrialization: The Impact of Industrialization on Two Rural Communities in Western Ireland*. London: Chapman.

Lucey, D.I.F., Walker, S. et al. (1987) *New Jobs in Mayo — A Study of Recent Major Employment Developments*. Castlebar: Mayo County Development Team.

Lyons, F.S.L. (1971) *Ireland since the Famine*. London: Weidenfeld and Nicolson.

McAleese, D. (1977) *A Profile of Grant-Aided Industry in Ireland*. Dublin: Industrial Development Authority.

McAleese, D. (1984) 'International trade, balance of payments and price stability'. In O'Hagan, J.W. (ed.) *The Economy of Ireland: Policy and Performance*, 4th ed. Dublin: Irish Management Institute.

McAleese, D. and Counihan, M. (1979) ' "Stickers" or "snatchers"? Employment in multinational corporations during the recession'. *Oxford Bulletin of Economics and Statistics*, **41**, 345–358.

McCashin, T. (1982) 'Social policy'. *Administration*, **30**, 203–223.

McCormack, D. (1979) 'Policy making in a small open economy: some aspects of Irish experience'. *Central Bank of Ireland Quarterly Bulletin*, **4**, 92–111.

McDermott, D. and Horner, A.A. (1978) 'Aspects of rural renewal in Western Connemara'. *Irish Geography*, **11**, 176–179.

McDonald, F. (1987) 'Bungalow blitz'. *The Irish Times*, Weekend Supplement, 12 September 1987.

McDowell, M. (1982) 'A generation of public expenditure growth: Leviathan unchained'. *Administration*, **30**, 183–200.

MacKeogh, K. (1983) 'The regional technical colleges and the changing geography of higher education in the Republic of Ireland'. *Irish Geography*, **16**, 120–125.

McKinsey and Company (1971) *Defining the Role of Public Transport in a Changing Environment*. Dublin: Stationery Office.

McKinsey International (1980) *The Transport Challenge: The Opportunity in the 1980s*. Dublin: Stationery Office.

MacLaran, A. and Beamish, C. (1985) 'Industrial property development in Dublin 1960–1982'. *Irish Geography*, **18**, 37–50.

McNulty, P. and MacLaran, A. (1985) 'High density, low-rise housing in inner Dublin'. *Irish Geography*, **18**, 73–76.

Maher, D.J. (1986) *The Tortuous Path: The Course of Ireland's Entry into the EEC 1948–1973*. Dublin: Institute of Public Administration.

Malone, P. (1981) *Office Development in Dublin 1960–1980*. Dublin: Department of Geography, Trinity College, Dublin.

Malone, P. (1983) *Office Development in Dublin 1960–1983*. Portsmouth: School of Architecture, Plymouth Polytechnic.

Matthews, A. (1984) 'Agriculture'. In O'Hagan, J. (ed.) *The Economy of Ireland: Policy and Performance*, 4th ed. Dublin: Irish Management Institute.

Mawhinney, K.A. (1975) *Survey of Outdoor Recreational Activities in Dublin City and County*. Dublin: Foras Forbartha.

Mawhinney, K.A. (1979) 'Recreation'. In Gillmor, D.A. (ed.) *Irish Resources and Land Use*. Dublin: Institute of Public Administration.

Meenan, J. (1970) *The Irish Economy since 1922*. Liverpool: Liverpool University Press.

Moore, B., Rhodes, J. and Tarling, R. (1978) 'Industrial policy and economic development: the experience of Northern Ireland and the Republic of Ireland'. *Cambridge Journal of Economics*, 2, 99–114.

Murphy, J.A. (1975) *Ireland in the Twentieth Century*. Dublin: Gill and Macmillan.

NESC (National Economic and Social Council) (1976) *Institutional Arrangements for Regional Economic Development*. Report 22. Dublin: Stationery Office.

NESC (1977a) *Service-Type Employment and Regional Development*. Report 28. Dublin: Stationery Office.

NESC (1977b) *Some Major Issues in Health Policy*. Report 29. Dublin: Stationery Office.

NESC (1977c) *Alternative Growth Rates in Irish Agriculture*. Report 34. Dublin: Stationery Office.

NESC (1978) *Rural Areas: Change and Development*. Report 41. Dublin: Stationery Office.

NESC (1979) *Urbanisation and Regional Development in Ireland*. Report 45. Dublin: Stationery Office.

NESC (1980a) *Personal Incomes by Region in 1977*. Report 51. Dublin: Stationery Office.

NESC (1980b) *Tourism Policy*. Report 52. Dublin: Stationery Office.

NESC (1980c) *Industrial Policy and Development: A Survey of the Literature from the Early 1960s*. Report 56. Dublin: Stationery Office.

NESC (1981a) *Urbanisation: Problems of Growth and Decay in Dublin*. Report 55. Dublin: Stationery Office.

NESC (1981b) *The Importance of Infrastructure to Industrial Development in Ireland — Roads, Telecommunications and Water Supply*. Report 59. Dublin: Stationery Office.

NESC (1982a) *A Review of Industrial Policy*. Report 64. Dublin: Stationery Office (Telesis Report).

NESC (1982b) *Policies for Industrial Development: Conclusions and Recommendations*. Report 66. Dublin: Stationery Office.

NESC (1983) *An Analysis of Job Losses in Irish Manufacturing Industry*. Report 67. Dublin: Stationery Office.

NESC (1986) *A Strategy for Development 1986–1990*. Report 83. Dublin: Stationery Office.

National Planning Board (1984) *Proposals for Plan 1984–87*. Dublin: National Planning Board.

Newman, J.J. (1967) *New Dimensions in Regional Planning, A Case Study of Ireland*. Dublin: Foras Forbartha.

O'Brien, J.A. (1954) *The Vanishing Irish*. London: W.H. Allen.

O'Brien, J.F. (1981) *A Study of National Wage Agreements in Ireland*. Paper 104. Dublin: Economic and Research Insitute.

O'Brien, R. (1986) 'Technology and industrial development: the Irish electronics industry in an international context'. In Fitzpatrick, J. and Kelly, J. (eds) *Perspectives on Irish Industry*. Dublin: Irish Management Institute.

O'Carroll, J.P., Passchier, N.P. and Van der Wusten, H.H. (1978) 'Regional aspects of the problem of restructuring use and ownership of agricultural land in the Republic of Ireland'. *Economic and Social Review*, 9, 79–106.

O'Carroll, N. (1984) *The Forests of Ireland*. Dublin: Turoe Press.

Ó Cinneide, M.S. and Keane, M.J. (1983) 'Employment growth and population change in rural areas: an example of the West of Ireland'. *Irish Geography*, 16, 108–112.

Ó Cinneide, M.S. (1986) 'Organising community involvement in the development process'. In Breathnach, P. and Cawley, M.E. (eds) *Change and Development in Rural Ireland*. Special Publications, 1. Dublin: Geographical Society of Ireland.

Ó Cinneide, S. (1980) 'Poverty in Ireland'. In George, V. and Lawson, R. (eds) *Poverty and Inequality in Common Market Countries*. London: Routledge and Kegan Paul.

O'Farrell, P.N. (1969) 'Continuous regularities and discontinuities in the central place system'. *Geografiska Annaler*, 52(B), 104–114.

O'Farrell, P.N. (1970a) 'Regional development in Ireland: problems of goal formulation and objective specification'. *Economic and Social Review*, 2, 71–92.

O'Farrell, P.N. (1970b) 'Regional development in Ireland: the economic case for a regional policy'. *Administration*, 18, 342–362.

O'Farrell, P.N. (1972) 'A shift and share analysis of regional employment change in Ireland, 1951–66'. *Economic and Social Review*, 4, 59–86.

O'Farrell, P.N. (1975) *Regional Industrial Development Trends in Ireland 1960–1973*. Dublin: Industrial Development Authority.

O'Farrell, P.N. (1976) 'An analysis of industrial closures: Irish experience, 1960–73'. *Regional Studies*, 10, 433–448.

O'Farrell, P.N. (1978) 'An analysis of new industry location: the Irish case'. *Progress in Planning*, 9, 129–229.

O'Farrell, P.N. (1980) 'Multi-national enterprises and regional development: Irish evidence'. *Regional Studies*, 14, 141–151.

O'Farrell, P.N. (1984) 'Components of manufacturing change in Ireland 1973–1981'. *Urban Studies*, 21, 155–176.

O'Farrell, P.N. and Cròuchley, R. (1983) 'Industrial closures in Ireland 1973–1981: analysis and implications'. *Regional Studies*, 17, 411–429.

O'Farrell, P.N. and Crouchley, R. (1984) 'An industrial and spatial analysis of new firm formation in Ireland'. *Regional Studies*, 18, 221–236.

O'Farrell, P.N. and O'Loughlin, B. (1980) *An Analysis of New Industrial Linkages in Ireland*. Dublin: Industrial Development Authority.

O'Hara, P. (1986) 'CAP structural policy — a new approach to an old problem?' In *The Changing CAP and its Implications*. Economics and Rural Welfare Research Centre, 13th Annual Conference. Dublin: Foras Taluntais.

O'hUiginn, P. (1972) *Regional Development and Industrial Location in Ireland*. Dublin: Foras Forbartha.

O'Malley, E. (1985) 'Industrial development in the North and South of Ireland'. *Administration*, **33**, 61–85.

O'Neill, H.B. (1971) *Spatial Planning in the Small Economy, a Case Study of Ireland*. New York: Praeger.

O'Sullivan, P.M. (1968) 'Accessibility and the spatial structure of the Irish economy'. *Regional Studies*, **2**, 195–206.

Orme, A.R. (1970) *Ireland*. London: Longman.

Paddison, R. (1970) 'Reorganisation of hospital services in Ireland'. *Irish Geography*, **6**, 199–204.

Paddison, R. (1976) 'Spatial bias and redistricting in proportional representation election systems: a case study of the Republic of Ireland'. *Tijdschrift voor Economische en Sociale Geografie*, **67**, 230–241.

Paddison, R. (1983) *The Fragmented State: The Political Geography of Power*. Oxford: Blackwell.

Parker, A.J. (1972) 'Ireland: a consideration of the 1971 Census of population'. *Area*, **4**, 31–38.

Parker, A.J. (1980a) 'Planned retail developments in Dublin'. *Irish Geography*, **13**, 83–88.

Parker, A.J. (1980b) 'Retail grocery price variations: a consideration of the structural and location characteristics of stores'. *Journal of Consumer Studies and Home Economics*, **4**, 35–49.

Parker, A.J. (1981) 'Planned retail developments in Cork City'. *Irish Geography*, **14**, 111–116.

Parker, A.J. (1982a) 'The 1981 and February 1982 general elections in the Republic of Ireland'. *Irish Geography*, **15**, 116–123.

Parker, A.J. (1982b) 'The "friends and neighbours" voting effect in the Galway West Constituency'. *Political Geography Quarterly*, **1**, 243–262.

Parker, A.J. (1983) 'Localism and Bailiwicks: the Galway West constituency in the 1977 general election'. *Proceedings of the Royal Irish Academy*, **83C**, 17–36.

Parker, A.J. (1986) 'Geography and the Irish electoral system'. *Irish Geography*, **19**, 1–14.

Perrons, D.C. (1981) 'The role of Ireland in the new international division of labour: a proposed framework for regional analysis'. *Regional Studies*, **16**, 81–100.

Pratschke, J.L. (1982) 'Aspects of agricultural incomes in Ireland'. *Irish Journal of Agricultural Economics and Rural Sociology*, **9**, 1–16.

Pratschke, J.L. (1984) 'Aspects of the redistribution of income in urban and rural Ireland 1973–1980'. *Irish Journal of Agricultural Economics and Rural Sociology*, **10**, 13–27.

Pringle, D.G. (1982) 'Regional disparities in the quantity of life: the Republic of Ireland, 1971–77'. *Irish Geography*, **15**, 22–34.

Pringle, D.G. (1986) 'Premature mortality in the Republic of Ireland, 1971–1981'. *Irish Geography*, **19**, 33–40.

Programme for Economic Expansion (1958) Dublin: Stationery Office.

Report of the Consultative Council on the General Hospitals Service (Fitzgerald Report) (1968) Dublin: Stationery Office.

Riordan, E.B. (1986) ' "Beef producers" stake in the evolution of CAP'. In *The Changing CAP and its Implications*. Economics and Rural Welfare Research Centre, 13th Annual Conference. Dublin: Foras Taluntais.

Roche, D. (1982) *Local Government in Ireland*. Dublin: Institute of Public Administration.

Ross, M. (1969) *Personal Incomes by County, 1965*. Paper 49. Dublin: Economic and Social Research Institute.

Ross, M. (1972) *Further Data on County Incomes in the Sixties*. Paper 64. Dublin: Economic and Social Research Institute.

Ruane, F. (1984) 'Manufacturing industry'. In O'Hagan, J.W. (ed.) *The Economy of Ireland: Policy and Performance*, 4th ed. Dublin: Irish Management Institute.

Sacks, P. (1970) 'Bailiwicks, locality and religion: three elements in the Irish Dail constituency election'. *Economic and Social Review*, 1, 531–554.

Sacks, P.M. (1976) *The Donegal Mafia: An Irish Political Machine*. New Haven, Connecticut: Yale University Press.

Scully, J.J. (1969) 'The development of Western Ireland'. *Irish Geography*, 6, 1–14.

Scully, J.J. (1971) *Agriculture in the West of Ireland*. Dublin: Stationery Office.

Seers, D. (1979) 'The periphery of Europe'. In Seers, D., Schaffer, B. and Kiljunen, M. (eds) *Underdeveloped Europe: Studies in Core–Periphery Relations*. Sussex: Harvester Press.

Sexton, J. (1982) 'Sectoral changes in the labour force over the period 1961–80 with particular reference to public sector and services employment'. *Quarterly Economics Commentary*, August, 36–45.

Siggins, L. (1987) 'The mackerel millionaires'. *The Irish Times*, Supplement, 17 January 1987.

Skidmore, Owings and Merrill et al. (1978) *Cork Land Use/Transportation Plan*. Cork.

Smyth, W.J. (1975) 'Continuity and change in the territorial organisation of Irish rural communities'. *Maynooth Review*, 1, 51–73 and 152–201.

Smyth, W.J. (1984) 'Social geography of rural Ireland: inventory and prospect'. In Davies, G.L.H. (ed.) *Irish Geography: The Geographical Society of Ireland Golden Jubilee 1934–1984*. Dublin: The Geographical Society of Ireland.

Soulsby, J.A. (1965) 'The Shannon Free Airport Scheme — a new approach to industrial development'. *Scottish Geographical Magazine*, 81, 104–114.

Stamp, L.D. (1931) *An Agricultural Atlas of Ireland*. London: Gill.

Stanton, R. (1979) 'Investment and host country politics: the Irish case'. In Seers, D., Schaffer, B. and Kiljunen, M. (eds) *Underdeveloped Europe: Studies in Core–Periphery Relations*. Sussex: Harvester Press.

Stationery Office (1972) *The Accession of Ireland to the European Communities*. Dublin: Stationery Office.

Stewart, J.C. (1976a) 'Linkages and foreign direct investment'. *Regional Studies*, 10, 245–258.

Stewart, J.C. (1976b) 'Foreign direct investment and the emergence of a dual economy'. *Economic and Social Review*, 7, 173–195.

190   *Ireland*

Stokes Kennedy Crowley, Peat Marwick and Davy Kelleher McCarthy (1987) *Tourism Working for Ireland: A Plan for Growth*. Dublin: Irish Hotels Federation.

Tansey, P. (1986) 'We're becoming Europe's banana republic'. *Sunday Tribune, Business Section*, 12 October 1986.

Tarrant, J.R. (1967) 'Recent industrial development in Ireland'. *Geography*, **52**, 403–408.

The Irish Times (1986) 'Urban renewal'. Supplement to *The Irish Times*, 26 November 1986.

Tussing, A.D. (1978) *Irish Educational Expenditures — Past, Present and Future*. Paper 92. Dublin: Economic and Social Research Institute.

Tussing, A.D. (1985) *Irish Medical Care Resources: An Economic Analysis*. Paper 126. Dublin: Economic and Social Research Institute.

Walsh, B.M. (1978) *The Unemployment Problems in Ireland*. Dublin: Kincora.

Walsh, B.M. (1984) 'Ireland and the European Monetary System'. In Drudy, P.J. and McAleese, D. (eds) *Ireland and the European Community*. Cambridge: Cambridge University Press.

Walsh, B.M. (1985) 'Youth unemployment: the economic background'. *Administration*, **33**, 151–166.

Walsh, B. and O'Leary, J. (1984) 'Demand management policy'. In O'Hagan, J. (ed.) *The Economy of Ireland: Policy and Performance*, 4th ed. Dublin: Irish Management Institute.

Walsh, F. (1976) 'The growth centre concept in Irish regional policy'. *Maynooth Review*, **2**, 22–41.

Walsh, F. (1977) 'The Navan zinc–lead mine'. *Irish Geography*, **10**, 95–100.

Walsh, F. (1979) 'The changing industrial structure of Northern and Southern Ireland'. *Maynooth Review*, **5**, 3–14.

Walsh, F. (1980) 'The structure of neo-colonialism: the case of the Irish Republic'. *Antipode*, **12**, 66–72.

Walsh, J.A. (1976) 'Spatial–temporal variation in crop production in the Republic of Ireland'. *Irish Journal of Agricultural Economics and Rural Sociology*, **6**, 55–74.

Walsh, J.A. (1979) 'Inmigration to the Republic of Ireland'. *Irish Geography*, **12**, 104–110.

Walsh, J.A. (1980) 'Principal components analysis of changes in agricultural patterns in the Republic of Ireland 1950–1971'. *Irish Journal of Agricultural Economics and Rural Sociology*, **8**, 73–95.

Walsh, J.A. (1986) 'Agricultural change and development'. In Breathnach, P. and Cawley, M.E. (eds) *Change and Development in Rural Ireland*. Special Publications, 1. Maynooth: Geographical Society of Ireland.

Went, A.E.J. (1979) 'Fisheries'. In Gillmor, D.A. (ed.) *Irish Resources and Land Use*. Dublin: Institute of Public Administration.

Whelan, C.T. and Whelan, B.J. (1984) '*Social Mobility in the Republic of Ireland: A Comparative Perspective*'. Paper 116. Dublin: Economic and Social Research Institute.

Whitaker, T.K. (1973) 'From protection to free trade — the Irish experience'. *Administration*, Winter, 405–423.

Whyte, J. (1971) *Church and State in Modern Ireland, 1923–1970*. Dublin: Gill and Macmillan.

Wright, M. (1967) *The Dublin Region: Advisory Regional Plan and Final Report*. 2 vols. Dublin: Stationery Office.

Wrigley, L. (1985) 'Ireland in economic space'. In Lee, J. (ed.) *Ireland: Towards a Sense of Place*. Cork: Cork University Press.

Yuill, D. and Allen, K. (eds) (1980) *European Regional Incentives: 1980*. Strathclyde: Centre for Study of Public Policy, University of Strathclyde.

Zimmerman, J.F. (1978) 'New town development in the Dublin area'. *Planning and Administration*, 5, 68–80.

Zimmerman, J.F. (1981) 'Health administration: aspects of reorganization'. *Administration*, 29, 153–170.

PLACE INDEX

SUBJECT INDEX

activity rates 16, 27
ACOT 30
Aer Lingus 33–4
agriculture xii, 4–5, 11, 15, 20–2, 30–
    1, 54, 59–61, 65–9, 76–7, 83, 85,
    98–104, 107, 122, 129–30, 169–
    70, 174
   and state 20, 30, 69, 102
   commercial 22, 30, 68, 77, 98, 111–
    2, 169–70
   duality 22, 30, 65–7, 77, 100–2,
    169–70
   mechanization 61, 67–8, 100, 116
   organization 15, 21–2, 30, 59, 65,
    68, 83, 100–2, 121, 174
   output 15, 20–2, 30, 66–8, 77, 83,
    98–100
   part-time 77, 83, 102, 111, 116, 124
   policies 20–2, 30–1, 103
   prices 20–1, 30, 68–9, 83, 85, 169–
    70, 174
   specialization 65, 67–8, 99, 102,
    169
Anglo-Irish Agreement 52–3
Anglo-Irish Free Trade Agreement 4
Anglo-Irish Treaty 2
aquaculture 131

balance of payments 4, 9–10, 19, 28,
   38
Bord Fáilte 116
Bord Iascaigh Mhara 108
Bord Na Móna 15, 106, 118
borrowing 8, 10, 18, 29, 175
'black hole' 9
branch plant xii, 24, 72, 74, 80, 120,

   170, 174
British Commonwealth 2–3
Buchanan Report 70, 149
budget 19–20, 28, 35, 37, 40, 42, 173,
   175
   deficit 18, 29, 35
building on reality 1984–87 28, 76
building societies 157
'bungalow blitz' 122

capital xiii, 1, 5–7, 9–12, 18, 20, 24,
   29, 31, 68, 71, 91, 104, 165, 174
car ownership 49, 91, 125, 160
catholic church 35–7, 41, 44, 49, 51
cattle 67–8, 77, 83, 99, 100, 102
cereals 67–9, 77, 83, 99
civil service 79, 146–7
class xii-xiii, 1, 35–7, 46, 51, 95, 99,
   117, 121, 123–7, 135, 150, 155–
   6, 161–4, 172–3, 176
   middle xiii, 35, 38, 46, 49, 95, 120,
    124, 155, 163–4, 171, 173
   working 36, 46, 50, 53–4, 95, 124,
    162–3, 170
coalition 11, 18–19, 28, 40, 43, 52–3
colonial xiii, 2, 3, 8–10, 59–60, 135–6
Common Agricultural Policy (CAP)
   xiii, 7, 20–2, 30, 76, 83, 102–3,
   169, 174
Common Fisheries Policy 108
community development 124–5, 128–
   9, 130–2
commuting 91, 99, 111, 120–1, 123–5,
   127, 129, 140, 154, 161–4, 171
consumption 11, 20, 25, 29, 36, 85,
   98–9, 172–3